War and Literature

War and Literature

Commiserating with the Enemy

Special Issue Editor

Rachel McCoppin

MDPI • Basel • Beijing • Wuhan • Barcelona • Belgrade

Special Issue Editor
Rachel McCoppin
University of Minnesota Crookston
USA

Editorial Office
MDPI
St. Alban-Anlage 66
4052 Basel, Switzerland

This is a reprint of articles from the Special Issue published online in the open access journal *Humanities* (ISSN 2076-0787) from 2018 to 2019 (available at: https://www.mdpi.com/journal/humanities/special_issues/war_literature).

For citation purposes, cite each article independently as indicated on the article page online and as indicated below:

LastName, A.A.; LastName, B.B.; LastName, C.C. Article Title. *Journal Name* **Year**, *Article Number*, Page Range.

ISBN 978-3-03921-910-0 (Pbk)
ISBN 978-3-03921-911-7 (PDF)

© 2019 by the authors. Articles in this book are Open Access and distributed under the Creative Commons Attribution (CC BY) license, which allows users to download, copy and build upon published articles, as long as the author and publisher are properly credited, which ensures maximum dissemination and a wider impact of our publications.

The book as a whole is distributed by MDPI under the terms and conditions of the Creative Commons license CC BY-NC-ND.

Contents

About the Special Issue Editor vii

Preface to "War and Literature: Commiserating with the Enemy" ix

Karol Zieliński
Women as Victims of War in Homer's Oral Poetics
Reprinted from: *Humanities* 2019, *8*, 141, doi:10.3390/h8030141 1

Bhushan Aryal
The Rhetoric of Krishna versus the Counter-Rhetoric of Vyas: The Place of Commiseration in the *Mahabharat*
Reprinted from: *Humanities* 2019, *8*, 154, doi:10.3390/h8040154 17

Yousef Deikna
Lucy Hutchinson and Margaret Cavendish: Civil War and Enemy Commiseration
Reprinted from: *Humanities* 2019, *8*, 43, doi:10.3390/h8010043 29

Danielle Johannesen
Depictions of American Indians in George Armstrong Custer's *My Life on the Plains*
Reprinted from: *Humanities* 2019, *8*, 56, doi:10.3390/h8010056 38

David Poynor
Meeting the Enemy in World War I Poetry: Cognitive Dissonance as a Vehicle for Theme
Reprinted from: *Humanities* 2019, *8*, 30, doi:10.3390/h8010030 47

Michael Sarnowski
Enemy Encounters in the War Poetry of Wilfred Owen, Keith Douglas, and Randall Jarrell
Reprinted from: *Humanities* 2018, *7*, 89, doi:10.3390/h7030089 64

Dario Marcucci
Enemy and Officers in Emilio Lussu's *Un anno sull'Altipiano*
Reprinted from: *Humanities* 2019, *8*, 26, doi:10.3390/h8010026 72

Allison Haas
Two 1916s: Sebastian Barry's *A Long Long Way*
Reprinted from: *Humanities* 2019, *8*, 60, doi:10.3390/h8010060 81

Robert T. Tally Jr.
Demonizing the Enemy, Literally: Tolkien, Orcs, and the Sense of the World Wars
Reprinted from: *Humanities* 2019, *8*, 54, doi:10.3390/h8010054 95

David Beard
How Can You Not Shout, Now That the Whispering Is Done? Accounts of the Enemy in US, Hmong, and Vietnamese Soldiers' Literary Reflections on the War
Reprinted from: *Humanities* 2019, *8*, 172, doi:10.3390/h8040172 105

Stephanie Callan
The Making of a Terrorist: Imagining Combatants' Points of View in Troubles Literature
Reprinted from: *Humanities* 2019, *8*, 27, doi:10.3390/h8010027 115

Steven K. Johnson
Translating the Enemy in the 'Terp': Three Representations in Contemporary Afghan War Fiction
Reprinted from: *Humanities* **2019**, *8*, 63, doi:10.3390/h8020063 . . . . **125**

Preface to "War and Literature: Commiserating with the Enemy"

The topic of war and literature has received much critical attention; however, this Special Issue focuses specifically on literary texts that discuss the topic of commiseration with the "enemy" within war literature. The articles included in this Special Issue show authors and/or literary characters attempting to understand the motives, beliefs, cultural values, etc. of those who have been defined by their nations as their enemies. This process of attempting to understand the orientation of defined "enemies" often shows that the soldier has begun a process of reflection about why he or she is part of the war experience. The texts included in this issue are arranged chronologically by their connection to a particular war. The two articles: "Women as Victims of War in Homer's Oral Poetics" by Karol Zieliński and "The Rhetoric of Krishna versus the Counter-Rhetoric of Vyas: The Place of Commiseration in the Mahabharat" by Bhushan Aryal show the existence of the theme of commiseration for one's proposed enemy even within ancient texts. Both Yousef Deikna's "Lucy Hutchinson and Margaret Cavendish: Civil War and Enemy Commiseration" and Danielle Johannesen's "Depictions of American Indians in George Armstrong Custer's My Life on the Plains" depict the issue of the topic within works of the Civil War era within America. Within the war poetry produced during World War I, again the topic of contemplation and then commiseration for those who have been identified as the enemy is analyzed in David Poynor's "Meeting the Enemy in World War I Poetry: Cognitive Dissonance as a Vehicle for Theme" and Michael Sarnowski's "Enemy Encounters in the War Poetry of Wilfred Owen, Keith Douglas, and Randall Jarrell." Dario Marcucci's article "Enemy and Officers in Emilio Lussu's Un anno sull'Altipiano" also addresses the issue topic from the perspective of the Alpine Front within World War I. Allison Haas' "Two 1916s: Sebastian Barry's A Long Long Way" focuses on both World War I and the 1916 Easter Rising in Ireland by examining Sebastian Barry's 2005 novel, A Long Long Way. The theme of commiseration for one's enemy is also shown to be a part of World War II literature, as discussed in the article "Demonizing the Enemy, Literally: Tolkien, Orcs, and the Sense of the World Wars" by Robert T. Tally, Jr.; it is also found in the literature of the Vietnam War, as discussed by David Beard in "How Can You Not Shout, Now That the Whispering Is Done? Accounts of the Enemy in US, Hmong, and Vietnamese Soldiers' Literary Reflections on the War." Additionally, Stephanie Callan's "The Making of a Terrorist: Imagining Combatants' Points of View in Troubles Literature" further shows the existence of the issue within the literature addressing the conflict between Protestant loyalists and Catholic nationalists during the Troubles (1968–1998) era within Ireland. Finally, the issue is also presented in Steven K. Johnson's "Translating the Enemy in the 'Terp': Three Representations in Contemporary Afghan War Fiction," showing that the concept of commiseration for one's enemy is still apparent in contemporary war literature. By analyzing literature from ancient to contemporary times, the articles within this collection show that when an author and/or literary character reflects against state-supported definitions of good/evil, right/wrong, and ally/enemy, the texts then present audiences an opportunity to reevaluate both the purposes of war and one's moral responsibility during wartime. As the threat of war is a consistent reality in our contemporary era, it is important to acknowledge the literary texts that reflect upon the political manipulation of belief during wartime and how it may cause one to embrace intolerance towards others by maintaining their designation as the enemy.

Rachel McCoppin
Special Issue Editor

Article

Women as Victims of War in Homer's Oral Poetics

Karol Zieliński

Institute of Classical, Mediterranean and Oriental Studies, University of Wrocław, 50-451 Wrocław, Poland; karol.zielinski@uwr.edu.pl

Received: 22 February 2019; Accepted: 31 July 2019; Published: 16 August 2019

Abstract: The article presents the problem of the empathy felt by the author or authors of the *Iliad* and *Odyssey* towards women depicted as victims of war. Understanding of the world in the Homeric poems may be misinterpreted today. Since Homer's works are a product of oral culture, in order to determine his intentions, it is necessary to look at them from the perspective of the tradition from which they derive. Furthermore, the author of an oral work can be deemed as creative because s/he shapes his/her story through interaction with the listening audience. The different aspects of the relationship of women as victims of war with their oppressors are, therefore, interpreted according to the use of traditional techniques adopted to evoke specific emotions in the audience.

Keywords: oral tradition; Homer; captive-women; Briseis; Andromache; funeral songs

---

It is above all through the perspectives of women that the poet exposes the brutality of war.

Barbara Graziosi, Johannes Haubold

In the world portrayed by Homer, women are special victims of war because they survive the downfall of the city.[1] At that point, their status changes and they become subjected to various sufferings, but they stay alive. Men do not. Nor do children. Full of wrath and hatred of the enemy, Agamemnon reprimands his brother Menelaus for showing mercy to his enemies.[2] In his opinion, they must not save anyone, not even fetuses in the wombs of mothers (VI 55–60). This means that women may also die in the conquest of the city, but it happens in a particular situation when they can carry male descendants in their wombs. The historical reality of this time was probably much more complex. It might have looked just like Homer depicts it or it may have been otherwise, that is, it might have been both less cruel and more cruel (Joshua captures Jericho sparing neither men nor women, nor children, nor older people, nor farm animals, Joshua 6:21). The decision to keep women alive is based on the perception of

---

[1] Graziosi and Haubold (2010, especially pp. 29–32) very aptly describe the functioning of the world of men and women in The Iliad.
[2] According to Kim (2000, pp. 57–58), Agamemnon represents a traditional attitude, that is, showing no mercy to enemies, which is judged positively in the *Iliad*. Hence, as Kim suggests, Menelaus receives a well-deserved admonishment from his brother. Blaming the Trojans for the entire war may be a justification for Agamemnon's atrocities (as the anonymous reviewer rightly pointed out). The Trojans' blame (collective responsibility for the immoral behavior of Paris) is undoubtedly a traditional element, i.e., present in all the songs whose subject was the Trojan War. In particular songs, however, this element could have been introduced and explained in different ways. In the *Iliad*, the collective blame of the Trojans is depicted as a violation of the truce. It seems, therefore, that there is no reason why the *Iliad*'s listeners should not have accepted Agamemnon's words with approval. The themes of cruelty and mercy are, however, much more subtly woven into the entire song. Achilles's excessive cruelty comes under criticism in the *Iliad*. The mercy shown to Priam is a breakthrough in his life, but it is also a return to the behaviors which preceded his conflict with Agamemnon, where he showed mercy to the Achaeans (by assisting them) and often the defeated enemies. The *Iliad* presents this matter somewhat paradoxically: Achilles, by killing his enemies and saving his community from extermination, fulfils the traditional role of a hero, but this does not bring him the expected glory, because he loses himself in the cruelty towards the enemy. Agamemnon's cruelty, which is also excessive, and just like his other behaviors, only seemingly legitimate and justified by the common good, is an implicit object of rebuke by the *Iliad*'s author (see Zieliński 2014, pp. 474–78).

their measurable value.³ They become part of the loot—like objects or animals—and, as in the case of objects and animals, they can be used later and they serve as status symbols.⁴

Research most often focuses on the historical and the sociological aspects of how the women of defeated enemies were treated. However, the question of what this issue meant to Homer, i.e., whether he acknowledged such treatment of women as expected behavior, necessitates an attempt to reconstruct the mental world of the people of that time. The poet addresses his audience with the expectation that they will accept his point of view, even when he relates to them tales of behavior deviating from the social norm.⁵ The most recognizable indication of this is Achilles's invitation to share a meal, extended to his enemy, the father of the detested Hector, whose corpse he continuously mangled, unable to satisfy his vengeance. For the Greeks, this behavior absolutely violates all the rules, because by breaking bread together, people establish a friendship so permanent that it should last through succeeding generations⁶ (the diners become *philoi* to each other, which means "their own kind" so "not strangers or enemies"). Hence, one does not dine with the enemy. Homer, however, expects his audience not to resent such behavior, but rather to understand fully or even to appreciate it.⁷

Identifying the author's intentions relies on the consideration on the nature of Homer's discourse. As is well known, Homeric poems are a product of oral culture; therefore, without understanding the circumstances of performance and the compositional techniques of this tradition, we are unable to judge them adequately. In the first decades of the research on the oral tradition, the focus was on the structure of the message and on its repetitive nature. This led to a particular perception of both the performers of traditional songs and of the works they performed. The repetition of the message served to preserve knowledge about the world and past events. Accordingly, this involved the development of tools for remembering and passing on this knowledge, in the form of stories, catalogs, proverbs, etc.⁸ The result, however, was a perception of the oral performer as being limited by a series of restrictions that forced him to replicate what he heard from others, and not to express his point of view or personality. Albert Lord emphasized that a writer of an epic composes his song during the performance;⁹ yet this may be perceived as a weakness of the performer for not remembering the story exactly as he heard it. The poor evaluation of the capabilities of the creators of oral culture was also due to the difficulties in its reception in the modern world and to different expectations from the text that emerged from the literary culture of the scholars' background. The contemporary reader simply becomes weary of the monotony of repetitive formulas, of lengthy, detailed descriptions of typical scenes and of standardized story-patterns.¹⁰ It is no wonder that some researchers in the Homeric

---

3   This issue is exaggerated, in my opinion, by Gottschall (2008), who makes women the main subject of disputes leading to manifestations of aggression (wars are supposedly fought as a result of a certain shortage of women). This is not how we should explain especially the conflict between Agamemnon and Achilles in the *Iliad*, which, contrary to appearances, is not about women, but about prestige and rivalry for the title of "the best from Achaeans," and the deeper, i.e., not explicitly disclosed, roots of the dispute go back to the blame for the incurring of extermination (Apollo's wrath) upon the Achaeans.
4   On the value of the war prize, see Van Wees (1992). More on the issue of violence, rape, and enslavement of women who are victims of wars according to ancient sources, see (Gaca 2011).
5   Progress of the narrative from the deviation of norms toward recovering the social, political and cosmic normalities is suggested by (Russo 1978, pp. 47–49; Elmer 2013, pp. 67–70).
6   Diomedes and Glaucus recognize that their grandfathers had established a relationship of hospitality, so they intend to abstain from fighting and avoid each other on the battlefield in the future. This relationship of friendship which prohibits hostility is renewed by exchanging gifts (VI 215–236).
7   I agree with the anonymous reviewer that this meal is depicted by Homer as "exceptional and difficult" (it is not clear if the characters are going to withstand their pain in contact with each other and if everything is going to happen as expected), which helps his audience to accept the non-conventional behavior of Achilles and "to allay any 'resentment' from them." It would probably be difficult to accomplish the acceptance of a hero's controversial behavior or belief by surprise given to the audience. Homer guides his listeners slowly, in a manner typical for oral narration, while building tension like a sinusoid of alternating horror and relief. The horror is extinguished every now and again and reconstructed anew. Thanks to this, the listeners' attention is permanently maintained.
8   This view is primarily exhibited by the works of Eric Havelock (Havelock 1963, 1982, 1986); also Ong (1982).
9   Lord (1960).
10 It is then not taken into account that in the oral reception, all these elements interact in a different way, stimulating the listener's imagination and involvement.

studies community have challenged the attribution of works that had laid the foundations of European culture to an oral artist. In one way or another it was asserted that the artistry of Homeric poems and the multitude of refined details must result from the possibility of using writing to shape these poems.[11] The problem, however, is that there is no basis for denying the creativity of a creator of oral art. In his research, anthropologist Jack Goody emphasizes the endless changeability of the oral tradition.[12] The oral tradition is not only about transmitting the story: the story itself is not as valuable as it is in literary culture. The epic singer tells the story not only as he remembers it, but, above all, as he understands it and how he wants it to be understood by his listeners. The listeners themselves, in turn, influence the shape of the story through their behavior and eagerness to listen. The story is produced through the interaction between the singer and his listeners.[13] The singer, in every way possible, tries to focus his attention on his story, taking into account their knowledge of tradition and their mentality and emotionality. The artistry of the Homeric poems developed in such dialogue with the recipients.[14]

I mention this because in the oral tradition, the use of standard techniques (e.g., repetitious formulas) can bear the characteristics of an individual artistic choice. On the other hand, the techniques that we tend to regard as innovations are still part of the oral tradition. New solutions constitute variant processing of the existing material. Thanks to this, the oral composer, Homer as well, not only recreates the world represented in the stories, but he also, by invoking it, constantly reinterprets it.

Repeatability does not exclude creativity and innovation, but from the perspective of tradition itself, these are, in a sense, indiscernible. Each performance occasions a modality of solutions, and the version of myth, stories, songs, etc. represented in the performance is the basis for the oral message's functioning in the consciousness of its recipients. The singer (sometimes in competition with other singers) endeavors to present the tradition familiar to him in a manner attractive to the audience, while employing narrative expansions or compressions of the story.[15] As a result, he constructs his own vision of the presented events. Therefore, when deciding to analyse Homer's legacy, we must determine his dialogue with tradition, unceasingly and from different vantage points. This is a difficult task because this oral tradition has virtually been lost.[16] Even when presenting a new episode, which the *Iliad* may well be, and when expanding it to monumental dimensions, the singer remains a part of this tradition and applies the tools that are characteristic of it.

Let us start with drawing the situation of captive women in the *Iliad*. The way they see their position and the way they behave may seem strange to the modern reader. Depriving Achilles of

---

[11] This view was expressed by: Bowra (1952); Lesky (1963, 1967); Parry (1966); Griffin (1980); West (2011, 2015).
[12] Goody (1977, 1986, 2010).
[13] The work of Scodel (2002) is pioneering in this matter. See also Ford (1992, 1997).
[14] Zieliński (2014) discusses more broadly the mechanism of influencing the emotions of listeners by the alternation of instilling horror and relief and taking advantage of the listeners' intellect and understanding the world through the use of tragic irony.
[15] The principle of expansion and compression in the composition of the oral epic is presented in Nagy (2010).
[16] The link between the Homeric poems and the oral tradition is primarily explored in the works of Gregory Nagy (Nagy 1996, 2010) and John M. Foley (Foley 1991, 1999). Their point of view differs from mine in many significant respects. Probably the main problem is the question of the allusions in Homer's epics. Foley's concept of traditional referentiality allows only for the understanding of individual elements of the composition thanks to their embedment in the tradition, i.e., thanks to their presence in similar contexts in other songs. The similarities between individual scenes in the Trojan cycle result, according to the classical understanding of orality, from the variation of using certain patterns. This theory has its supporters and opponents. Cairns (2011, p. 113, n. 26) sees "no evidence for the view that audiences always activate knowledge of the totality of a multiform tradition, but much evidence for their activation (or suppression) of their knowledge of specific tales and episodes". In his opinion traditional referentiality makes unsustainable claims about cultural differences in cognitive capacity (See also Cairns 2001). He is right, I think, because we should not fall into the trap of L. Lévy-Bruhl's error. However, there are many specificity in orally presented narrations, the story is presented in a different way than when the text is being created in written. First of all, we should think about the every performance in oral tradition as an adjustment of traditional patterns to the given situation. The system of allusions present in Homeric poems does not mean a departure from the oral tradition, but it constitutes, in my view, a typical element of this tradition. The author of the *Iliad*, however, does not refer to other songs, as suggested by neoanalysts, but to images perpetually functioning within the tradition: perpetually—despite the multiple variants of their use. One could say in a nutshell that the *Iliad* is one of the ways of recounting the myth about the Trojan war (Zieliński 2014).

Briseis triggered off his anger, so she may seem to be important to him. But how close was she to him and who was he for her? Is the behavior of the both sides understandable to us?

In Homer Briseis is not a virgin. Perhaps some affection for Achilles comes into play (IX 335–343), but this does not matter in the dispute between him and Agamemnon. Briseis is given a voice by Homer only when she sees Patroclus's corpse. She grieves for him because she lost a loved one, who was especially close to her. Achilles killed her three brothers and her husband, whom she had just wedded: Patroclus promised that Achilles would become her husband.[17] How could a modern viewer become convinced that a woman so wronged could cherish hope for a marriage with the murderer of her loved ones? At best, she would be accused of suffering from Stockholm Syndrome.

It is, therefore, necessary to look at how Briseis is represented in the *Iliad* and what role she plays in the text. We could proclaim with horror that she is being objectified: she is a victim of a war that took her family, she is a captive and the victim of quarrels among her oppressors, transferred from hand to hand like a commodity, passed around between Achilles and Agamemnon. It must be stated, however, that treating a girl as a commodity is not something that was only true for slaves. Girls were married in exchange for property measured in heads of cattle handed over to their families.[18] The maidens who danced during the holidays were identified with the epithet ἀλφεσίβοιαι "those who supply oxen" (XVIII 593). In this cultural context, they may be rather proud of such a term, because it suggests girls that are beautiful and happy,[19] and not humiliated in any way. They can, therefore, joyfully take on the cultural role that is imposed on them.

The subjection of women in this world is symbolized, in some way, by Helena. Her circumstance exemplifies two methods of winning a wife: buying her or kidnapping her. In both cases, she legally becomes a wife. In the mythical version, the contract between the father and the groom (and often the family of the groom) materializes in the setting of a competition[20] in which the winner gets the girl's hand as a prize (even then, it is difficult to call it her choice). Kidnapping, in turn, is nothing reprehensible: it is a widespread custom for obtaining a wife in many cultures. Paris is disapprovingly portrayed by Homer not because he acquired his wife through kidnapping, but because he violated the law of hospitality: he acted as an enemy against someone who offered him friendship. That is why it makes sense to have the fight between Menelaus and Paris happen at the beginning of the war: the winner takes Helena and the treasures because he deserves them as the stronger opponent. After the death of Paris, Helena is inevitably promised to one of his brothers, Deiphobus. By taking Helena as a wife, he takes command of the Trojans. It can thus be inferred that Helena fulfills the function of a magical talisman in the epic of the Trojan tradition: whoever possesses her has the power.[21]

Briseis is brought back to the tent of Achilles, along with the seven girls from Lesbos, who Agamemnon had previously offered to Achilles as part of a canny game between them. Their magnificence is beyond doubt, as Agamemnon comments, stating that he chose them himself,[22] because they were those (IX 130)

... αἳ κάλλει ἐνίκων φῦλα γυναικῶν

who surpassed other women in their beauty.

---

[17] Dué (2002, pp. 67–81) delineates a change in the attitude of Briseis to Achilles, who, from the murderer of her family, becomes a person desired by her in an erotic sense and as a future husband.
[18] McInerney (2010); Walcot (1979).
[19] I borrowed this expression from Andrew Dalby (2006, p. 7): they are beautiful and lucky.
[20] Jamison (1999, esp. pp. 243–258) points out the parallels in the Old Indian epic to this way of acquiring a wife (*vīryaśulka svayamvara*) and concludes about the common Indo-European origin of these ritual, ceremonial and epic structures.
[21] What seems to have an analogous function in the epic about the Argonauts' expedition is the golden fleece, while in the epic about the Theban war, it is the necklace given to Eriphyle by Polyneikes. There are more magical items of this importance, see (Zieliński 2014, pp. 234–41).
[22] The spoils were common property of the group and were distributed among all men in accordance with hierarchy of rank and merit. It should be noted that choosing something from the spoils is a special privilege, which in *The Iliad* is confirmed to have been reserved for Agamemnon and Achilles.

Gregory Nagy suggests that the word φῦλα, not translated above, means not so much a group of women as such, but a group of girls taking part in the singing and dancing agons on Lesbos, where the inhabitants, the Aeolians, gathered.[23] In Nagy's interpretation, these are girls who had won the competition against others, so they were the most eligible maidens, but the war thwarted their youthful plans: Achilles conquered the island and their fate changed completely; they became slaves, intended for sexual bondage and housework. To some extent, one can assume, their aristocratic status was, nevertheless, preserved, because usually the epic poem and the Attic tragedy mention only spinning and weaving as the chores awaiting those aristocratic female captives.[24] It is difficult to say whether and to what extent this reflects the historical reality and whether, in this case, the ability to weave is not synonymous in an epic poem with women's work in general. In any event, in the Homeric world, women are always portrayed at work. Men can rest while sitting and feasting. In the *Odyssey*, Helena, despite the ongoing wedding reception of her daughter, only leaves the women's rooms for a moment to talk to her husband and Telemachus, and even then she spools the thread, so as not to waste time.

In front of Achilles's tent, Briseis discerns the body of Patroclus and laments over it. The lament has a ritual character (XIX 284–286):

ἀμφ' αὐτῷ χυμένη λίγ' ἐκώκυε, χερσὶ δ'ἄμυσσε
στήθεά τ'ἠδ' ἁπαλὴν δειρὴν ἰδὲ καλὰ πρόσωπα.
εἶπε δ'ἄρα κλαίουσα γυνὴ ἐϊκυῖα θεῆσι

she flung her arms around him and gave out a shrill shriek, then she tore with her nails

her breasts, her soft neck and her lovely face.

Wailing, this goddess-like woman said ...

Women's lamentation is mandatory in the Greek funeral ritual. The loud wailing and crying are accompanied by ritual gestures. The entire assortment of these gestures is never listed. The economy which is characteristic for the Homeric technique manifests itself in the mere mention of only some behaviors adapted to the situational context.[25] Richard Seaford explains women's self-mutilation gestures as a message directed to other men. The laceration of the breasts, neck and face disfigures women, so their sexual attraction becomes compromised. The death of a man in a family, especially a sudden and violent one, is a threat to women: by overstating their mourning, they demonstrate that they have been deprived of a defender. Consequently, with their crying, women prompt other men of their family to take revenge on the killer.[26] The explosion of feelings manifested by women causes the men to share rapidly these feelings. In the *Iliad*, this situation is better visible in the scene of the lamentation of women in Troy over the body of Hector. There are no warriors' families in the Achaean camp. The role of the women related by blood is played by the captives, who are Agamemnon's compensation for the harm done to Achilles. Their presence, then, signals a restoration of the hero's reputation, but they actually appear there only to perform rituals over the body of Achilles's friend.[27]

When Briseis finished the mourning speech for Patroclus, the other women joined her, XIX 301–302:

---

[23] (Nagy 2010).
[24] See (Rabinowitz 1998, pp. 56–68; Dué 2006, pp. 27, 109; Nagy 2010, pp. 241–50, 285). On more about the importance of weaving see Nagy (2010, pp. 273–308). In reference to Andromache, however, carrying water (VI 457) is also mentioned, which is undoubtedly hard work.
[25] Hitch (2009) shows that there is not one template of a scene depicting the entire sacrifice ritual, but that each time only selected elements of this typical scene are exposed, depending on the requirements of the narrative.
[26] Seaford (1994, chp. 3, especially pp. 86–92). The first observations on the role of lamentation and self-mutilation of women in order to provoke men's revenge were made by Alexiou (2002, pp. 21–22).
[27] These are not the only captive women owned by Achilles. When the hero refuses to take part in the fight and sends away the ambassadors sent to him, he beds down with Diomede, also captured from Lesbos, and Patroclus with Iphis, captured from Skyros (IX 663–668). However, it seems that Homer does not mention them in the context of funeral laments.

Ὣς ἔφατο κλαίουσ' ἐπὶ δὲ στενάχοντο γυναῖκες
Πάτροκλον πρόφασιν, σφῶν δ' αὐτῶν κήδε' ἑκάστη.

That's what she said while weeping and the women moaned

over Patroclus, and each of them had her own cause for distress.

It is typical for the choral song developed within the Greek oral culture to be performed by one person, while others repeat the ritual patterns and quasi-choruses after him or her. The antiphonal character of the song is typical of primitive cultures[28] and we can assume that this form of expression in the song has been present in human culture from its very beginnings. The song, i.e., rhythmical and often melodized speech, is primarily a way of conveying emotions to the other members of the group. C.M. Bowra noticed that in primitive cultures, virtually every powerful emotion is directly articulated in a song, be it in a public or a private situation.[29] In my opinion, the group's response to the expression of emotions by the person who performs the song is the token of an emotional contagion spreading to others. It involves the gradual "infection" with feelings of the people to whom the expression is addressed. These people gradually fall into a trance that allows them to share the feelings articulated by the "coryphaeus," whether plunging with him into grief or sinking into exaltation caused by joy. A choral song of a ritual nature, both a funeral and a wedding song, will, therefore, have the same sense. This is also true for a song which constitutes a dramatic re-enactment of a myth, in which the protagonist embodies a mythical character experiencing what happened to the hero in a time of the beginning; and the group does not look at this as spectators, but becomes the community of their ancestors accompanying the protagonist in his actions. Just as he talks about what happens to him, they respond by giving him emotional support or commenting on his behavior.

Similarly, the women gathered over the corpse of Hector, taking turns to praise the deceased (using a Greek word, they "start' gr. *arkhein*): Andromache, his wife, Hecuba, his mother, and Helena, his sister-in-law, while the other Trojans respond with laments (XXIV 721–775). The groaning and wailing of the Trojan women are also heard after each relative speaks about the dead man:

XXIV 745

Ὣς ἔφατο κλαίουσ' ἐπὶ δὲ στενάχοντο γυναῖκες

So she said weeping and the women added their groans

XXIV 760

Ὣς ἔφατο κλαίουσα, γόον δ' ἀλίαστον ὄρινε

So she said weeping, and unceasing lament [goos] was stirred up

XXIV 776

Ὣς ἔφατο κλαίουσ', ἐπὶ δ' ἔστενε δῆμος ἀπείρων.

So she said weeping, and the innumerable crowd join in the moaning

In the case of lamentation over Patroclus, Homer allows himself to remark that each of the women had her own reason to express despair. Their lament cannot be spontaneous, because they are not related to the dead through kinship, so they are somehow forced to play the role of the mourners,

---

[28] Antiphonal form and structure of the Greek dirges are described by Alexiou (2002, pp. 131–40). She finds that both the antiphonal structure and often present in it dialogues where identifications with the dead or tomb appear are primitive in character.
[29] Bowra (1962).

even though such coercion was not expressed *expressis verbis*.[30] Briseis is not a relative either, so she justifies her wailing with the fact that Patroclus had always been good to her, even the best of all because he gave her hope for a better life.[31] The laments are honest, because each of the women remembers her misfortune: instead of a wonderful marriage and family they now have bondage and the sight of the death of their loved ones in front of their eyes.[32]

Let us note, then, that women perform a ritual function here, that is, they express what constitutes an indispensable element of the tradition: a fallen warrior, a hero must be properly mourned. The author of the *Iliad* can, however, grasp the circumstances of their fate and indicates that their gesture is, on the one hand, a formality, and on the other hand, the evocation of feelings alone inspires the experiencing of the feelings and linking them with one's own motives. We could say that Homer, when evoking the traditional image of a warrior's funeral,[33] capitalizes on the opportunity to emphasize the particular nature of the situation in which the characters, including background characters, find themselves. He is also able to empathize not only with the situation of the heroes, but also the victims of their wars and disputes.

It would be premature to treat this remark as a typical expression of the author's individual style. In the further part of this scene, only the most important Achaean chiefs (Agamemnon, Menelaus, Odysseus, Nestor, Phoinix and Idomeneus), stay with Achilles at the body of Patroclus and do their utmost to comfort him (XIX 312–313). Their efforts are ineffective, because only bloody revenge can heal Achilles's wound. Now, in turn, Achilles expresses his grief with weeping and a speech (XIX 315–337), and the lament of the chiefs accompanying him joins in:

Ὣς ἔφατο κλαίων, ἐπὶ δὲ στενάχοντο γέροντες

μνησάμενοι τὰ ἕκαστος ἐνὶ μεγάροισι ἔλειπον

He said so weeping, and the old men moaned

Each mentioning something that he had left in his palace

Achilles, when mourning the death of Patroclus, recalls his family home, juxtaposing the present loss with hypothetical news about the death of his father, whom he left at home, or the death of his son Neoptolemus, whom Patroclus was supposed to bring to his homeland after the war (he knew about his death at Troy, but did not predict the death of his friend). The chiefs, companions for the expedition, were called γέροντες, i.e., "elders" here. Usually, this term refers to their rank as members of the council (their high command, so to speak), but in this instance it can also take on the meaning of the hypothetical members of the family who are grieving.[34] Achaean chiefs have far more reasons to

---

[30] Tyrtaeus fr 7 testifies that in Sparta, the Helots (the people conquered and subjugated by the Dorians), were expected to attend the funeral lamentations in honor of their oppressors. Similarly, Hippias from Erythrai says the analogous was true for the inhabitants of Erythrai (Athenaios 259e). Alexiou (2002, p. 10) notes that alongside the family, strangers, often hired or forced to perform lamentation and other behaviors, participated in funeral ceremonies throughout antiquity. This is how she evaluates the use of the women captives to mourn Patroclus. Alexiou, however, does not seem to notice the problem of substitution which is visible in the *Iliad*, and which must have been the basis of the habits of using strangers in funeral rituals.

[31] However sincere the comforting assurances by Patroclus were, Achilles's next statement shows that the hopes for their coming true were vain. Achilles knew he could not return home and must die at Troy, so the future marriage to Briseis turns out to be an illusion created for the sake of the girl, an illusion which Achilles did not really believe in. However, we cannot accuse him of insincerity because it was his friend that had beguiled her with false hope.

[32] Alexiou (2002, p. 41) emphasizes the commitment and even the genuinity of the lamentation of rented mourners in modern Greece. He gives an example of one of them (Sophia Lala), who confesses that when wailing for the dead, she expresses his pain after the loss of her relatives. This means that the behavior of the women captives in the *Iliad*, who express pain over the body of Patroclus, should be considered typical. They do their duty, on the one hand, by stimulating the despair of relatives, and on the other, by absorbing the misery experienced by the family of the dead, which releases their own pain resulting from their own ordeals.

[33] There are many indications that the spectacular funeral of Patroclus corresponds to the traditional image of the funeral of Achilles, to which the *Iliad* refers allusively and which the *Odyssey* mentions. The mention of Oedipus's funeral (XXIII 679–680) seems to testify to the traditional nature of the motif of the spectacular burial of the hero in the Greek epic tradition.

[34] This may be suggested by listing in one verse the names of Nestor and Phoinix, who appear in the plot of *The Iliad* as old, together with Idomeneus, who is described with the epithet γέρων "old" (XIX 311). Also Aias, son of Oileus (XXIII 476) points out euphemistically that Idomeneus is not of the youngest age (XXIII 476).

mourn for Patroclus than the captives from Lesbos do, and yet they also employ the same lamentation formula: that each of them had, in fact, his own private sorrows and reasons for the manifestation of grief. Thus, Homer's innovation which exhibits the traits of an individual style still remains an element of the conventional construction of the oral narrative. The "performance" of a woman "starting her song" among other women has its counterpart in the "performance" of a man "starting to sing" among other men. Their moans are divided by gender, reflected in the order of speeches. Reality may not have been so clear, and this division may reveal an epic tendency to separate the masculine world of heroes, who embark on warfare, from the female world, associated with the situation of peace, because they belong to families left at home. This female world is represented here by the women captives—prizes of war. It seems that, mourning over the body of Hector, brought to the palace of Priam, depicts a situation closer to reality, in which the moans of both sexes are not so separated, XXIV 719–724:

οἳ δ' ἐπεὶ εἰσάγαγον κλυτὰ δώματα, τὸν μὲν ἔπειτα
τρητοῖς ἐν λεχέεσσι θέσαν, παρὰ δ' εἷσαν ἀοιδοὺς
θρήνων ἐξάρχους, οἳ δὲ στενόεσσαν ἀοιδὴν
οἳ μὲν ἄρ' ἐθρήνεον· ἐπὶ δὲ στενάχοντο γυναῖκες.
τῇσιν δ' ἀνδρομάχη λευκώλενος ἦρχε γόοιο
Ἕκτορος ἀνδροφόνοιο· κάρη μετὰ χερσὶν ἔχουσα

they [Priam and Idaios], when they had brought him to the glorious house, laid him

on a corded bedstead,[35] and by his side set singers, *aoidoi*,

"leaders" of the dirge, and [the men] started the song of lamentation[36]—

they [*aoidoi* and men] chanted the dirge, and the women moaned.

And among these [women] white-skinned Andromache started the wailing [*goos*],

holding in her hands the head[37] [of Hector? Her head?]

---

[35] Most probably other men, probably younger than them, members of Priam's family had to undertake this.

[36] I would venture such a translation of this excerpt because of the placement of the "men" and "de" particles which is confusing when you think of the traditional interpretation of this fragment (cf. Richardson 1993, p. 351). In the traditional reading, the pronoun "hoi" from verse 721, is interpreted as dat.sg., which would mean: "the *aoidoi* were singing to him as a dirge [or in the form of a dirge] (*ethrēneon*) a mourning song." These particles, however, signify a contradiction, so you could interpret this pronoun as nom.pl. (adding accent), so it would refer to the men who carried Hector's body, so you can expect them to be family members.

[37] It is commonly understood that Andromache holds Hector's head, which would express her great love and attachment to her husband (see N. Richardson, op cit., 352). Alexiou (2002, p. 6) assesses that the gesture of placing one's hands on the deceased is part of the funeral ritual: "Andromache leads off the dirge at Hector's *próthesis* by laying her hands around his head, and Achilles laments by laying his hand on Patroklos' breast" (XXIV 724; XVIII 317). The gesture of a woman holding dead man's head during a lament performed over the dead is confirmed by iconographic sources, Boardman (1955, pp. 56–57). However, the text is not so unambiguous. This formula follows the formula that describes Andromache's husband, and this, first of all, suggests the link with this image. In the vase paintings of the geometric period depicting a *prothesis* (laying out a dead body on a bed), women either ritually raise their hands above their heads or hold their heads in a similar ritual gesture (see geometric vase, Karlsruhe, Badisches Landesmuseum 2674). A few lines above, Hecuba and Andromache embrace Hector's body when it is still in front of the gates of Troy, holding their heads. However, a different verb is used: ἁπτόμεναι κεφαλῆς, which means holding your head, and it is also sometimes suggested that it denotes tearing hair out. It is possible that in both cases we are dealing with the same gesture. In Alexiou's opinion, op.cit., p. 8: "Perhaps the more ecstatic attitude of the mourner at the tomb can be explained by the nature of the ritual. The *próthesis* was a formal affair, with a large number of people grouped round the bier in more or less set positions. Lamentation at the tomb on the other hand was at once more restricted and more personal, involving the direct communication between the relatives and the dead." The iconography on which this opinion is based, however, dates back to the period when public display of emotions at funerals was subject to far-reaching restrictions. The Homeric description refers to the clan structure, where displaying the feeling of despair and influencing others in this way is perceived as still beneficial and appropriate. Hence, no matter how we interpret Andromache's gesture, we should assume the naturalness of showing and stimulating the emotions aroused in the participants of the ceremony at all its stages.

Men join in the singers who "lead" the singing of the dirges (*thrênoi*) and women join in Andromache who "leads" the lament (*goos*).[38] However, as evidenced by subsequent (already quoted) reactions to Hecuba and Helena's (XXIV 760 and 776) lamentations/dirges, lament is contagious and overcomes all participants of the funeral.[39]

Thus, it can be seen that the author of the *Iliad* is able to use conventional narrative structures to describe unusual situations, whose individual shape results from the specificity of this particular plot. This individuality is noticeable; nevertheless, it is not entirely innovative. Applying this to the topic of our discussion: recognizing the suffering of the victims of war—the captive women enslaved by the Achaeans—is a function of compliance with the conventions found in the oral tradition and of the possibility of adapting those patterns to the current needs of the narrative. Adapting a repetitive message to a particular situation is the guiding principle of the functioning of communication in oral culture, regardless of what form of poetic and non-poetic speech we might consider. The conventionality and the schematicism allow the singer to move his story forward, but when making choices within the matter of the epic tradition, variable by nature as it is, he takes into account the effects of plot denouements as they are applied at a given moment.

So we come to the question of on what grounds we can make judgments about Homer's humanitarianism. The author of the *Iliad* undoubtedly tells the recipient to take into account the miserable fate of the captive women, but this results from the adaptation of the oral techniques to the needs of the narrative. Listeners probably regarded sanctioning the honesty of the laments of the women captives and the Achaean "old men" through their own sufferings as natural, but this does not change the fact that realizing the existence of an analogous source of evoked despair in "their own kin" and "strangers" means forcing the recipients to ponder on the suffering of strangers in the same terms as they think about the suffering of their own kin.[40]

The issue of the fate of women who are held captive is raised several times in Homer's poems. The most extensive description, of course, can be found in the speech of Andromache addressed to her husband Hector (VI 407–439). Her situation is analogous to Briseis's situation: Achilles had previously killed her father and seven brothers.[41] Andromache makes her husband aware of what will happen to her and their child when he dies and the city is captured. She says this to stop Hector from heading to the battlefield, but in the narrative strategy this speech performs the function of anticipating events that will inevitably follow and which will not be presented in the song. This is a special strategy of the oral poet, who refers to the audience's knowledge of tradition. Although in the plot structure of the song there will be a place for Andromache lamenting over the dead body of her husband, this speech becomes her lamentation over herself and her child. Hector accounts for this possibility and foresees the defeat of the Trojans. He spends a moment unfolding a vision of her fate in captivity, and the

---

[38] Tsagalis (2004b, p. 32) postulates the interpretation of the *goos* as a kind of a ritual song, analogous to the dirge and the epic song. Cf. Dué (2006, pp. 1–56).

[39] Dué (2007, p. 235) accentuates the separateness of the performances of women's and men's songs. The joining in the *gooi* by the people of Troy after Helena's "performance" ("not with antiphonal wailing of the women") is explained by the fact that she is perceived as the cause of the war. Indeed, women can be hostile to Helena (it seems that no Trojan woman addresses her during the whole epic), but I do not think this matter is important here where common weeping unites everyone as a kind of collective hysteria (note the gradation of mood present in the quoted verses XXIV 745, 760, 776).

[40] Perhaps the sympathy of the audience can be evoked easier thanks to the fact that they treat the captive girls as their country people. Dué (2002) shows that the character of Briseis was characterized in the *Iliad* as clearly 'Aeolian'. If we accept G. Nagy's concept of the Homeric poems being shaped within the Aeolian, Ionic and Athenian traditions, and determine the first of them to be the oldest one, we get a picture in which the Aeolian hero, Achilles conquers the Lesbos island which, at the time when the epic tradition of the Trojan War was being shaped, was already inhabited by the Aeolians. The Aeolians who colonize the depopulated Troy from the eighth century BC, feel themselves to be the guardians of the Trojan tradition and the heirs of the legacy of the epic poem that they had most likely shaped. Nagy notices how individual elements fit the Aeolian tradition, including the reference to the ritual of the beauty contest of women organized in Lesbos, confirmed by other sources (Nagy 2010, pp. 241–250). Dué (2006), however, extensively shows that in classical Athens, the Trojan War was presented not so much as a victory over strangers, but as a horror of war, very often from the perspective of the defeated Trojans.

[41] However, he showed respect for them: he buried the father with his armor (VI 416–419) and then he bought the mother out of captivity (VI 425–428).

thought of this is more distressing for him than that of the fate of his parents and brothers who will have to perish (VI 450–465). He firmly rejects his wife's pleas to continue fighting behind the walls of Troy. The audience of the epic does not get the impression that they are dealing with a hysterical woman[42] when listening to how assuredly Andromache speaks of the inevitable destiny of herself, her husband and son. The consciousness of the listeners that such a fortune really awaits them invites them to perceive her lament as real.[43] The singer motivates the audience to remember the facts that are known to them from tradition and that go beyond the knowledge of the heroes of the song.[44]

What is missing in Andromache's complaints is the fear of rape. This matter is not mentioned in either Homeric poem, although it is always a nightmare experienced by women during the conquest of the city.[45]

The fate of Andromache is surprisingly similar to the fate of the woman who is mentioned in a simile evoked in the *Odyssey* (viii 523–531):[46]

ὡς δὲ γυνὴ κλαίῃσι φίλον πόσιν ἀμφιπεσοῦσα,

ὅς τε ἑῆς πρόσθεν πόλιος λαῶν τε πέσῃσιν,

ἄστεϊ καὶ τεκέεσσιν ἀμύμων νηλεὲς ἦμαρ·

ἡ μὲν τὸν θνῄσκοντα καὶ ἀσπαίροντα ἰδοῦσα

ἀμφ' αὐτῷ χυμένη λίγα κωκύει· οἱ δέ τ' ὄπισθε

κόπτοντες δούρεσσι μετάφρενον ἠδὲ καὶ ὤμου

εἴρερον εἰσανάγουσι, πόνον τ' ἐχέμεν καὶ ὀϊζύν·

τῆς δ' ἐλεεινοτάτῳ ἄχεϊ φθινύθουσι παρειαί·

ὡς Ὀδυσεὺς ἐλεεινὸν ὑπ' ὀφρύσι δάκρυον εἶβεν.

When a woman laments, embracing the body of her husband

who fell defending his city and people,

The immaculate [man] died on the merciless day for his city and children,

and she, seeing him dying in convulsions,

embraces him, and wails with piercing cries, but [the victorious men] from behind

beating her back and shoulders with their spears

escort her to be a slave and have toil and misery,

and with the most pitiful grief her cheeks waste away,

So Odysseus shed a pitiful tear beneath his eyelid.

---

[42] Andromache's speech has the characteristics of a funeral lament (Tsagalis 2004a, p. 119; Stoevesandt 2016, p. 168). Murnaghan (1999, p. 209) points out that the majority of women's statements in the *Iliad* are structurally or thematically related to lamentation. Andromache does not act as a concerned wife, but as a wife already lamenting over her dead husband. The situation corresponds to Thetis and Nereid mourning Achilles as being dead, although he is still alive in the *Iliad's* narrative.

[43] On the links between this scene and the cycle see Anderson (1997, p. 193). Nagy (2010, pp. 203–11, 321–25) assesses the version of the *Iliad*, in which Astyanax—Scamandrius is the only son of Hector and Andromache, whom inevitable death awaits after the Achaean conquest of the city, as an Attic version—intentionally breaking with the Ionic and with the Aeolian version. This circumstance has a significant impact on the tragic undertone of this scene.

[44] On accounting for and stimulating the knowledge of tradition among the listeners, see (Zieliński 2014, pp. 295–430). This is a stance discordant with the position of Scodel (2002), who assumes minimal knowledge of the audience about the characters and events under Troy as sufficient.

[45] However, this subject was present in the Greek epic tradition in the motif of change this the rape of Ajax, son of Oileus, raping (not on) on Kassandra. Seaford (1994) indicates that Homer deliberately avoids eliciting the graphic images of atrocities present in the tradition, such as incest or matricide. Nagler (1974, pp. 43–63) interprets Achilles's metaphorical definition of the capture of the walls of Troy as a tearing of the *krēdemna*, or the face veil used by married women (xixi 100), as suggesting a picture of rape. The image of the ornaments worn by married women—including the *krēdemna* (XXII 468–472)—being cast off the head of Andromache as she faints at the sight of the death of her husband is also a symbolic sentence.

[46] Nagy (2010, p. 243ff.).

Odysseus listening in the palace of Alcinous, one of kings of the Phaeacians, to the singer Demodocus, is compared to a woman suffering a painful loss of her husband, a widow whose future is cruel captivity. The singer is singing about the capture of Troy, emphasizing Odysseus's outstanding merits in this war. This song is, therefore, a song of praise for Odysseus. Instead of the hero's pride of his own achievements (the song about the Wooden Horse is performed at the request of Odysseus), Odysseus responds by secretly bursting into tears. He also weeps clandestinely when, in his first song, Demodocus conjures up another Trojan incident involving the protagonist. Homer's text assumes two different perspectives for the reception of it: an emotionally involved perspective, where the listener strongly identifies with the suffering of the heroes and a more relaxed perspective, where the viewer is intrigued only by the course of events.[47] The story is not presented as an audacious adventure, but as a series of misfortunes, which, in the case of Odysseus, hinder his return home.

What is surprising, however, is not only the reaction of Odysseus, but, above all, the simile itself. At the moment in which a reference is made to the heroic deeds of the hero, the narrator develops an analogy between the hero and the victims of his actions.[48] Of all the victims of the capture of the city, Homer chooses the situation of a woman (which is understandable, since men were usually murdered), who is the wife of the most important defender. In the tradition of the Trojan War entwined around the *Iliad*, this role is played by Andromache, not mentioned elsewhere in the *Odyssey*. Whether this, however, is an allusion to her specific fate, is not certain, because contrary to what one might expect, there are very few indications that the author of the *Odyssey* knew the story of the *Iliad* familiar to us. In the plots of the songs from the Trojan cycle other than the *Iliad*, the role of the main defender of the Trojans—Priam's son—is ascribed to other heroes. The most important of them, Paris/Alexander, seems to be presented in an unfavorable light in the *Iliad*. He is, however, Helena's husband, and her fate after the fall of Troy differs from the fate of Andromache. Demodocus's song about the siege of Troy mentions the scene which is crucial in Odysseus's praise, a scene in which the hero, together with Menelaus, defeats the son of Priam, Deiphobus, who had been Helena's husband since the death of Paris. Therefore, it would be quite embarrassing to refer to the character of Andromache at this point. The simile rather presents a hypothetical situation, which could have appeared many times in the broadly understood oral tradition.[49]

For the author of the *Odyssey*, the widow of the hero, the city's defender seems to be the most worthy of pity. The image which is evoked in the simile is intended to arouse the listeners' compassion for the unfortunate woman. The extent of her sorrow is revealed by emphasizing the magnitude of her husband's heroism, in whom, just like their children and the entire community, she had lost her support and rescue. Such a hyperbolization of the value of a departed man is typical of women's funeral lamentations. This compassion, however, is also aimed at attaining the compassion of the listeners for the hero to whom the simile refers. One could say that in order to obtain the right emotion for his listeners, the author of the *Odyssey* alludes to the most typical compassion-arousing image in

---

[47] Ford (1997, pp. 413–14) discerns impropriety in his behavior, because a poet's song is supposed to bring joy, pleasure and is so perceived by the gathered Phaeacians. Odysseus's reaction is due to the fact that it is a story about his life, and so he is touched by the mere mentioning of the experienced events. All of them contributed to his current regrettable situation (the reaction of Odysseus has an analogy in the reaction of Penelope to Phemius's song on the Return of Achaeans). In turn, Segal (1994, p. 130ff.) notes that the purpose of the tale in the *Odyssey* is to provoke tears: listeners feel sorry for everyone who talks about their misfortunes, identifying in them the common fate of all mortals (an example is Odysseus's story in Eumaeus's hut). Greene (1999) assesses that inducing tears is a kind of mystical communion of the described past and present for the listeners.
[48] See (Nagy 1999, pp. 100–1).
[49] Let us note that verse VIII 527 contains the phrasing which appears in the aforementioned verse XIX 284, that is when the despair of Briseis over the body of Patroclus is described. Gaca (2008) suggests that Achilles's comparison of Patroclus to a little girl (XVI 7–11) refers to the situation of conquering a city in which the fleeing mother abandons her child. However, it is difficult for me to agree with this interpretation; it seems to me to distort the meaning of Achilles's speech.

this culture.[50] However, using such a simile for this purpose may seem drastic, and even shocking. It is surprising that such a clear reversal of roles should occur: a man is compared to a woman, a victor to a victim, and a war hero to a war captive. In Homer's poems, however, we find another example of similarly extreme reversals of meanings within similes. This may, therefore, point to a characteristic feature of Homeric technique,[51] that is, reaching for such surprising combinations at crucial moments in order to evoke intense emotions in the recipients. Here is one of the most important scenes of the *Iliad*, when the old king Priam arrives to Achilles to beg him to release the body of his dead son. His behavior is illustrated by means of an astounding simile, XXIV 480–484:

ὡς δ' ὅτ' ἂν ἄνδρ' ἄτη πυκινὴ λάβῃ, ὅς τ' ἐνὶ πάτρῃ

φῶτα κατακτείνας ἄλλων ἐξίκετο δῆμον

ἀνδρὸς ἐς ἀφνειοῦ, θάμβος δ' ἔχει εἰσορόωντας,

ὣς Ἀχιλεὺς θάμβησεν ἰδὼν Πρίαμον θεοειδέα·

θάμβησαν δὲ καὶ ἄλλοι, ἐς ἀλλήλους δὲ ἴδοντο.

As when a man is gripped by dense blindness, and in his native country

kills a man, and seeks refuge in a foreign country

in a wealthy lord's house, and amazement overwhelms those looking at him,

so Achilles was astounded when he saw god-like Priam

and the others were astounded as well and looked around at each other.

Priam appears in Achilles's hut suddenly. The simile actually refers only to the surprise which his unexpected arrival engenders among the men present. Meanwhile, it acquires more significance due to the message behind the whole scene. Moments later, Priam humiliates himself in front of Achilles (according to the king of Troy, like no one before him in history), begging for the mercy of his most terrible enemy and kissing the hands of the murderer of his sons. In the image constructed in the simile, the roles are reversed: it is Priam who is represented as a murderer, but one seeking help. The situation of such a man is desperate: he drew down upon himself the vengeance of a family, whose blood he shed, that is why he must leave his country; this deprives him of all protection and dooms him to the fate of an outcast. An outcast is a man of no value: no one respects his judgement (social respect is a measurable indicator of human value), and the lack of family bonds which would protect him expose him to the greatest danger everywhere. So he is forced to plead for protection, completely relying on someone's favor. The then recipient of Homer understood the gravity of the situation in which such a beggar found himself, and the comparison with Priam's lot must have led him to discover how pitiful the position of the Trojan ruler was at the moment and how threatened his life was. Priam's status in Achilles's hut is considerably different from the status he enjoyed when he was leaving the palace. To show us this change in Priam's situation, Homer resorted to portraying the reversal of the roles of both protagonists of this scene: the victim is compared to the murderer, submitting himself to the mercy of the one who is defined as the murderer of his children.

However we are limited to Homeric examples, employing a reversal of meanings in similes seems to be part of tradition.[52] To some extent, one can speak of the automatic and instrumental use of these

---

[50] We can find the same juxtaposition in the above mentioned statement of Hector, in which he anticipates the dire fate of Andromache in captivity—VI 455–463: it will be particularly painful for her, according to Hector, when she is called the ex-wife of Hector, the bravest of the Trojans.

[51] This technique is characteristic for the author of the *Iliad* and the author of the *Odyssey*. Perhaps it means that also other authors used this method, and although the technique is extraordinary, it could also be considered as belonging to the tradition.

[52] Foley (1984) interprets the reverse similes present in the *Odyssey*, in which the reversal of gender roles is shown: men are compared to women and women to men, as an image of the breakdown of social order on Ithaca, which will be restored by

comparisons by the poet-singer. They occur in the strategic moments of the plot, as perceived from the perspective of the task of the singer, which is to represent the hero's glory. There is no doubt that this is true in the case of Achilles's meeting with Priam in the *Iliad*, but perhaps this is less obvious when it comes to the situation described in the *Odyssey*: after all, Odysseus is safe on the island of the Phaeacians, treated like a guest of honor. The aim, however, of each epic is to present the glory of the hero, which he gains by performing a heroic act. Demodocus's song about the Wooden Horse shows the fullness of the glory of the hero, which he deserved, by contributing the most to the capture of Troy. But this is an act whose glory will not survive in human memory, if Odysseus does not return to Ithaca and does not perform a new heroic deed, that is, free his home from the suitors. Demodocus's song reminds him of that glory, but the simile used to describe Odysseus's reaction nullifies it. It rather exposes all the misfortunate circumstances of the hero, simultaneously paving the way for the glory that the hero partakes in this song about Odysseus and which is expressed directly in the apology of Odysseus that follows, and then in his deeds on Ithaca.

However, the above-presented broader analysis of the significance of the comparison of Priam with a murderer does not lead to the conclusion that the poet employs it only in order to describe the surprise of Achilles and his companions, thus acting almost mechanically. The comparison of Priam to a murderer was also shocking for Homer's audience, but it enabled them to appreciate the scale of the king's humiliation. Priam is the king of Troy, so an enemy; therefore there is no reason for the recipients of the *Iliad* to identify with him. This unexpected comparison, however, serves as a catalyst for arousing pity for the king in the listeners. As we have seen, the same role of the catalyst for arousing pity for the hero was played by the comparison of Odysseus to an unfortunate victim of war. The presented comparisons affect the emotional reception of songs in the listeners. And this is not a coincidence. The feeling of pity is the ideological dominance of the *Iliad*, as well as the *Odyssey*.[53]

Conclusions

The evaluation of the attitude towards women enslaved by war in Homeric poems depends on the understanding of what the epic oral tradition is. Homer uses many unique techniques, which are very precisely adapted to the context, and researchers often conclude that these techniques constitute the innovations of the poet who comes beyond the tradition from which he originated. I would like to emphasize that I do not share this way of reasoning. Yet the oral tradition does not mean mechanically reproduced material. Even repetitive elements are subject to constant redistribution and selection. By telling the story, the singer chooses one of the options he follows for a time, which does not mean that he cancels others. In the oral tradition, all elements have an equal meaning, and often co-exist side by side. The constant adaptation of the variety of elements found in the tradition to the context proves the creativity of the oral artist, who repeats what is known, but in a way that he considers to be suitable. Thus, particular songs can acquire individual features associated in the tradition with the name of a particular singer. There is not enough room here, nevertheless, for an in-depth consideration of this issue.

Each time, particular formulas or scenes assume such shape which the author of the *Iliad* or *Odyssey* deems appropriate for expressing his thoughts. It is not true or it is only partially true that the singer cannot omit these repeatable elements and must always evoke them. By conjuring them up at selected moments, he emphasizes what he would like his audience to see. He also tries to gain acceptance of the audience even if this concerns a matter that is not obvious for them, like a familiar,

---

Odysseus reintroducing order into his home (p. 60: "these similes can be interpreted as the most important part of the larger disruption and restoration in the epic"). Foley notices that compared to the fairy-tale worlds visited by Odysseus, it is only in Ithaca that the social roles are properly assigned to both sexes. Thus, the typical mission of the hero, which is to restore the cosmic order, is carried out in the *Odyssey* in the form of restoring order within the *oîkos* and *dêmos*, where this situation is being presented as complicated and multifaceted, largely by means of the unique 'reverse similes'.

[53] Kim (2000).

common belief. One example of such unobvious reactions stimulated in the audience is recognizing one's own reasons for grieving by the victims forced to mourn for a fallen hero with whom the audience identifies. Similarly, the comparison of a hero with a widow led into captivity is not an obvious angle to take. A sense of pity is aroused in the listeners for strangers suffering from misfortune, while the enslaved woman plays an almost symbolic role. However, Homer's goal does not seem to be to present the universal truth about human fate. The hardship of the strangers, especially the calamity of the enslaved and family-deprived women, ultimately serves to depict the scale of the adversity of a hero (likewise in the case of Patroclus, Achilles and Odysseus). The fate of the hero is always the essence of the epic story.

In the world of Homer, the woman captive is treated as a commodity or, phrasing this in terms closer to Homeric axiology, as a measurable expression of respect within the community of conquerors–warriors. In any case, their fate is irrelevant in the context of disputes and wars in which the heroes engage. Nevertheless, appealing to the unfortunate fate of the female victims of war in order to incite the desired sense of pity shows that the poet-singer and his audience shared a sensitivity to the wrongs experienced also by others: not only by men, but also by women. When Homer gives voice to women, they mourn their fate, pointing to the loss brought about by the deaths of the men who used to look after them. The same way of expressing their misfortune is present in women's funeral lamentations. The power of this means of expression, called *goos* in the Greek tradition, is immense. This is due, in my opinion, to the scale of their impact on others, not only women, but even and above all on men, achieved through communicating the most intense emotions of despair and grief. I believe that this explains the persistence of women's lamentations, which—as Alexiou points out[54]—survived up to modern times despite the change of religion to Christianity. The striking or even overwhelming effectiveness of women's lamentations is also a reason why there were the constant attempts to limit this form of feminine expression since antiquity to the present. For as the song should, in my opinion, be regarded as the most effective way of conveying emotions, then measured by the yardstick of effectiveness, the feminine funeral dirge should be considered the most effective of all because it arouses the strongest feeling of despair leading to uncontrolled outbursts of manhood aggression that take the form of revenge. So, in this primordial way men are defenseless against women's crying.

Funding: The research received no external funding.

Conflicts of Interest: The author declares no conflict of interest.

References

Alexiou, Margaret. 2002. *The Ritual Lament in Greek Tradition*, 2nd ed. Revised by Dimitrios Yatromanolakis and Panagiotis Roilos. Lanham, Boulder, New York and Oxford: Rowman & Littlefield Publishers.

Anderson, Michael John. 1997. *The Fall of Troy in Early Greek Poetry and Art*. Oxford: Clarendon Press.

Boardman, John. 1955. Painted Funerary Plaques and Some Remarks on Prothesis. *Annual of the British School at Athens* 50: 51–66. [CrossRef]

Bowra, Cecil Maurice. 1952. *Heroic Poetry*. London: Macmillan.

Bowra, Cecil Maurice. 1962. *Primitive Song*. Cleveland: World Pub. Co.

Cairns, Douglas L. 2001. Introduction. In *Oxford Readings in Homer's Iliad*. Edited by Douglas L. Cairns. Oxford: Oxford University Press.

Cairns, Douglas L. 2011. Ransom and Revenge in the Iliad. In *Sociable Man. Essays on Ancient Greek Social Behaviour in Honoour of Nick Fisher*. Edited by Stephen D. Lambert, Nicolas R. E. Fisher and Douglas L. Cairns. Swansea: Classical Press of Wales, pp. 87–116.

Dalby, Andrew. 2006. *Rediscovering Homer. Inside the Origins of the Epic*. New York and London: W.W. Norton & Company.

---

[54] Alexiou (2002, esp. pp. 49–51).

Dué, Casey. 2002. *Homeric Variations on a Lament by Briseis*. Lanham: Rowman and Littlefield.
Dué, Casey. 2006. *The Captive Woman's Lament in Greek Tragedy*. Austin: University of Texas Press.
Dué, Casey. 2007. Learning Lessons from the Trojan War: Briseis and the Theme of Force. *College Literature* 34: 229–62. [CrossRef]
Elmer, David Franklin. 2013. *The Poetics of Consent. Collective Decision Making and the Iliad*. Baltimore: John Hopkins University Press.
Foley, Helene P. 1984. "Reverse Similes" and Sex Roles in the Odyssey. In *Women in the Ancient World. The Arethusa Papers*. Edited by John Peradotto and John Patrick Sullivan. Albany: State University of New York Press, pp. 59–78.
Foley, John Miles. 1991. *Immanent Art: From Structure to Meaning in Traditional Oral Epic*. Bloomington: Indiana University Press.
Foley, John Miles. 1999. *Homer's Traditional Art*. University Park: The Pennsylvania State University Press.
Ford, Andrew. 1992. *The Poetry of the Past*. Ithaca: Cornell University Press.
Ford, Andrew. 1997. Epic as a Genre. In *A New Companion to Homer*. Edited by Ian Morris and Barry B. Powell. Leiden, New York and Köln: Brill, pp. 396–414.
Gaca, Kathy L. 2008. Reinterpreting the Homeric Simile of Iliad 16.7-11: The Girl and her Mother in Ancient Greek Warfare. *The American Journal of Philology* 129: 145–71. [CrossRef]
Gaca, Kathy L. 2011. Girls, Women, and the Significance of Sexual Violence in Ancient Warfare. In *Sexual Violence in Conflict Zones. From the Ancient World to the Era of Human Rights*. Edited by Elizabeth D. Heineman. Philadelphia: University of Pennsylvania Press, pp. 73–88.
Goody, Jack. 1977. *The Domestication of the Savage Mind*. Cambridge: Cambridge University Press.
Goody, Jack. 1986. *The Logic of Writing and the Organisation of Society*. Cambridge: Cambridge University Press.
Goody, Jack. 2010. *Myth, Ritual, and the Oral*. Cambridge: Cambridge University Press.
Gottschall, Jonathan. 2008. *The Rape of Troy: Evolution, Violence, and the World of Homer*. Cambridge: Cambridge University Press.
Graziozi, Barbara, and Johannes Haubold. 2010. *Homer Iliad: Book VI*. Cambridge: Cambridge University Press.
Greene, Thomas M. 1999. The natural Tears of Epic. In *Epic Traditions in the Contemporary World: The Poetics of Community*. Edited by Margaret Beissinger, Jane Tylus and Susanne Wofford. Berkeley: University of California Press, pp. 189–202.
Griffin, Jasper. 1980. *Homer on Life and Death*. Oxford: Clarendon Press.
Havelock, Eric Alfred. 1963. *Preface to Plato*. Cambridge: Belknap Press, Harvard University Press.
Havelock, Eric Alfred. 1982. *The Literate Revolution in Greece and its Cultural Consequences*. Princeton: Princeton University Press.
Havelock, Eric Alfred. 1986. *The Muse Learns to Write: Reflections on Orality and Literacy from Antiquity to the Present*. New Haven: Yale University Press.
Hitch, Sarah. 2009. *King of Sacrifice: Ritual and Royal Authority in the Iliad*. Washington: Centre for Hellenic Studies, Trustees for Harvard University, Cambridge: Distributed by Harvard University Press.
Jamison, Stephanie W. 1999. Penelope and the Pigs: Indic Perspectives on the Odyssey. *Classical Antiquity* 18: 227–72. [CrossRef]
Kim, Jinyo. 2000. *The Pity of Achilles: Oral Style and the Unity of the Iliad*. Lanham, Boulder, New York and Oxford: Rowman and Littlefield.
Lesky, Albin. 1963. *Geschichte der Griechischen Literatur*. Bern: De Gruyter.
Lesky, Albin. 1967. Oral Poetry als Voraussetzung der Homerischen Epen. In *Homeros*. Albin Lesky, Sonderausgabe der Paulyschen Realencyclopädie der Klassischen Altertumwissenschaft, Supplement-Band IX. Stuttgart: A. Druckenmüller, pp. 7–18.
Lord, Albert. 1960. *The Singer of Tales*. Cambridge: Harvard University Press.
McInerney, Jeremy. 2010. *The Cattle of the Sun. Cows and Culture in the World of the Ancient Greeks*. Princeton: Princeton University Press.
Murnaghan, Sheila. 1999. The Poetics of Loss in Greek Epic. In *Epic Traditions in the Contemporary World*. Edited by Margaret Beissinger, Jane Tylus and Susanne Wofford. Berkeley: University of California Press, pp. 203–20.
Nagler, Michael. 1974. *Spontaneity and Tradition: A Study in Oral Art of Homer*. Berkeley: University of California Press.
Nagy, Gregory. 1996. *Poetry and Perfomance: Homer and Beyond*. Cambridge: Cambridge University Press.

Nagy, Gregory. 1999. *Best of the Achaeans: Concepts of the Hero in Archaic Greek Poetry*, 2nd ed. Baltimore: Johns Hopkins University Press.

Nagy, Gregory. 2010. *Homer the Preclassic*. Berkeley, Los Angeles and London: University of California Press.

Ong, Walter Jackson. 1982. *Orality and Literacy: The Technologizing of the Word*. London and New York: Methuen.

Parry, Adam. 1966. Have We Homer's Iliad? *Yale Classical Studies* 20: 175–216.

Rabinowitz, Nancy Sorkin. 1998. Slaves with Slaves: Women and Class in Euripedean Tragedy. In *Women and Slaves in Greco-Roman Culture: Differential Equations*. Edited by Sandra Rae Joshel and Sheila Murnaghan. London: Routledge, pp. 56–68.

Richardson, Nicholas. 1993. *The Iliad: A Commentary*. Cambridge: Cambridge University Press, Vol. VI, pp. 21–24.

Russo, Joseph. 1978. How and what does Homer communicate? The Medium and Message of Homeric Verse. In *Communication Arts in the Ancient World*. Edited by Eric Alfred Havelock and Jackson P. Hershbell. New York: Hastings House.

Scodel, Ruth. 2002. *Listening to Homer: Tradition, Narrative, and Audience*. Ann Arbor: University of Michigan Press.

Seaford, Richard. 1994. *Reciprocity and Ritual. Homer and Tragedy in the Developing City-State*. Oxford: Clarendon Press.

Segal, Charles. 1994. *Singers, Heroes, and Gods in the Odyssey*. Ithaca: Cornell University Press.

Stoevesandt, Magdalene. 2016. *Homer's Iliad: The Basel Commentary*. Book 6. Berlin and Boston: De Gruyter.

Tsagalis, Christos. 2004a. *Epic Grief: Personal Laments in Homer's Iliad*. Berlin and New York: De Gruyter.

Tsagalis, Christos. 2004b. The Poetics of Sorrow: Thetis' Lament in "Iliad" 18. *Quaderni Urbinati di Cultura Classica* 76: 9–32. [CrossRef]

Van Wees, Hans. 1992. *Status Warriors. War, Violence and Society in Homer and History*. Amsterdam: J.C. Gieben.

Walcot, Peter. 1979. Cattle Raiding, Heroic Tradition, and Ritual. The Greek Evidence. *History of Religions* 18: 326–51. [CrossRef]

West, Martin Litchfield. 2011. *The Making of the Iliad: Disquisition and Analytical Commentary*. Oxford: Oxford University Press.

West, Martin Litchfield. 2015. *The Making of the Odyssey*. Oxford: Oxford University Press.

Zieliński, Karol. 2014. *Iliada i jej tradycja epicka. Studium z zakresu greckiej tradycji oralnej*. Wrocław: Wydawnictwo Uniwersytetu Wrocławskiego.

© 2019 by the author. Licensee MDPI, Basel, Switzerland. This article is an open access article distributed under the terms and conditions of the Creative Commons Attribution (CC BY) license (http://creativecommons.org/licenses/by/4.0/).

Article

The Rhetoric of Krishna versus the Counter-Rhetoric of Vyas: The Place of Commiseration in the *Mahabharat*

Bhushan Aryal

Liberal Arts and Education Department, University of Minnesota Crookston, Crookston, MN 56716, USA; aryalb@umn.edu

Received: 13 February 2019; Accepted: 17 September 2019; Published: 23 September 2019

Abstract: In the context of the mixed perception among scholars whether the *Mahabharat* is a pacifist or a militant text, this paper analyzes the rhetorical project of the epic to examine its position on violence. Highlighting the existence of two main arguments in the *Mahabharat*, this paper argues that the author has crafted a grand rhetorical project to question the dominant war ideology of the time that Krishna presents as the divine necessity. Historically, the emergence of Krishna—one of the major characters of the epic—as an incarnation of Lord Vishnu in Hindu tradition and the extraction and elevation of the *Bhagavad Gita* from the epic as an independent text have undermined the complexity of Vyas' rhetoric. This paper places Krishna's argument within the broad rhetorical scheme of the epic and demonstrates how Vyas has represented Krishna's rhetoric of 'just war' only to illustrate its pitfalls. By directing his narrative lens to the devastating consequences of the war in the later parts of the epic, Vyas problematizes Krishna's insistence on the need to suppress human emotions to attain a higher cognitive and ontological condition. What emerges is the difference between how Vyas and Krishna view the status of feeling: the scientist Krishna thinks that human emotions and individual lives are trivial, incidental instances in the cosmic game—something not worthy of a warrior's concern; Vyas' rhetoric, this paper argues, restores the significance of ordinary human emotions. It is a war—not human life and feeling—that arises as a futile enterprise in Vyas' rhetoric.

Keywords: rhetoric in the mahabharat; krishan's rhetoric; vyas' rhetoric; commiseration in arjun; south-asian rhetoric

---

As the battle in the *Mahabharat* is about to begin, the epic's most skilled archer is overwhelmed when he sees the prospect of killing his relatives fighting against him from the enemy battalion.[1] In this, one of the most unanticipated dramatic moments in this classical South Asian epic, Arjun finds the war futile when compared to the death and destruction that it would bring. Disarming himself, he informs his charioteer Krishna about his decision to not fight the war anymore:

> O Krishna, I have no desire for victory, or for a kingdom or pleasures. Of what use is a kingdom or pleasure or even life, if those for whose sake we desire these things—teachers, fathers, sons, grandfathers, uncles, in-laws, and others with family ties—are engaging in this battle, renouncing their wealth and their lives. Even if they were to kill me, I would not want to kill them, not even to become the ruler of the three worlds.[2]

Responding to this agonized warrior, Krishna—the revered spiritual master—delivers the long sermon encapsulated in the *Bhagavad Gita*, where he convinces Arjun to resume the war, despite the disciple's

---

1   The epic is available on public domain here: http://www.gutenberg.org/files/15474/15474-h/15474-h.htm (accessed on 13 January 2019).
2   *Gita*, 1: 32–35. For the *Gita*'s citation, the articles uses the following text: Eknath Easwaran, trans., *The Bhagavad Gita* (Easwaran 1985).

constant questioning of the war's ultimate advantage.[3] Indeed, Krishna has tried to avert the war before, but he does not use this opportunity to explore the possibilities of peace further. This condition leads to the question: why does he not stop the impending carnage? Given the *Mahabharat's* cultural capital in the South Asian subcontinent, this question has been raised for centuries, primarily to examine the epic's position on the appropriateness of the use of violence and the value of human emotions.[4]

One dominant interpretation has been that the war is preordained in the *Mahabharat*. Built on what Krishna states at one point, that he has incarnated himself to restore the balance in the world through the religious war, this perspective presents Krishna's birth as a fact of the war's inevitability; he is at the scene not to stop the war but to direct it to the desired outcome. So, whatever attempts he carries out to broker the peace between Pandav and Kaurav represent merely playful pretenses, not serious endeavors. The Kaurav brothers are evil, and the only way to get rid of the evil in them is to destroy them through the war. No language of compromise works for them.

This paper begins by questioning the total truth of this interpretation. When all incidents and events in the epic are analyzed together, the war emerges as the product of unresolved negotiations, not an inevitable occurrence. Accepting the predetermination of something precludes the power of rhetorical exchanges to make a difference in the world. Attributing the value of representing Krishna's true intentions to some of his words and actions while relegating others to meaninglessness by characterizing them as playful pretenses may assist his admirers in creating a more favorable image of him, but it fails to accord justice to the whole rhetorical and literary project incorporated in the *Mahabharat*. This paper is a small attempt to change that approach by foregrounding Vyas' rhetorical lens.

Because the issue is central to the Vyas' rhetorical project, this article primarily participates in the scholarly conversation about the use of violence in the *Mahabharat*. Simultaneously, the paper also aims to contribute to the academic discussion of non-western, particularly South Asian, rhetorical tradition. The article should add a new dimension to the scope of South Asian rhetoric by establishing how the *Mahabharat* is a lofty rhetorical project, where the author takes up a celebrated teacher's ethos and argument for 'just war' only to dissect them by presenting their shocking material corollaries.[5]

About the use of violence in the *Mahabharat*, commentators hold divided opinions. Wendy Doniger captures this division succinctly when she highlights how the same book has been used historically both for pacifist and militant purposes. Reviewing Richard H. Davis' *The Bhagavad Gita: A Biography*, she writes, "we might divide [the interpretations of the book] into two broad groups: what I would call the warrior's *Gita*, about engaging in the world, and the philosopher's *Gita*, about disengaging."[6] Commenting on whether the *Gita* incites violence, Eknath Easwaran points us to Gandhi: "Gandhi had a practical answer: just base your life on the *Gita* sincerely and systematically and see if you find killing or even hurting others compatible with its teaching."[7] While Easwaran does not foreground this part, Dipesh Chakrabarty and Rochona Majumdar demonstrate that Gandhi's pacifist interpretation of the *Gita* in itself was a strategic deployment of the text to counter its militant reception by some early

---

[3] Widely distributed as a separate book, the *Bhagavad Gita* comes from the *Mahabharat*. Suspecting that such a long discourse at the battlefield could not have been a logical part of the narrative, many commentators think of the *Gita* as a later interpolation; see (Pandit 1992). Critics also insist on the integrity of the *Gita* with the epic, emphasizing how the ideas in the *Gita* are thoroughly interwoven throughout the larger text: See (Upadhyaya 2000).

[4] For the broad impact and reception of the text, see this work: Richard H. Davis, *The Bhagavad Gita: A Biography* (Davis 2015).

[5] While the epic has generated substantial literary studies, not much rhetorical analysis of the text exists; few existing works within the broad rhetorical field is limited to the *Gita* that mainly highlight on the nature of philosophy and argumentation. One notable reception of the epic in the field recently has been Iswari Pandey's book, *South Asian in the Mid-South: Migrations of Literacies* (Pandey 2015). Although the work is not entirely about the rhetoric in the *Mahabharat*, Pandey demonstrates how the literacy practices of recent Hindu immigrants to the United States from South Asia have used the stories from the epic as the heritage for their cultural preservation and identity formation.

[6] (Doniger 2014).

[7] Easwaran, "Introduction," *Gita*, 20.

twentieth-century Indian revolutionaries, such as Bal Gangadhar Tilak and Sri Aurobindo.[8] Given the epic's grand and layered narrative, it is not surprising that the *Mahabharata* lends itself to multiple, often contradictory, interpretations, but the same complexity should not deter us from posing the question of whether the text has a more coherent view on the use of violence.

1. Foregrounding Vyas's Rhetorical Project

In this context, I argue that an analysis of the author's rhetoric can elucidate the mixed reception highlighted in the previous paragraph.[9] The different opinions, I contend, emanate from the fact that the *Mahabharata* has two separate major arguments about war—those of Krishna and Vyas.[10] Their difference arises from where they place the emotion in the hierarchy of significance. Characterizing emotions as fleeting and irrelevant phenomena in the cosmic scheme of things, Krishna downplays the value of commiseration or other human emotions, whether felt during or in the aftermath of the war. Krishna's argument is so sophisticated and comes with such prominence in the epic that he may appear to be the authorial mouthpiece, but the whole point of the *Mahabharat*, I argue, is to expose the devastating consequences of Krishna's logic and to restore the value of commiseration and non-violence. For that purpose, Vyas probes the rhetoric of 'just war' embedded in Krishna's oratory.

The doctrine of just war has multicultural, multi-religious, and secular roots and practices—a reason I am characterizing it as having a universal resonance.[11] Any war, whether it is carried out to expand one community's influence or resist their enemy, demands a justification because of the inherently problematic nature of violence. At the core of the 'just war' rhetoric rests the notion that a fair-minded humane culture or community should not go for war unless it is absolutely necessary, without any alternative course of action. In a way, the doctrine of just war sets limits within a culture or a country, instilling an anti-militant value system. However, as this paper discusses, the same value system is often used to initiate a war and mobilize people. While the rhetoric of just war found in different religious, national, and historical contexts may include context-specific content, they mostly have in common a reference to some lofty ideal, an explanation of the absence of other options, and the characterization of the other as evil. Just war rhetoric assigns appropriate reasons for war, eliciting war-supporting emotions among followers, believers, or citizens. Since there is not a non-discursive indicator to determine exactly when and whether the condition for the war has become an absolute necessity, the rhetoric of just war comes into play, depending on participants' motivations, power dynamics among the parties in conflict, and philosophical resources available to the rhetoricians making a case for or against the war.

As this article demonstrates, questioning the ideology of 'just war' imprinted in the collective human unconscious, something that is expressed through various religious and patriotic forms and fought for centuries after centuries, required the double eyes—the eyes that could feel the logical throbs of the charismatic leader like Krishna, and also could render the subtlest of human emotions with an artist's sensitivity. Vyas brings forth both of them by first creating the rhetoric of Krishna and then by laying bare its devastating consequences. Using the Rogerian rhetorical approach long before Carl Rogers hinted at it and communication scholars later theorized it, Vyas first portrays

---

[8] See (Chakrabarty and Majumdar 2010).
[9] This article is not about Vyas the sage who plays different roles at various moments in the epic. The Vyas the author that this article discusses is the collective of those scribes and bards who churned this epic over many centuries and gave humanity one of the most powerful texts.
[10] Indeed, the current trend of transforming Hinduism into an organized religion has inspired many religious activists to historicize Krishna, particularly to match the historical provenances of Buddhism and Christianity. It is possible that a historical figure might have inspired the creation of the Krishna character, but I'm treating him primarily as a character developed by the collective authorship of Vyas. And, for those who object to this characterization of Krishna, here is an idea: a powerful character (as all gods and goddesses are) can have more influence on reality-production than a historical person. For the complexity of establishing the historical authorship of the *Mahabharata*, see (Satchidanandan 2009).
[11] For the doctrine of just war in the Christian tradition, see (Johnson 1975).

Krishna and his argument credibly, developing Krishna as the most admirable person of the epic.[12] Krishna gets represented as what their admirers would perceive any cherished war hero. So, instead of automatically slandering the idea that he was going to interrogate, Vyas gives Krishna and his views their due place, letting their strengths speak for themselves. Because of this strategy, readers get to see Krishna in a complete form with all his logical, personal, and divine manifestations. In this rhetorical maneuver, Vyas thus sets up Krishna to be loved by his readers in the way they would admire a captivating commander of any war.

However, the epic does not end there, and that is where Vyas' counter rhetoric comes into play. In *Stri Purva* and *Shanti Purva* (*Books of Women* and *Book of Peace*, respectively), Vyas zooms his narrative lens on the scenes in the aftermath of the war with such searing graphic detail that readers come to question the wisdom of the war. The wailing women and children, dismembered warriors, and widespread hopelessness pervade the atmosphere. In these books, which I am arguing we should accord the same significance allotted to the *Gita*, Vyas juxtaposes the catastrophic consequences of the war with the amazing ideology that encouraged it.

2. Krishna's War Rhetoric and Its Universal Resonance

Before analyzing how Vyas treats Krishna and his argument further, let us contextualize Krishna's argument first[13]. At the outset of the battle between the Pandav and Kaurav at Kurukshetra, Pandav Prince Arjun generates a sense of empathy for his cousins, uncles, and teachers, who have grouped to war against him.[14] Seeing the futility of winning a war by slaying his relatives, he throws away his bow. Krishna, whom Arjun deeply respects, delivers the long discourse demonstrating how fighting—instead of being governed by commiseration and other flippant emotions—was the best course of action for a Kshatriya warrior like him.[15] Besides reminding Arjun of his Kshatriya Dharma, Krishna also uses various philosophies dominant at the time to persuade Arjun back to the battle.[16] However, when Arjun remains adamant in his resolve by questioning everything Krishna stated, he equips Arjun with a spiritual vision, where he reveals his divine selfhood and the operating mechanism of the cosmos.[17]

Through that vision, Krishna initiates Arjun to the cosmic vision said to have been experienced by deep meditators, a mystic experience that Krishna presents as pure ontology.[18] In this vision, the differences among people and things appear as a phenomenal illusion; the deeper reality opens as an undifferentiated wavelike whole, with the Brahman spirit pervading the existence. All beings and things—as if there were a difference between them—are thus automatically the parts of that spirit, emanating from the same source and plunging back into the same eternal omnipresence. While the Atman migrates from one being to another in the transformative cosmic process, the phenomenal beings themselves are impermanent.[19] Commenting on this vision, Barbara Stoler Miller writes, "the aspect of himself that Krishna reveals to Arjun on the battlefield embodies time's deadly destructiveness: a fearsome explosion of countless eyes, bellies, mouths, ornaments, and weapons—gleaming like

---

[12] For Rogerian argument, see (Ede 1984). Ede's article highlights the complexity of correspondence between Carl Rogers' psychological theories and its use in communication and writing studies. By characterizing Vyas' rhetoric as Rogerian, I'm emphasizing on his respectful representation of Krishna's argument.
[13] Thapar (2009) argues that the *Mahabharata* represents the transitional moment of ancient Indian society from clan to caste system.
[14] *Gita*, 1: 31–32.
[15] *Gita*, 2: 31–37.
[16] *Gita*, 2: 39–53.
[17] *Gita*, 3:1; 4:4; 6: 33–34.
[18] For the philosophical dimension of *Gita*, see (Stroud 2005). Also see (Maitra 2006).
[19] Krishna's ontological vision may have some parallel with modern quantum physics. See (Capra 1975).

the fiery sun that illuminates the world."[20] Using the terms of modern science, Krishna presents his understanding of the time-space puzzle of the universe in its most churning physiological dimension.[21]

In this cosmic context—Krishna continues—Arjun should not let his feelings debilitate his resolution for action. The people, for whose sake he wants to abandon his Kshatriya Dharma, existed in the current form momentarily. The truth is he could neither kill them nor could bring them back to human forms.[22] Since their death was merely a small part in the transformative cycle of the world, he should internalize this cosmic picture, and thus not permit his momentary emotion to cloud his judgment. Abandoning his duty would not save his relatives as they were destined to die whether or not Arjun becomes a vehicle in the process. The argument continues like this: If Arjun could do anything meaningful and dignified in this context, it would be combatting the evil for the restoration of righteousness.

This explanation of how the world operates dissociates Arjun from his "consubstantiality" with his Kaurav cousins. As rhetorician Kenneth Burke has defined, consubstantiality is that fabric of connection between two distinct people, where one identifies another as made up of the same substance, promoting confidence and desire for mutual protection.[23] Theorized in the context of World War II, the notion of consubstantiality helped Burke understand why in the chaos of the war Allies and Axis powers placed all their energy to obliterate one another while keeping the cohesion of disparate forces within them intact. In this theorization, consubstantiality—or its absence thereof—determines who commiserates with whom.

In the case of Arjun, he indeed has trained his whole life to build a war-appropriate body and mind so that no enfeebling emotions would perturb him during the war. However, when faced with the prospect of the death of his cousins and teachers in his hand, the fundamental human desire for connection intervenes into his trained temperament, failing him to maintain his composure. He feels a human connection with them; at that moment he could not visualize them as an abstract embodiment of evil as theorized by Krishna; they remain standing before him as the flesh-and-blood people with whom he has grown. This experience disrupts his mental disposition that is essential to a fighter governed by the Kshatriya code.

In that context, it becomes Krishna's challenge to unsettle that connection so that Arjun could restart seeing his relationships using the same abstract values such as good and evil prevailing in the warrior's code. But, as stated above, the problem is that Kshatriya Dharma or the duty recognized by the tradition alone does not suffice to persuade Arjun. Krishna thus has to show "the ultimate truth" of the existence, a vision that asks him to see his enemies in theoretical terms as chemical/biological compositions that transform continuously from one state to another. In this formulation, attaching emotional connection with momentarily living bodies would mean falling under the spell of Maya—not knowing the law that governs the universe. So, Krishna asks Arjun to see how the human relationship formed between himself and his enemies was merely a small incidence in the eternity of time, and thus not worthy of a warrior's emotional investment. Therefore, as Krishna explains, Arjun is required to detach himself emotionally from his relatives so that he could contribute to Krishna's campaign of restoring justice and righteousness in the world.

This kind of rhetoric of 'just wars' has a universal resonance. War leaders use it as a rhetorical ploy as contemporaneously now as Krishna deployed it in the *Mahabharat* time. They justify wars with abstract noble ideas. This kind of war narratives portray the deaths of ordinary people, including soldiers, as a necessary sacrifice for achieving or maintaining a larger common good. This line of

---

[20] (Miller 1986).
[21] I write this note in the afternoon of April 10, 2019, the day when scientists have revealed a new picture of the black hole. The picture reminds me of the mouth that Krishna describes in the *Gita*. The mouth as he says is the all-powerful physical phenomenon that engulfs planets and other heavenly bodies.
[22] *Gita*, 2: 12.
[23] See (Burke 1969).

Manichean argumentation characterizes the enemy—sometimes justifiably—as evil time and again. It is not problematic that evil is spotted and fought; what is concerning is that this kind of rhetoric does not value common lives in and for themselves.[24] What loses in this process is the significance of emotional fabrics, connections, and joys of common life—the extraordinary traits of humanity.

3. Vyas's Rhetorical Design: The Double Eyes Representing and Critiquing Krishna

Given the universal resonance of the rhetoric of just war, the questions then become these: How does Vyas confront Krishna's rhetoric? What exactly does he do? What does his rhetoric have to do with the fundamental human attributes such as commiseration and empathy? Vyas uses a two-part strategy to expose the consequences of the rhetoric of the just war. The first part of his rhetorical approach represents Krishna's rhetoric—particularly the Kshatriya war code—authentically, so that all of its valid points and shining observations on existence receive due credit. The discussion up to this point in this article has largely covered the first part of Vyas' rhetorical process. In his second part of the strategy, he shows the devastating impact of that ideology by focusing his attention on the conditions of people in the aftermath of the war, when the Kshatriya war code has unfolded in its full intensity. He does that particularly by highlighting the condition of women in the *Book of Women* and Yudhishthira's state of mind in the *Book of Peace*. What emerges from these two books is Vyas's denunciation of Krishna's indifferent view about human emotion, a forceful revelation that empathy and commiseration are not human limitations standing on the road to Dharma as Krishna argues, but the soul of it.[25]

In *Stri Parva* (*Book of Women*), Vyas critiques Krishna's rhetoric graphically. Instead of weaving his counterargument with a different set of reasoning, he concentrates his narrative lens on the shattered landscape strewn with dismembered corpses, the disfigured rivers deluged with fresh blood, and the frightening silence reigned by a cruel death.[26] In place of Krishna's transcendental cosmic vision abstracted from daily human reality, Vyas paints a catastrophe picture for the mortals to see and contemplate. At the end of the war, in suffering and death, both sides lose the sense of their difference. In this picture of stunning unison, all the talks of bravery, duty, and enlightenment that led to the devastation of common lives sound preposterously chilling. The scene is that of death, wailing, and human senselessness. Following is a passage from that context for your perusal:

> At that time a loud wail of woe arose from every Kuru house. The whole city, including the very children, became exceedingly afflicted with grief. Those ladies that had not before this been seen by gods were now helpless ... Seizing each other by the hand, they uttered loud wails after their sons and brothers and sires. They seemed to exhibit the scene that takes place on the occasion of the universal destruction at the end of a Yuga. Weeping and crying and running hither and thither, and deprived of their senses by grief, they knew not what to do. Those ladies who formally felt the blush of modesty in the presence of even companions of their own sex, now felt no blush of shame though scantily clad, in appearing before their mothers-in-law. Formally, they used to comfort each other while afflicted with even slight causes of woe. Stupefied by grief, they now, O king, refrained from even casting their eyes upon each other.[27]

---

[24] Sometimes, the way evil is framed/defined can be problematic.
[25] There are many translations of the *Mahabharata*. This paper uses Vyasa (1883). The citations of the *Mahabharata* in this paper are from the web link included above. Since the web link does not state specific pages effectively, I will refer to the Parva (the book) and will include URLs to locate the source.
[26] Indeed, Kurukshetra has surviving intellectuals such as Bidur still propagating the dominant ideology that justified the war even now in the aftermath. However, those statements that inspired lofty passions before and during the war are so out of the place now that they look absurdly hypocritical among the corpses and bereaving souls.
[27] *Mahabharata*, Book of Women. (http://www.sacred-texts.com/hin/m11/m11010.htm).

This description, read in connection with the larger context of the epic, particularly in juxtaposition to Krishna's teaching in the *Bhagavad Gita*, inverts the essence of Dharma. As Krishna expounded, treading on the path of Dharma (the dominant ideology of the Kshatriya Caste) required Arjun to detach his "true self" from his emotions, so that he could follow the Dharma and participate in the righteous war. Since the fight is internal as much as the one fought on the external physical realm, his suppression of emotion would transform the flesh-and-blood human enemies that were antithetical to the religious order into abstracted objectified others. In this description, stunned by the calamity of the war, the mass of women and children has lost their ability to feel the basic emotions. Also missing is their ability to maintain social dignity, the common Dharma expected of them by their customs and culture, including the habit of caring for each other during the difficult moments of life. It is ironic that Krishna's call for the detachment from one's emotions for the sake of a higher duty of justice results in shock and terror among the most vulnerable sections of society.

Vyas's interrogation of Krishna's war rhetoric continues in the *Book of Peace* (*Shanti Purva*), as the narrator places his attention on the mental state of the victors. Unlike in the previous book—the *Book of Women*—the critique now is more discourse driven. In this book, Vyas makes a strategic rhetorical decision by choosing to tell the story from Yudhishthira's perspective, because Yudhishthira's high reputation for his adherence to justice and righteousness is of paramount significance for Vyas' rhetorical project. Yudhishthira may speak from within the dominant intellectual and cultural framework that justified the war, yet his cultural capital provides Vyas a character with a unique upright ethos for the final assessment of the war ideology. That the war has come to an end, and all of its impacts have been laid bare before eyes, Yudhishthira's discourse now must include his reflection on the facts from the ground instead of merely repeating the lofty words from the ideology of just war. The book presents the new king Yudhishthira finding his victory pointless as he questions the arguments and interests that supported the war in the context of death and destruction surrounding him.

In this book, Yudhishthira condemns the fundamental attributes of Kshatriya Dharma: "fie on the usages of Kshatriyas, fie on might and valor, and fie on wrath, since through these such a calamity hath overtaken us."[28] He realizes that the esteemed qualities such as might, bravery, and wrath had failed the warriors to recognize the thin fabrics of empathy and commiseration. Now, with the consequences of the war with them, the otherwise prized assets emerge merely as pretexts used by them to fulfill a subliminal human urge for blood. He states, "like a pack of dogs fighting one another for a piece of meat, a great disaster has overtaken us! That piece of meat is no longer dear to us."[29] With a cruel revelation, an intuitive understanding dawns onto Yudhishthira that what they had fought for was not a clean and sophisticated ideal but an enactment of the brutish impulse lodged in them.

The idea of commiseration runs deep in Yudhishthira's lamentation. For instance, he states how an ordinary beggar's life would have been preferable for him now to the king's wealth and power. He says to Arjun, "if, O Arjun, we had led a life of mendicancy in the cities of the Vrishnis and the Andhakas, then this miserable end would not have been ours in consequence of having exterminated our kinsmen."[30] Not only is such a state emotionally deranging, but Yudhishthira also finds it morally disturbing as well. He continues, "our foes, the Kurus, have gained prosperity, while we have become divested of all the objects of life, for what fruits of righteousness can be ours when we have guilty of self-slaughter?"[31] As Yudhishthira starts making sense of what had just happened for the last 18 days of the war, the guilt of not acting on finer emotions overwhelms him.

Another recurrent theme in Yudhishthira's discourse is war's emotional toll on participants, including the victors themselves. As his state of mind suggests, the unbearable loss of friends and relatives, many of them in the prime of their youth, deprives the survivors a general joy of life.

---

[28] *Mahabharata*, Book of Peace, Section VII. (https://www.sacred-texts.com/hin/m12/m12a007.htm).
[29] *Mahabharata*, Book of Peace, Section VII. (https://www.sacred-texts.com/hin/m12/m12a007.htm).
[30] *Mahabharata*, Book of Peace, Section VII. (https://www.sacred-texts.com/hin/m12/m12a007.htm).
[31] *Mahabharata*, Book of Peace, Section VII. (https://www.sacred-texts.com/hin/m12/m12a007.htm).

Yudhishthira captures the irony of the situation: "alas, having slain, for the sake of the earth, such lords of the earth as deserved not to be slain by us, we are bearing the weight of existence, deprived of friends and bereft of the very objects of life."[32] Going to the war, they had aimed for a slice of earth, but they have returned with the unbearable "weight of the existence" and "bereft of the very objects of life."

To understand the futility of the war suggested in Yudhishthira's lamentation, we have to attend to the phrase "object of life" that he uses repetitively in the book. Examining his past and present contexts, he feels and states how the whole discourse of 'just war' misunderstood and misrepresented proper "object of life." As Krishna presented in the *Gita*, the dominant ideology of the time interpreted the attainment of selfhood liberated from the shackles of worldly connections as the true "object of life." The object of life, the argument continues, should be the realization of pure rational spirituality so that the self could unite with the elemental cosmic essence. Not attaining that union is a sheer waste of precious human life and its high cognitive capacity. For that union, as Krishna frames, a Karma Yogi like Arjun, who has followed the path of action for spiritual liberation, is not required to renounce social obligations, as practiced by other traditional seekers of that essence, but could realize it by observing their responsibilities, particularly by disengaging themselves emotionally from the results of their action.

Embedded within this thought tradition, Yudhishthira lacks the intellectual resources or courage to deconstruct the logical sophistication of Krishna's rhetoric.[33] Therefore, the book does not contain comparably developed counter-rhetoric in Yudhisthira on the "object of life". However, that deficiency does not stop Yudhishthira from making the case of a thorough reevaluation of the dominant ideology of Kshatriya Dharma, because he finds a misalignment between the ideology and the proper "object of life." It is in this connection, the chaos and collapse of the war remind him of the maternal instinct and their nurturing efforts: "by fasts and sacrifices and sacred rites and auspicious ceremonies mothers conceive."[34] However, what the war has done to their sons must make us think of the "object of life" in a different fashion: "alas, since their sons, youth in years and resplendent with ear-rings, have been slain, therefore, those expectations of theirs rendered fruitless, have been abandoned by them."[35] For him, this becomes the question: should not the good feelings and simple joys amidst the beauty of nature be the "objects of life?" Framing the debate in this way, Vyas contrasts his views on the significance of human commiseration from Krishna's teaching. From Krishna's perspective, human lives—no matter how refined within the biological system—ultimately vanish in the biochemical drama of the physical world. Little human lives and their emotions do not factor substantially in the larger ontological stratum, a position that does not depart vastly from our prevailing scientific worldview, consisting of the ever-expanding universe as a journey between the big bang and the singularity crunch.[36] For Krishna, the mantra becomes "follow the current warrior code". Krishna's encounter with Gandhari for the first time after the war further illustrates this point. When asked why he let the bloodshed happen by this blind-folded bereaving mother, Krishna smiles back at her, instead of sympathizing with her grief. He is indifferent, almost absurdist about human emotion.[37] For him,

---

[32] *Mahabharata*, Book of Peace, Section VII. (https://www.sacred-texts.com/hin/m12/m12a007.htm).
[33] I'm using the word rhetoric in the broadest sense of the term. Rhetoric, as used here, is a totality of discourse incorporating the elements far beyond argumentation and delivery.
[34] *Mahabharata*, Book of Peace, Section VII. (https://www.sacred-texts.com/hin/m12/m12a007.htm).
[35] *Mahabharata*, Book of Peace, Section VII. (https://www.sacred-texts.com/hin/m12/m12a007.htm).
[36] Easwaran, *Gita*, 164.
[37] The use of the term "absurd" to interpret the *Gita* may elicit an opposition, especially in light of how the twentieth-century European absurdist movement defines the word that negates the existence of anything supreme beyond human consciousness and thus the possibility of any providential meaning of human life. The *Gita* is a paramount spiritual text that emphasizes the presence of the supreme consciousness and unique human capacity to enlightenment in contact with that Supreme Being. While the *Gita* firmly establishes the god's existence, it also presents the human life more from an elemental scientific view that characterizes human emotions as the products myopic human perspective without much consequences on the broader world. Thus, human emotions, while significant for human beings themselves, do not appear to be of any effect in the cosmic ontology envisioned in Krishna's teaching.

battle and death are insignificant in the grand scheme of things. From his perspective, Gandhari's emotions—while deep and devastating in themselves—are merely the transitory outpouring from a mother without an intellectual capacity to distinguish between the worldly attachment and the true spirit of the existence. In the transformative wheel of the universe, deliberate human actions do not make a significant difference; while the attainment of spiritual liberation would place a person closer with the ultimate reality, even that achievement does not make much of a difference in the totality of the essence. In this context, it is important to note that while Krishna offers the soaring rhetoric persuading Arjun to take up his arms again, an examination of his actions and expressions suggests that a particular result, or even whether the war takes place, does not make much of a difference for him. That Krishna gives his army to Duryodhana, although he is counseling Arjun, suggests that the charismatic master is not totally for one side; he could maintain an equanimity irrespective of the battle. As he states, when Krishna is the cosmos himself, nothing remains to be gained or lost at the battlefield at Kurukshetra. Krishna's response to Gandhari should therefore be placed within the larger theory of detachment that he transmitted to Arjun earlier.

Unquestionably, detachment and equanimity are central characteristics cultivated by seasoned mystics and meditators, which help them rise above the temporary sensory fluctuations. The attainment of these characteristics means that one has developed the witnessing selfhood, free from a normal moment-to-moment response-prone human disposition. Of course, these characteristics are also esteemed as the mark of objectivity in the Western Enlightenment tradition. However, the whole point of this analysis is that when placed in the furnace of rigorous rhetorical scrutiny, Vyas finds these prized qualities fail to serve humanity well.

This analysis demands a note on the difference between the rhetorical styles of Krishna and Vyas.[38] Krishna's rhetorical style is direct: as he tries to dissuade Arjun from running away from the impending war, Krishna openly addresses Arjun, using his knowledge, experience, and ethos that comprised the dominant belief system of the time. Composed by Vyas, Krishna's discourse, indeed, is one of the best expressions of human eloquence, which blends a complex system of ideas, from ethics to metaphysics. Because of this rhetoric created in the epic, Krishna subsequently emerges as one of the ten incarnations of Lord Vishnu in the Hindu Pantheon. Vyas's rhetoric, on the other hand, is more nuanced, both because it includes Krishna's discourse and also counteracts to the persuasive prowess built-in Krishna's rhetoric. Vyas needed to represent Krishna authentically if his rhetorical enterprise were to be up to the mark of his design. Not portraying the object of his analysis precisely with all its beauty and power would not have allowed him to dissect it. After all, he was aiming at exposing something that was considered to be beautifully almost universally.

In a sense, through this complex rhetorical design, Vyas attends to the fault line between the philosophical and theological preference for logos and ethos and the cost of human pathos entailed in such preference. While logos, ethos, and pathos are not always strictly separable, the dominant philosophical tendency has been its preference for logos. Plato's call for the banishment of poets from his republic and his insistence on the installation of the philosopher-king at the throne therein represents a prime anecdote of this tendency. Ethos is the backbone of major religions, where speakers establish the integrity of their teaching either by claiming themselves godheads or by presenting themselves as the true spokespersons of the god. Indubitably, philosophies and theologies also evoke certain emotions, but they do this by giving short shrift to the fundamental human pathos. For instance, Krishna criticizes artists and the people engrossed in the beauty and power of the world in a very Platonic tone. He states, "There are ignorant people who speak flowery words ... Their hearts are full of selfish desires, Arjun. Their idea of heaven is their own enjoyment, and the aim of all their activities

---

[38] Krishna's rhetoric itself is created by Vyas the author. My argument is that Krishna's argument was the dominant ideology of the time, and the genius of the author lies not only representing this ideology so eloquently but also in exposing its devastating consequences when it is used to support wars.

is pleasure and power. The fruit of their actions is a continual rebirth."[39] In this statement, Krishna is not denouncing hedonism: he finds fault in people's preoccupation with common human emotions. For him, if there is anything worth doing as a human, it is the transcendence from the cycle of births and rebirths. In the epic, Vyas—I am arguing—presents his artist's take on this transcendence-seeking charismatic war leader. As analyzed throughout this paper, whether to value and act upon finer human emotions such as commiseration is the main difference between these two rhetorical projects.

To appreciate the monumentality of Vyasa's rhetorical project, we have to comprehend the idea that Krishna's teaching was not radical within the historical and cultural context of the epic. Krishna represented the dominant ideology of the time eloquently, because of which he garnered widespread admiration across the spectrum of warriors from Bhisma to Duryodhana. He embodies the basic creed governing the faith system of the time. What distinguishes Krishna from other major figures of the epic is not the idea that he propagates, but his ability to embody and explain that ideology in its radically pure form.

An ideology serves as a fabric of life and is sustained through individual performances.[40] While it may harm certain or sometimes all people participating in the system of its operation, requiring them to conform to its restricting norms, an ideology works as a way of life, mostly explaining the societally and ethically sound course of action for someone in crisis. Ideology also serves as a ready-made handbook for its inhabitants' daily operation. Opposing an ideology is therefore an enormous mission, not only because it is difficult for someone to see through the cracks of ideology, but also because some of the best intellectual and cultural resources within the territory of the ideology's influence are used to bolster it.

To confront the dominant ideology of his time, Vyas creates Krishna as an admirable character. If Vyas's purpose were to create a ridiculous, questionable character, the author could have created Krishna in whatever form he wanted—maybe someone full of flaws. Indeed, there are such characters in the *Mahabharata*—full of intelligence but filled with malice and revenge—whom readers automatically disapprove of, and the author does not have much to expose of them. Vyas is undertaking a bigger rhetorical task: demonstrating the destructive capacity of a commendable leader through the character of Krishna. Thus, Krishna is a celebrated, charismatic leader. The most effective war leaders are like that, and thus converting Krishna into something negative would not have served the author's purpose of countering the major war ideology of the *Mahabharat*. For that purpose, the *Mahabharat* has Duryodhana, the anti-hero—the blood-thirsty warmonger without any limits to his greed. That kind of figure and tendency has already been shamed and thus does not inspire idealistic masculine wishes. For Vyas, the problem does not lie in the Duryodhana- figure and tendency because they are treated as abhorrent within the dominant ideological imagination; the problem rests on the veneer of virtuosity represented by the Krishna-figure and its ability to inspire self-righteous proclamations. Lodged within human racial memory, this archetypal war hero is conceived fundamentally as a lover of peace, who must wage war only as the last recourse in the absence of other alternatives. So, if this dominant archetypal figure were to be questioned effectively, Vyas had to present it in its ideal form without compromising its authenticity.

4. Vyas' Interrogation of the War Rhetoric and Its Contemporary Relevance

What is the relevance of this analysis? What can we gain by foregrounding an artist's exposure of a celebrated divine figure, especially at a time when the wars described in the ancient epics look old-fashioned without much resemblance to the wars fought in our time? While it is true that some forms of wars have become antiquated with the ever-expanding use of new technology, what has not become outdated is the persistence of the rhetoric of 'required and just war'. This form of rhetoric

---

[39] *Gita*, 2: 42–43.
[40] My understanding of ideology primarily comes from Marxist theorists such as (Althusser 1978). (Laclau 1977).

presents wars at the last recourse by associating them with some noble ideas, in which the human cost of such wars is touted as a necessary sacrifice for the restoration of order and normalcy. At the core of this 'required and just war' rhetoric lies the idea that fighters should detach themselves from their feelings so that they can kill their fellow human beings robotically, without themselves being harmed emotionally by the experience in the process.[41]

As Arjun's emotional outburst at the beginning of the war suggests, killing ruthlessly in an organized fashion is challenging for a human. However, that is what war machines need from fighters—a reason countries set up an arduous training process for soldiers to develop their mental and physical habits for decimating foes mechanically. In a sense, Arjun's eruption of commiseration at the battlefield represents the failure of that training from Krishna's perspective. From Vyas's perspective, however, Arjun's empathy stands for the fundamental human desire for connection with fellow human beings. What Vyas shows is that even the rigorous Kshatriya war code that structured the worldview of warriors such as Arjun could not function in absolute terms in the presence of people before him. In such an occurrence, the whole theory of detachment and associated penances and training lose their command.

The nature of war has changed dramatically in the centuries following the composition of the *Mahabharata* and other similar epics, such as the *Iliad*. Unlike in the ancient epics, the leaders making the war decisions do not directly participate in most twenty-first-century wars, a condition that automatically detaches them from the messiness and emotional turmoil of their battles. For them, war therefore becomes a political calculus, sanitized from the muddle of death and destruction. Detachment defines their state of mind. Interpreted in this context, the idea of detachment as expressed in the *Gita*—while important from a particular spiritual perspective—can have devastating consequences. The concept of detachment not only dehumanizes and objectifies a warrior by turning them into battling robots, but it also makes them oblivious to the suffering of their enemies brought about by their actions. The ideology of Kshatriya Dharma and its modern descendants may celebrate the bravery of such detached work, but such heroism comes at the cost of humanity. Humanity should entail the cultivation of more delicate feelings and the enhancement of more in-depth relationships among human beings, if not upholding of the value of biosphere by expanding one's sense of care into the realms of animals, insects, and plants.

With his counter-rhetoric, specifically by the inclusion of the *Stri Purva* (the *Book of Women*) and *Shanti Parva* (the *Book of Peace*) in the *Mahabharata*, Vyas directs us to expand our horizons in that direction. His rhetoric certainly challenges the prevailing war ideology of his time, which asked the most intelligent members of his society to detach themselves from their bodies and fellow humanity for the sake of abstract notions of justice and righteousness. However, the logic of his monumental work transcends his context, as the *Mahabharat*—when analyzed in its totality as a sophisticated rhetorical undertaking—asks us to see through the rhetoric of 'required and just wars'.

Funding: This research received no external funding.

Acknowledgments: The author thanks three anonymous reviewers and the editor for their comments throughout the revision process of this paper.

Conflicts of Interest: The author declares no conflict of interest.

References

Althusser, Louis. 1978. *Lenin and Philosophy*. Translated by Ben Brewster. New York: Monthly Review Press.
Burke, Kenneth. 1969. *A Rhetoric of Motives*. Berkeley: University of California Press.

---

[41] As recent statistics and national conversation demonstrate, war veterans suffer significant post-traumatic stress disorder (PTSD) because their experience in wars is unhealthy from the normal human psychological structure.

Capra, Fritjof. 1975. *Tao of Physics: An Exploration of the Parallels between Modern Physics and Eastern Mysticism*. Boulder: Shambhala Publications.

Chakrabarty, Dipesh, and Rochona Majumdar. 2010. Gandhi's Gita and politics as such. *Modern Intellectual History* 7: 335–53. [CrossRef]

Davis, Richard H. 2015. *The Bhagavad Gita: A Biography*. Princeton: Princeton University Press.

Doniger, Wendy. 2014. War and Peace in the Bhagavad Gita. *The New York Review of Books*. December 4. Available online: https://www.nybooks.com/articles/2014/12/04/war-and-peace-bhagavad-gita/ (accessed on 4 December 2014).

Eknath Easwaran, trans. 1985, *The Bhagavad Gita*. Tomales: Nilgiri Press, Reprinted in 2007.

Ede, Lisa. 1984. Is Rogerian Rhetoric Really Rogerian. *Rhetoric Review* 3: 40–48. [CrossRef]

Johnson, Jame Turner. 1975. *Ideology, Reason, and Limitation of War 1200–1740*. Princeton: Princeton UP.

Laclau, Ernesto. 1977. *Politics and Ideology in Marxist Theory*. London: Macmillan.

Maitra, Keya. 2006. Comparing the Bhagavad-Gita and Kant: A Lesson in Comparative Philosophy. *Philosophy in the Contemporary World* 13: 63–67. [CrossRef]

Miller, Barbara Stoler. 1986. Introduction. In *The Bhagavad-Gita: Krishna's Counsel in Time of War*. New York: Bentham Books.

Pandey, Iswari. 2015. *South Asian in the Mid-South: Migrations of Literacies*. Pittsburg: University of Pittsburg Press.

Pandit, Nalini. 1992. Ambedkar and the *Bhagavad Gita*. *Economic and Political Weekly* 27: 1063–65.

Satchidanandan, K. 2009. Reflections: Vyasa and Ganesh. *Indian Literature* 53: 6–8.

Stroud, Scott R. 2005. Ontological Orientation and the Practice of Rhetoric: A Perspective from the *Bhagavad Gita*. *Southern Communication Journal* 70: 146–60. [CrossRef]

Thapar, Romila. 2009. War in the *Mahabharata*. *PMLA* 124: 1830–33. [CrossRef]

Upadhyaya, Kashi Nath. 2000. *Early Buddhism and the Bhagavadgita*. Delhi: Motilal Banarsidass Publishers.

Vyasa, Krishna-Dwaipayana. 1883. The Mahabharata of Krishna-Dwaipayana Vyasa. Translated by Kisari Mohan Ganguli. Originally Published between 1883 and 1896. Available online: http://www.sacred-texts.com/hin/maha/index.htm (accessed on 12 January 2019).

© 2019 by the author. Licensee MDPI, Basel, Switzerland. This article is an open access article distributed under the terms and conditions of the Creative Commons Attribution (CC BY) license (http://creativecommons.org/licenses/by/4.0/).

Article

Lucy Hutchinson and Margaret Cavendish: Civil War and Enemy Commiseration

Yousef Deikna

English Department, Idaho State University, Pocatello, ID 83209, USA; deikyous@isu.edu

Received: 11 January 2019; Accepted: 19 February 2019; Published: 1 March 2019

Abstract: Lucy Hutchinson (1620–1681) and Margaret Cavendish (1623–1673), prolific writers from the seventeenth century, came of age in one of the most difficult times in British history. Blair Worden, an eminent historian, writes, "The political upheaval of the mid-seventeenth century has no parallel in English history," and none of the previous conflicts "has been so far-reaching, or has disrupted so many lives for so long, or has so imprinted itself on the nation's memory" (2009, p. 1). Hutchinson and her husband, John, were on the side of the parliamentarians in the Civil War while Cavendish and her husband, William, were stout royalists. Instead of showing aggressive stances against their enemies, Hutchinson and Cavendish engaged expansively in a language of empathizing with the enemy in order to lessen the extreme partisanship of that period. Focusing specifically on Hutchinson's *Memoirs of the Life of Colonel John Hutchinson*, and Cavendish's *Sociable Letters*, among other writings, I argue that during the political impasse which characterized the English Civil War writings, the perspectives advanced by Hutchinson and Cavendish highlight the valuation of human life regardless of political allegiance, augmenting the odds for peaceful co-existence, in which empathy is foregrounded over, and at times alongside, loss and agony as a result of the Civil War aftermath. Suzanne Keen's groundbreaking research in *Empathy and The Novel* draws upon examples from the Victorian period to illustrate her understanding of empathy, but she also states that "I feel sure they also pertain to the hopes of authors in earlier periods as well" (2007, p. 142), which is a position taken wholeheartedly in this article. Using a cognitive literary approach where authorial empathic constructions are analyzed, Hutchinson's and Cavendish's closely read texts portray an undeniable level of commiseration with the enemy with the goal of abating violence and increasing cooperation and understanding.

Keywords: English Civil War; Lucy Hutchinson; Margaret Cavendish; empathy

---

During partisan politics of Civil War England, and the dehumanization and vulgarity associated with war rhetoric, Hutchinson's and Cavendish's constructions of empathic scenarios necessarily devised strove to support a world of civility and reasonableness, especially in a polemic atmosphere in which people fought not only with swords and muskets but with "paper, appealing to the nation with indignant ripostes to each other's declarations and messages and protests" (Worden 2009, p. 40). When commiserating with the enemy by helping or advancing their agenda in any way was considered high treason with no less than capital punishment awaiting those involved, yet, over and over again, Hutchinson and Cavendish did invest in writing about the miseries of their people even if they were from the other side of the war, as the examples below will demonstrate. It is worth keeping in mind that at the time, politics and war were polemic subjects though Norbrook (1997) points out that for Hutchinson at least, "the personal and the political are never clearly separable" (p. 470). In her writings, Cavendish too engaged in topics of religion, war, governorship, and other controversial topics, yet she kept mitigating her writings with reader epistles to lessen societal sanctions against feminine expression. Both authors though present empathic constructions of "enemy" situations and characters in order to mitigate anxiety and fear, as well as to lessen violence and increase livability for all. More importantly, for Hutchinson and Cavendish as the examples below show, they buttress a vision of civilized English society as one that has built-in social justice even for one's enemies, as it is the one way to progress as a country. Mia Szalavitz and Bruce Perry, well-known scholars of empathy, explain that "Not only will frightening circumstances promote inhumane behavior, they will also tend to minimize intellectual capacity, as the fear that results from being under constant threat remodels the brain" so that "individuals who are always threatened cannot reason to their maximal capacity" (Szalavitz and Perry 2010, p. 116). Hutchinson, though benefiting during the first eight years of the Interregnum as her husband John Hutchinson became one of the leading parliamentarians in the commonwealth, suffered tremendously in the last two years of the Interregnum followed by the Restoration period. They lost their estates, and her husband was first considered highly suspect, and eventually died imprisoned in Sandown Castle, one of the worst prisons at the time in England, indicating how the Hutchinsons fell out of favor during the Restoration period after being high gentry class in the years before and during the Civil War. Similarly, Cavendish's relatives were killed and forced to go to exile during the Civil War. Her brother Charles Lucas was executed and her mother lost her estates and died shortly after feeling the misery of her loss[1]. Cavendish herself fled to exile with Queen Henrietta Maria, serving in her court, even though her family objected to the idea. Under this duress, Hutchinson and Cavendish were in fact able to pen their works, but it was through engaging imaginatively with the trauma their families were experiencing. Martin Hoffman, a long time empathy researcher, argues that "Empathy can thus be aroused when observers imagine victims: when they read about others' misfortunes, when they discuss or argue about economic or political issues, or even when they make Kohlbergian[2] judgements about hypothetical moral dilemmas" (Hoffman 2000, p. 91).

In the early modern period, there are no defined boundaries of genre. For example, even though Hutchinson's *Memoirs of Colonel Hutchinson* (hereafter *Memoirs*) might sound like a historical text with myriad historical events pertinent to the Hutchinsons' lives, it uses a lot of literary characteristics. For example, Susan Cooke argues that the *Memoirs* should be considered a protonovel, saying, "Her very subjectivity, while perhaps detracting from the value of the *Memoirs* as a factual document (though on the whole its history is accurate) looks towards the development of the novel, which demands a presentation of a story to an audience, and the communication of one continuum to another" (Cooke 1993, p. 276). Hutchinson's *Elegies*, discovered by David Norbrook in 1997, uncovers Hutchinson's agency as a writer with a clear personal voice eulogizing her husband's legacy and his attributes in verse. Similarly, Cavendish, the first early modern women writer to publish her work during her life, achieved literary acclaim for her fictional and philosophical writings, including *Sociable Letters*, which are mostly imaginative correspondence between Cavendish and other characters, though historians have confirmed the reality of some of those addressees.

The relationship between and the civilizing process and the production of written material especially by women of the gentry class and above in the early modern period "saw a significant growth in the rates of female literacy, particularly in the cities" (Barker-Benfield 1992, p. 163), leading to fashioning a feminine expression that highlights new emphatic sensibilities to reform society. What accelerated the civilizing process is the constant questioning of the status of women in society as well as the genesis of women writers in the period, according to Graham Barker-Benfield (1992,

---

[1] In summarizing the war aftermath, Cavendish writes in *True Relation*, "But not only the family I am linked to is ruined, but the family from which I sprung, by these unhappy wars, which ruin my mother lived to see, and then died . . . . These unhappy wars forced her out, by reason she and her children were loyal to the King, for which they plundered her and my brothers of all their goods, plate, jewels, money, corn, cattle, and the like, cut down their woods, pulled down their houses, and sequestered them from their lands and livings; but in such misfortunes my mother was of an heroic spirit, in suffering patiently where there is no remedy (Newcastle et al. 2000, pp. 48–49).

[2] Lawrence Kohlberg, a preeminent American psychologist whose "six stages of moral development" in light of Jean Piaget's work on morality, sparked an important achievement in the field of moral development. Hoffman, on the other hand, focuses on ways of internalizing empathy in the development of a human being in a society. While both scholars account for ways of how moral behaviors develop, Hoffman's criticism of Kohlbergian theory shadows many similar observations that Kohlbergian theory projects many inconsistencies in terms of how humans form moral judgements, and it is limiting to human diversity of thinking, a point with Hoffman's work opposes, showing humans, instead, capable of reasoning at diverse situations without any contradictions or inconsistencies.

p. 278). For this article, Hutchinson and Cavendish are chosen to represent a case where empathy for the other is clearly a distinguishable occurrence as members of warring groups in the Civil War period, who, according to Nigel Wheale, "was the elite which had most to lose in the periods of crisis" (Wheale 2007, p. 25), resulting in anxieties throughout both Hutchinson's and Cavendish's chosen writings; yet, the authors could be empathizing not just to support a peaceful living for all, but they might also be seeing the value of bipartisanship at the time, a quality which is not always present at times of war. This research illuminates the writings of Hutchinson and Cavendish, both of whom created voices that reject tribalism for a more empathic society where reasonable contestations should be heard even if they are against one's ideals.

Recent insights from cognitive science that are relevant to Hutchinson's and Cavendish's writings focus on "empathy's role in pro-social and altruistic behavior" (Coplan and Goldie 2011, p. xxii), which specifically looks at the moral significance of empathy and its ethics of care, which include insights from researchers like Martin Hoffman, Steven Pinker, Amy Coplan, and Peter Goldie, among others. These researchers provide the scientific cognitive material for empathy based on experimental analyses, gaining insights about perspective-taking, which is the ability to feel and think from other points of view; mind-reading, or empathic accuracy, which is the ability to accurately guess someone's mind via physical or language cues; emotional contagion, which is a process of communicating one's feelings and inner emotions to surrounding environment; familiarity bias, which is the human tendency to feel empathy for people similar to oneself and to withhold empathy from those outside one's group; and authorial strategic empathizing, which is instigating readers' empathy through devised situations, among other cognitive processes. For example, Hoffman "highlights the role of empathy in moral emotion, motivation, and behavior" (Hoffman 2000, p. xxv). This emphasis on empathy as an ethic to be valued by all during difficult times resonates with arguments about the civilizing process as described by Norbert Elias, Steven Pinker, and Keith Thomas. Despite differences, these scholars argue that the civilizing process such as the increased practice of perspective-taking through the increased literacy rates gradually decreased violence and increased the value of, trade, tolerance, just practices, and human cooperation. The civilizing process is not linear, and rather went through different setbacks; nevertheless, the process hascontinued till this very day. Norbrook points out many instances in the *Memoirs* where Hutchinson is engaged in scathing attacks against those who used their wit in a way that frustrated the cause of the parliamentarians like Dr. Huntingdon Plumtre (Hutchinson and Keeble 1995, p. 96) and James Chadwick (ibid., 1994, p. 97). In both cases, these vicious attacks on these characters were unavoidable as they violated civil conduct of breaching trust given to them by her husband, and the parliamentarians in general. Hutchinson cannot be considered for advancing feminist ideals, where in her Memoirs, she projects herself as subservient to her husband's. Likewise, Deborah Boyle argues that Cavendish sees the absolutism of the King as "necessary to promote peace, it seems reasonable to infer that she thought Patriarchal marriage was also necessary to promote peace", which dislodges the parliamentarian strife for limiting the powers of the monarchy (Boyle 2013, p. 528).

Of particular importance is the involvement of Hutchinson and Cavendish with the public sphere, which is a key part of the civilizing process. The steady increase in reading practices, especially for women noticeably starting from the 1650s and dramatically increasing by the 1700s in England (Pinker 2012, p. 174), greatly increased the consumption of perspective-taking, and accepting of others' viewpoints. Pinker rightly argues that, "the cognitive process of perspective-taking and the emotion of sympathy must figure in the explanation for many historical reductions in violence," pointing out that empathy cannot be the only solution to world problems, and it has to be accompanied by institutional reforms to take an effect (Pinker 2012, pp. 590–92). Still, to see these writers engage in empathic manifestations sheds new light on the development of nobler sensibilities during the seventeenth century.

Although Hutchinson is a republican and Cavendish is a royalist, both showed empathy and concern for the other warring group, promoting understanding and peace. News pamphlets and petitions calling for specific declarations proliferated dramatically during the Civil War period corresponding with an uptick of printing houses (Pinker 2012, pp. 172–75). For women writers in the early modern period, the changing patterns of work, according to Graham Barker-Benfield, "allowed more women to find more time for literacy in the seventeenth and eighteenth centuries, and therefore, with women's ability to leave the historian a record of their wishes on an unprecedented scale, albeit one still largely confined to the bourgeoisie" (Barker-Benfield 1992, p. 161).

Sarah Ross stresses that for women who circulated their work for readership in manuscript form starting from the sixteenth century with Elizabeth Melville, Anne Southwell, and concluding with the latter part of the seventeenth century with Jane Cavendish, Putler Hester, and Lucy Hutchinson, all of whom "engaged in unique and particular social, ideological, and geographical networks defined not by gender but by family, community, and religious and political affiliation." Ross sees a continuum of early modern women writing "in the sense that clear commonalities can be identified in the poetic tropes, genres, and material forms in which they articulate their politics" (Ross 2015, p. 6). Manuscript networks offered Putler and Hutchinson a venue "in which they were active participants who were vital to seventeenth century literary production, and were potent literary and socio-political arenas, continuing to flourish into the first half of the eighteenth century" (Ross 2015, p. 23). Even if Hutchison has not published her work during her life time, the circulation of the material in manuscript form indicated a certain type of readership acknowledged during the period.

Empathy has long occupied English literary consciousness. T.S. Eliot famously said in 1921 that "the dissociation of sensibility" he experienced when comparing early seventeenth-century poetry with latter periods leads one to "look into the cerebral cortex, the nervous system, and the digestive tracts" (p. 250 qtd in Keen 2007, p. 57) in the poetic lines, and he especially valued the empathic connection that these poets create between themselves and their readers (Keen 2007, p. 57). Empathy came under renewed investigation recently especially in the literary domain. Coplan and Goldie (2011) identify empathy as "a complex imaginative process in which an observer simulates another person's situated psychological states (both imaginative and affective) while maintaining clear self-other differentiation" (p. xxxiv). Or as Martin Hoffman puts it, "empathy is the cognitive awareness of another person's internal states, that is, his thoughts, feelings, perceptions, and intentions" (Hoffman 2000, p. 29). Empathy is more noteworthy in conditions where those mentioned are not relatives, but strangers who do not belong to the same ideological group. There have been many studies of empathy that focus on the theory of mind, which is "our ability to recognize others' mental states as different from our own and to understand their beliefs, desires, and intentions" (Jaén and Simon 2013, p. 20). This later develops further into what is called "simulation theory", which affirms that readers of literary texts, especially novels, tend "to replicate, mimic, or impersonate the mental life of the target agent" either in a real life story or an imaginative fictional one (Gallese and Goldman qtd. in Jaén and Simon 2013, p. 21).

Such learned experience could be transferred to real-life situations originating from the connection created with the emotions of the literary characters (ibid., p. 21). Thus, this emphasis on empathy helps critics understand literature both at the individual or ontogenetic level and at the species evolution or the phylogenetic level (ibid., p. 21). Jaén and Simon further state that empathy is essential in understanding affective responses to literary readings, and could offer answers to why readers cry or laugh when deeply immersed in the act of reading. Stories learned from a literary work could be seen as an adaptive mechanism of survival where readers could learn valuable lessons about life without endangering themselves (ibid., p. 21), boosting readers' mental functions of empathizing via the intermental thinking of the other (Jaén and Simon 2013, p. 22). This could explain why people today, who are way more literate than people in the Renaissance, are more sensitive to violence in all of its forms. It is this development of intermental thinking that drives people into standing up for those who are in need of help.

Now turning to works of Cavendish that employ empathy, in *Sociable Letters*, specifically *Letter 16*, Cavendish offers a compelling empathy inducing language for those who differ from her own politics. She says,

> I Hope I have given the Lady D.A. no cause to believe I am not her Friend; for though she hath been of Ps. And I of Ks. Side, yet I know no reason why that should make a difference betwixt us, as to make us Enemies, no more than cases of Conscience in Religion, for one may be my very good friend, and yet not of my opinion ... (Newcastle and Fitzmaurice 2012, p. 60)

The empathic accuracy that Cavendish shows to addressed friend who has a republican ideology foregrounds the need for human cooperation across partisan ideological boundaries. In fact, the above instance of empathy happens in more than one fictional letter that Cavendish composed. In *Letter 9*, she clearly states that women should not interfere in politics of the country as they cause Civil Wars. This is an important letter as Hutchinson and other republicans accuse Charles I's queen Henrietta Maria of promoting her own politics in England. Hutchinson, in her *Memoirs*, calls Charles I an uxorious husband, who does not know how to control his country as his letters that the parliamentarians uncovered show (Hutchinson and Keeble 1995, p. 200). Ann Hughes, however, indicates that Hutchinson's evaluation of the King as too effeminate to rule the country, and succumbing to his wife's demands instead of his country, is a common allegation against the royalists as Parliamentarians see that a family matter in the King's house is spewing out of control and affecting the whole country (Hughes 2012, pp. 61–62). Nonetheless, Cavendish's opinion that political partisanship should not confine people's lives is a significant advancement in the way people imagined their political allegiance at the time. She compares politics with matters of religion, which is personal between the individual and God, and could only be judged by God himself. Cavendish acquiring this position on republicans as a royalist herself clearly identifies an act of empathy to the other side of the war and to acquire their position even fictionally will create an atmosphere of altruism and peace as Pinker indicated (Pinker 2012, p. 590).

Yet in *Letter 120*, Cavendish furthers her opposition to violence in general without pointing fingers. She states, "for in a Civil War, Brothers against Brothers, Fathers against Sons, and Sons against Fathers, become Enemies, and Spill each others Blood, Triumphing on their Graves" (Newcastle and Fitzmaurice 2012, p. 174). Like the previous letter, the loss of the war is inflicted on everybody, not just her side. In fact, Cavendish goes on to give her own theory of what drives violence. It is a "Fever of Fury, or a Furious Fever of Cruelty ... the Plague of the Mind" (ibid., 2012, p. 174). Cavendish's view of the situation of an individual who engages in unjustified violence is similar to Hoffman's hot cognition where the emotional side of the brain takes over, thus leading a human being into acts of irrationality. The drive to this continuous violence in her view is something deeply seated in the minds of those who continue the violence from either side. In cognitive terms, the identification and experience of war that she had been through enabled her to see all of the causes of the mayhem, especially when she admits that "Unwise Government, where many Errours gather into a Mass" (ibid., 2012, p. 175), among other causes she proposes for why wars start. Katie Whitaker, Cavendish's biographer, stresses that in many of her writings, Cavendish "envisaged groups of people gathering to read her plays aloud and discuss the choices and actions and the moral and intellectual issues presented" (Whitaker 2003, p. 211). In an epistle to *The Blazing World*, for example, Cavendish contemplates why fictions are important for human beings. It is important to "recreate the mind, and withdraw it from its more serious contemplation" (Newcastle and Lilley 1994, p. 124), and she hopes that no one will blame her for this art creation because "it is in every one's power to do the like" (1994, p. 124). As Sara Mendelson reminds us, Renaissance women writers have to be both modest and reserved, but also leaders in mainstreaming civil manners (Mendelson 2000, p. 117). Thus, Cavendish could be both a moralizer and modest woman, yet at the same time making a paragon of reasonableness and justice through her special royalism. Jacqueline Broad and Karen Green stress that "Cavendish's political thought is a critical response to the horrors of civil war, and her central problem is how to secure the obedience of subjects and maintain peace and order in civil society" (Broad and Green 2009, p. 200).

Other instances highlight empathizing with the poor as the real noble people, e.g., *Letter 55*, various tragic issues faced by married women, e.g., *The Convent of Pleasure* act III scene II to X, and other instances of empathy inducing situations that are designed to invoke empathic distress on the readers. All such instances represent what Barker-Benfield calls the "new emphasis on sensation and feeling as the true basis for a claim to moral consideration" (Barker-Benfield 1992, p. 231) during the seventeenth century.

Now moving to Hutchinson's *Memoirs* is similarly rife with examples of empathy. Hutchinson indicates how royalist close relatives helped her husband while in regicide trial after the Restoration like Sir Richard Biron and Allen Apsley, who both fought as captains in the Royalist army in the battle of Edgehill (Hutchinson and Keeble 1995, p. 282). However, the list of royalists who stood by his side in court includes others who were stout enemies during the war, like the Duke of Newcastle-William Cavendish who acted humanely with the Colonel and was really an important point of contact in the royalist side whom Hutchinson is really grateful for (Hutchinson and Keeble 1995, pp. 300–2). Whenever Hutchinson mentions William Cavendish, the information is objective even in her narration of his involvement in the Civil War, and the intimacy towards him increases after the Restoration as Cavendish was reinstated to some of his previous positions held in the North of England where the Hutchinsons now live. In one instance, Hutchinson narrates that her husband was being fetched, for new accusations of plotting against the King, to talk to "the Marquess of Newcastle, who treated him very honourably; and then falling into discourse with him, 'Colonel,' saith he, 'they say you desire to know your accusers, which is more than I know'" (Hutchinson and Keeble 1995, p. 300). Even with the seriousness of the accusation, Hutchinson is left alone to leave his property without guards as per orders from Cavendish. What is apparent from Hutchinson narrations of Cavendish is civility shown to her husband from this royalist neighbor who was also in exile and his estates confiscated and sold during the Interregnum. Hutchinson sees that empathy towards her husband here is a natural right afforded to them by their equal empathic treatment of royalists in the war years. Other royalists like Mr. Palmer, Sir George Booth, came to testify positively on behalf of her husband in court. Hutchinson states "Although they knew his principle contrary to theirs, yet they so justified his clear upright carriage, according to his own persuasion, as was a record much advancing his honour, and such as no man else in that day received" (Hutchinson and Keeble 1995, p. 282). This instance paints a picture of a true Independent who does not depend on court connections to support his cause even though they disagree with him at the ideological level. Mia Szalavitz and Bruce Perry tell us that if one's kin are involved in a dangerous situation, it could impact one's nervous system negatively, as it is wired in human brains and genetics to feel with kin (Szalavitz and Perry 2010, p. 14), but the example of those men standing up for the Colonel in trial is possible through a social bonding similar to what Pinker calls "communal relationships" that results in "mutual sympathy" (Pinker 2012, p. 585) as both Hutchinsons see positivity from those royalists. These unexpected allies must also have experienced something positive from the Hutchinsons in the past. It is one of the most remarkable kinds of empathy: perspective-taking to minimize conflict based on mutual respect.

Another great example of empathy is to be found early on in the *Memoirs*, where she mentions how her husband, once appointed as the commissioner from the high court of the Parliament, prevented royalist prisoners accused by the court from facing persecution as he thinks that it is enough that those in high positions faced the penalty. Hutchinson says, "His unbloody nature desiring to spare the rest of the delinquents after the highest had suffered, and not delighting in the death of men when they could live without cruelty to better men" (Hutchinson and Keeble 1995, p. 237). These aforementioned lines are repeated over and over throughout the *Memoirs*, where Hutchinson sees that most of those in the lower ranks who joined either side in the conflict were driven by economic reasons to support their families rather than really seeking to support one side over the other for ideological reasons (e.g., Hutchinson and Keeble 1995, pp. 307–8). There are other similar explications of soldiers from lower social classes in the *Memoirs* whom Hutchinson highlights positively as a shared emotional response to the violent conditions in the country. These moments of conveying empathic concerns highlight the Renaissance's turn to prose writings to plainly convey emotions of the role-taking imagination in order to reach out to as many readers as possible (Keen 2007, p. 41).

The Hutchinsons, in fact, were treating royalists well, especially during the Protectorate where Hutchinson and her husband retired from political activities, going back to the countryside after objecting to Cromwell's Protector status, and the dissolution of Parliament. Hutchinson was relieved of his duties in 1653 and was forced out of London after official appointment as a governor to Nottingham Castle in 1643, and sitting in the Counsel of State. Norbrook (2003) indicates that the Hutchinsons during this retirement period enjoyed many activities similar to royalist ones, like collecting paintings, teaching children music and dancing, and translating Lucretius's *On the Nature of* Things (qtd. in Richards 2003, pp. 72–73). Even the physical appearance of John Hutchinson, a Parliamentarian with long hair, was not appealing to fellow republicans who thought it is not a sign of allegiance to their cause (Bryson 1998, p. 217). In fact, Hutchinson quotes a line from John Cleveland's satire "Hue and Cry" mocking the way the Puritan minsters looked as "something ridiculous to behold" (Hutchinson and Keeble 1995, p. 87). Norbrook indicates that this is an important aspect of the way the Hutchinsons' civility to royalists materialized as they were accused of using a "cavalier like language" by other republican groups (p. 72 qtd. in Richards 2003), indicating how the solidary of these social relations that the Hutchinson's enjoyed cut through divisions caused by ideology (ibid., p. 73). Within- group familiarity bias which should have been directed against royalists is not part of Hutchinson's structure of feeling throughout her narrations of the Civil War incidents where Norbrook sees a general positive trend in the way Hutchinson views royalists.

The last example of empathy comes from Hutchinson's *Elegies*, where Norbrook indicated that Hutchinson is much more direct and personal in these twenty-three numbered poems (Norbrook 1997, p. 469). In *Elegy 4*, Hutchinson presents an account of her husband as both a magnificent, stout soldier, and very honorable religious man. She says: "Shuch killing weapons too he wore/Not to destroy but to restore;/Which done he threw ye sword aways/Embraceing Those who prostrate Lay;/" (4.6–10). Though showing mercy for vanquished foes is a heroic trope, it could also be read as:I don't want to be in this person's situation or If I were to be put in this situation like this defeated foe, I would appreciate being set free. Although, it is clear here that the second reading into these lines is stronger from the word choice like "throw ye sword away" and "embracing" it is her husband's civil practices during the unjust war being described here where a word like 'embracing' is an indication of fellow feeling towards friends rather than just heroism to a defeated foe. Similarly in *Elegy 5*, she states, "He flung his sword & with it hate away/Releiuing vanquisht foes whoe prostrate lay; Brauely he Armd more brauely he lay armes downe/Thinking it more to win than to weare a Crowne" (5.57–60). Hutchinson in these poems tries to show that her husband's arms were used in a noble way—namely, to protect, and defend himself rather than just acting as a violent perpetrator in the war; although this is a common position to take for those siding with the Parliamentarian forces, it still gives a reason why arms have to be used in the first place (Walters 2013, p. 218). Being involved in the military, as Norbrook comments, was only a regrettable necessity (p. 69 qtd in Richards 2003, p. 69). Further, her husband showed mercy to those enemies who "prostrate Lay," which is repeated twice in these poems. The Colonel's arms too are put down once chance happened to stop the bloodshed, and allow for peace and justice to take effect. The word "bravery" which appears in these poems indicates what Johnathan Barry claims as an important moral development during the seventeenth century as more and more people started to associate civility with "possession of specific cultural attributes" (Barry 2000, p. 196), including highlighting empathic concerns during difficult times. Mannerisms do change from one age to another. For example, Barker-Benfield states that in the seventeenth century, "honor," for example, experienced meaning change from "title of rank" to "goodness of character," which is "a shift corresponding to the evolution of the fluidity of sensational psychology, but corresponding, too, to the promises Protestantism and its sequelae (as well as civic humanism) held for women"

(Barker-Benfield 1992, p. 289). Civil practices are essential to empathy as they lead the way for a nobler society driven by empathic distress. Patricia Patrick notes how Hutchinson was adamant in treating the wounded royalists even when Captain Palmer vociferously objects to Hutchinson's "favour to the enemies of God," and she responds by saying that she is performing "her duty in humanity to them, as fellow-creatures, not as enemies" (p. 129 qtd. in Patrick 2015, p. 351). This took place at a time when other Parliamentarians were unjust and cruel to the defeated royalists (Hutchinson and Keeble 1995, p. 129). Sympathizing with the victims of the war by helping them heal is an altruistic act to alleviate their suffering whether Hutchinson enjoys it or not regardless of social class, or ideological affiliation of those affected. The motivation behind this act is to promote peace and tranquility as the empathizer does not benefit in any shape or form. Pinker argues that such acts of empathy are necessary even if one does not intentionally believe in doing a certain empathic act (Pinker 2012, p. 584). Hutchinson and Cavendish are undoubtedly participating in a mission to reform men's sensibilities as Barker-Benfield notes, "The culture of sensibility wished to reform men, to make them conscious of women's minds, wishes, interests, and feelings, in sum, their sensibility (Barker-Benfield 1992, p. 249). Hutchinson towards the near end of the *Memoirs* when her husband in Prison and she was appealing on his behalf in the court, directly states how her discourse enabled her to negotiate a deal for her husband from his jailor at the Tower of London (Hutchinson and Keeble 1995, pp. 307–10). This indicates a discourse sensibility that her husband was not able to make on his own-the ability to forge solutions based on empathic language constructions.

Similarly, Lopes (2011) argues that empathy is always involved with some sort of motivation, and empathy is a skill that could be improved (qtd in Coplan and Goldie 2011, p. 119). Hutchinson and Cavendish deployed empathy on different ways to put brakes on warrior practices like honor culture, and other war-related cultural themes including martial glorification of winning, and other manly virtues that eventually lead to bloodshed and more children becoming orphaned as a result of the conflict (Pinker 2012, pp. 686–87). Early modern women writers therefore, could be understood within the framework of larger civilizing process that allowed for an emphasis on civil discourse. Sarah Ross indicates that there "was 'a major shift' between 1660 and 1750 from women's domestic, devotional, and coterie poetic practice to 'the emergence of the professional woman poet within an expansive print culture" (Ross 2015, p. 3). Clearly Hutchinson is leaving her works for her connections, and possibly she thought of us too reading her work, and she probably thought of teaching us of these empathic moments and how one could benefit from them through empathic contagion that allows one to experience how it feels to be in someone else's position. While Hutchinson wrote the *Memoirs* to clear her husband's name, it also offers a record of empathy and community beyond political affiliation and the wounds of war.

Funding: This research received no external funding.

Acknowledgments: Special thanks to my advisor Curtis Whitaker for assistance with finding sources and conducting such research on this area. I would also like to thank Matthew VanWinkle for his continuous support in making this work come to light. In addition, my sincere thanks go to the editors of this journal who helped in editing this paper.

Conflicts of Interest: The author declares no conflict of interest.

References

Barker-Benfield, Graham. 1992. *The Culture of Sensibility: Sex and Society in Eighteenth-Century Britain*. Chicago: University of Chicago Press.

Barry, Johnathan. 2000. Civility and Civic Culture in Early Modern England: The Meanings of Urban Freedom. In *Civil Histories: Essays Presented to Sir Keith Thomas*. Edited by Peter Burke, Brian Harrison, Paul Slack and Keith Thomas. Oxford: Oxford University Press.

Boyle, Deborah. 2013. Margaret Cavendish on Gender, Nature, and Freedom. *Hypatia: A Journal of Feminist Philosophy* 28: 516–32. [CrossRef]

Broad, Jacqueline, and Karen Green. 2009. Margaret Cavendish, Duchess of Newcastle. In *A History of Women's Political Thought in Europe, 1400–1700*. Cambridge: Cambridge University Press.
Bryson, Anna. 1998. *From Courtesy to Civility: Changing Codes of Conduct in Early Modern England*. Oxford: Clarendon Press.
Cooke, Susan. 1993. "The Story I most Particularly Intend": The narrative Style of Lucy Hutchinson. *Critical Inquiry* 5: 271–7.
Coplan, Amy, and Peter Goldie, eds. 2011. *Empathy: Philosophical and Psychological Perspectives*. New York: Oxford University Press.
Hoffman, Martin. 2000. *Empathy and Moral Development: Implications for Caring and Justice*. New York: Cambridge University Press.
Hughes, Ann. 2012. *Gender and the English Revolution*. London: Routledge.
Hutchinson, Lucy, and Neil H. Keeble. 1995. *Memoirs of the Life of Colonel Hutchinson*. London: Dent.
Jaén, Isabel, and Julien J. Simon. 2013. *Cognitive Literary Studies: Current Themes and New Directions*. Austin: University of Texas.
Keen, Suzanne. 2007. *Empathy and the Novel*. Oxford: Oxford University Press.
Lopes, Dominic. 2011. An Empathic Eye. In *Empathy: Philosophical and Psychological Perspectives*. Edited by Amy Coplan and Peter Goldie. New York: Oxford University Press.
Mendelson, Sara. 2000. The Civility of Women in Seventeenth-Century England. In *Civil Histories*. Edited by Brain Harrison Burke and Paul Slack. Oxford: Oxford University Press, pp. 111–25.
Newcastle, Margaret C., and James Fitzmaurice, eds. 2012. *Sociable Letters*. New York: Routledge.
Newcastle, Margaret C., and Kate Lilley. 1994. *The Description of the New Blazing World and Other Writings*. New York: Penguin Group.
Newcastle, Margaret, Sylvia L. Bowerbank, and Sara H. Mendelson. 2000. *Paper Bodies: A Margaret Cavendish Reader*. Peterborough: Broadview Press.
Norbrook, David. 1997. Lucy Hutchinson's "elegies" and the Situation of the Republican Woman Writer (with Text). *English Literary Renaissance* 27: 468–521. [CrossRef]
Norbrook, David. 2003. 'Words More Than Civil': Republican Civility in Lucy Hutchinson's 'the Life of John Hutchinson'. In *Early Modern Civil Discourses*. Edited by Jennifer Richards. Houndmills, Basingstoke and Hampshire: Palgrave Macmillan.
Patrick, Patricia. 2015. "All That Appears Most Casuall to Us": Fortune, Compassion, and Reason in Lucy Hutchinson's Exploratory Providentialism. *Studies in Philology* 112: 327–52. [CrossRef]
Pinker, Steven. 2012. *The Better Angels of Our Nature: Why Violence Has Declined*. New York: Penguin.
Richards, Jennifer. 2003. *Early Modern Civil Discourses*. Houndmills, Basingstoke and Hampshire: Palgrave Macmillan.
Ross, Sarah. 2015. *Women, Poetry, & Politics*. New York: Oxford University Press.
Szalavitz, Mia, and Bruce Perry. 2010. *Born for Love: Why Empathy Is Essential, and Endangered*. New York: HarperCollins.
Walters, Elizabeth. 2013. Gender and Civil War Politics in Margaret Cavendish's "assaulted and Pursued Chastity". *Early Modern Women* 8: 207–40.
Wheale, Nigel. 2007. *Writing and Society: Literacy, Print and Politics in Britain 1590–1660*. New York: Routledge.
Whitaker, Katie. 2003. *Mad Madge: The Extraordinary Life of Margaret Cavendish, Duchess of Newcastle, the First Woman to Live by Her Pen*. New York: Basic Books.
Worden, Blair. 2009. *The English Civil Wars 1640–1660*. London: Weidenfled & Nicolson.

© 2019 by the author. Licensee MDPI, Basel, Switzerland. This article is an open access article distributed under the terms and conditions of the Creative Commons Attribution (CC BY) license (http://creativecommons.org/licenses/by/4.0/).

Article

Depictions of American Indians in George Armstrong Custer's *My Life on the Plains*

Danielle Johannesen

Department of Liberal Arts & Education, University of Minnesota Crookston, Crookston, MN 56716, USA; johan259@crk.umn.edu

Received: 8 February 2019; Accepted: 10 March 2019; Published: 14 March 2019

Abstract: General George Armstrong Custer remains one of the most iconic and mythologized figures in the history of the American West. His infamous defeat at the 1876 Battle of the Little Bighorn largely defines his legacy; historical scholarship and popular representations of Custer consistently focus on his "Last Stand." However, Custer was also a writer with a keen appreciation for arts and culture. This article analyzes Custer's descriptions of American Indians in his memoir *My Life on the Plains* (1874). I trace how Custer's descriptions of Indians and Indian culture clearly reveal a colonial mindset; yet, Custer regularly reflects on Indians and Indian culture with interest, curiosity, and even respect. I analyze these moments of potential commiseration and question whether these moments depart from a colonial mindset. Additionally, I analyze how Custer constructs Indians as the "enemy" and show how these constructions are problematic, yet critical for Custer's aestheticizing of military conflict. Ultimately, I argue that Custer's memoir is deserving of increased attention as a literary text and show how to reveal complexities and contradictions with literary and historical implications.

Keywords: Indian Wars; George Armstrong Custer; war narratives; colonialism; settler-colonialism; Western American literature; frontier literature

---

War narratives are an important part of world and American history. From a literary perspective, war narratives are powerful in their engagement with historical events of the utmost dramatic magnitude. War is an arena where questions of mortality, comradery, heroism, and humanity are situated within complex sociopolitical contexts and global power structures. War is often defined by an overarching story founded on a basic dramatic premise where a protagonist battles an antagonist as a way to resolve political conflict. Of course, war is sometimes perpetuated upon participants who are subsequently forced to defend themselves against foreign invaders or external threats. For example, when used as an arm of colonialism, war typically involves the conquest of indigenous lands; this conquest is often justified by an overarching narrative pitting European conquerors and settlers as civilized and aligned with God against indigenous peoples characterized as uncivilized and savage (Callahan et al. 2006, p. 556). Colonialism depends on the construction of a war narrative wherein an antagonistic enemy must be defeated in the name of civilization. The North American Indian Wars were perpetuated by colonial, governmental, and military forces inspired by this very logic.

As one of the most iconic and mythologized figures in the history of the American West, General George Armstrong Custer was a major participant in the North American Indian Wars. His infamous defeat at the 1876 Battle of the Little Bighorn largely defines his legacy; historical scholarship and popular representations of Custer consistently focus on his "Last Stand". However, Custer was also a writer with a keen appreciation for arts and culture. Beginning in 1872, Custer began publishing accounts of his frontier experiences in *The Galaxy*, a magazine "which contained better-class fiction along with articles dealing with history and biography and some verse" (Custer [1874] 1976, p. xxiii). These accounts were collected and published in 1874 as *My Life on the Plains, or Personal Experiences with Indians*. Custer's *My Life on the Plains* is a war narrative. The memoir not only includes Custer's accounts of actual armed conflicts, including the Battle of the Washita, but the book also reflects how the Indian Wars more broadly hinged on depictions of Indians as the cultural enemy of white Europeans. Custer's memoir provides a powerful example of a soldier reflecting on cultural differences as a way to justify war. The complex and often contradictory depictions of Indians and Indian culture throughout *My Life on the Plains* have literary and historical implications in terms of how scholars and students reflect on Custer's legacy and the broader history of the American West.

While Custer's descriptions clearly reflect a colonialist mindset, depictions of Indians as the violent, "savage" enemy are sporadically countered with passages where Custer reveals an interest in and respect for Indians and Indian culture. Custer's reflections reveal curiosity and interest in Indian culture and an appreciation for Indians as necessary actors in the theater of war. Additionally, brief moments emerge in *My Life on the Plains* where Custer arguably commiserates with Indians. This article analyzes how Custer expresses curiosity in and appreciation for Indians and questions the implications of brief commiserations with Indians. Further, this article shows how curiosity in and descriptions of the indigenous "enemy" are difficult to separate from colonialist ideology. Ultimately, despite an apparent interest in Indian life and a complex and often contradictory attitude toward Indians, Custer's memoir fails to reveal a genuine sense of justice or mercy toward Indians who continue to resist colonization.

Custer had lofty ambitions in all areas of his life. While renowned for his military achievements and exploits, Custer also aspired to gain respect as an intellectual. Although Custer was unremarkable as a student at West Point, he possessed a keen interest in culture, history, and the arts. Custer greatly enjoyed New York City, frequenting the theater and engaging with newspaper reporters and editors, several of whom expressed interest in his talents as a writer (Stiles 2016, pp. 419–20). As Edgar I. Stewart writes in his introduction to *My Life on the Plains*, "Custer had always been interested in writing, and although he had been nothing better than an average student at the Military Academy ... he developed into a serious student after the close of the Civil War, very likely through the influence of his wife, Elizabeth Bacon Custer. His special interests were history and literature" (Custer [1874] 1976, p. xxiii). Custer also wrote articles for *Turf, Field and Farm* magazine, which were published between 1871–1873 (Stiles 2016, p. 365). Additionally, Custer's letters to his wife, Libbie, are often quoted and studied for their descriptions of Custer's military and frontier exploits and for their intimate personal reflections. Custer's letters offer firsthand documentation of Civil War and frontier history as well as detailed accounts of a marriage situated in the context of some of the most significant historical events in American history. *My Life on the Plains* is, therefore, an important text, both for its engagement with frontier history and as an example of Custer's literary abilities. Although opinions differ as to the literary quality of Custer's writing, the memoir aspires to be a respected literary text.

Custer immediately puts his memoir in conversation with literary depictions of Indians and Indian life. Early in the memoir, Custer expresses a desire to counter inaccurate and romanticized depictions of Indians such as those found in the works of novelist James Fenimore Cooper. Custer writes,

> Stripped of the beautiful romance with which we have been so long willing to envelope him, transferred from the inviting pages of the novelist to the localities where we are compelled to meet with him, in his native village, on the war path, and when raiding upon our frontier settlements and lines of travel, the Indian forfeits his claim to the appellation of the "*noble red man*". (Custer [1874] 1976), p. 13)

The implication is that Custer's firsthand experiences, which he goes on to document in the memoir, provide a more realistic and accurate record of Indian life than what might be found in "the inviting pages of the novelist." Specifically, the passage shows Custer's desire to counter depictions of Indians as "noble savages". Custer attempts to strip the idea of "nobility" from the Indian and implies that the reality of what he terms the "Indian character" (Custer [1874] 1976, p. 19) coincides with a serious threat to settlement and civilization. Throughout his memoir, Custer consistently describes Indians as savage, violent, and uncivilized. Establishing Indians as "savage" and impossible to civilize is central to Custer's construction of Indians as the "enemy". Custer regularly describes Indians as "infesting" the landscapes and territories of the American West. He uses similarly dehumanizing terminology throughout the book, describing Indians as "the most cruel, heartless, and barbarous of human enemies" (Custer [1874] 1976, p. 274) and later notes the "red man's bloodthirsty and insatiable vengeance" (Custer [1874] 1976, p. 289). These types of descriptions, which permeate the memoir, serve as simplistic generalizations seemingly aimed at providing evidence of the threats Indians posed to white settlers as they moved into the lands west of the Mississippi River. Those Indians who resisted moving to the reservations were viewed as especially dangerous (Kreyche 1994, p. 89), and this view is reflected in Custer's memoir.

Custer's depictions of Indians as the barbarous and uncivilized enemy reflect an obvious and predictable colonial mindset. It is important to note that the memoir participates in and encourages what Dunbar-Ortiz (2014) terms the "settler-colonialist context of US history" (p. 6). According to Custer, Indians who continued to resist reservation life—those who continued to fight for their lands and traditional ways of life—posed the most serious threat to white settlement; this Indian resistance necessitated the Indian Wars. Configuring those Indians as the "hostile enemy" surfaces as an important element of Custer's logic, and of the broader logic of settler-colonialism, which Cox (2017) defines as "an ongoing system of power that perpetuates the genocide and repression of indigenous peoples and cultures. Essentially hegemonic in scope, settler-colonialism normalizes the continuous settler occupation, exploiting lands and resources to which indigenous peoples have genealogical relationships." The memoir establishes a spectrum of sorts where "peaceful" Indians who acquiesce to the government's demands by moving to the reservations are essentially harmless, whereas those Indians who continue to resist must be defeated in order to enable white settlement. In many ways, the memoir reveals how Indians are defined as the "enemy" largely because their ways of life did not conform or cater to the logic of white supremacy.

Although Custer's memoir clearly reflects a racist and hegemonic ideology rooted in settler-colonialism, *My Life on the Plains* includes many passages and reflections where Custer expresses keen curiosity and interest in Indian life. The most well-known of these passages appears early in the memoir where Custer reflects on the lives of reservation Indians as compared to those who remain "free": "If I were an Indian, I often think I would greatly prefer to cast my lot among those of my people adhered to the free open plains rather than submit to the confined limits of a reservation, there to be the recipient of the blessed benefits of civilization, with its vices thrown in without stint or measure" (Custer [1874] 1976, p. 22). Interestingly, this passage reveals a brief moment where Custer questions the supremacy of civilization, romanticizing the "free open plains" as preferable to the "confined limits" of a reservation. Custer further reflects on how Indians do not, realistically, have the ability to control their own destinies. He notes that Indians can act and behave in ways as long as their actions do not "run contrary to the requirements of civilization in its advancing tread" (Custer [1874] 1976, p. 22). This passage shows Custer's awareness of the inevitability of white settlement and of the destruction of indigenous autonomy. Of this inevitability, Custer goes on to write, "Destiny seems to have willed it, and the world looks on and nods its approval" (Custer [1874] 1976, p. 23). These passages expose a potential contradiction underlying Custer's construction of Indians as the enemy. On one hand, Custer consistently portrays hostile Indians as dangerous foes who must be eliminated by means of warfare. Conversely, the passages quoted above reveal how Custer views the defeat of the Indians as inevitable, with the forces bringing about this defeat being "destiny" and the "requirements of civilization" rather than military force. This is important because it exposes a point where Custer falls short of genuine commiseration; although he seems to understand why Indians would resist colonization in favor of the "free open plains", at no point does this understanding cause him to question his own actions as a military officer.

Custer reveals great curiosity and interest regarding Indians and Indian culture. Throughout *My Life on the Plains*, Custer regularly uses the words "interest" and "interesting" when reflecting on Indian culture. Early in the book, Custer writes, "In studying the Indian character, while shocked and disgusted by many of his traits and customs, I find much to be admired and still more of deep and unvarying interest. To me, Indian life, with its attendant ceremonies, mysteries, and forms, is a book of unceasing interest" (Custer [1874] 1976, p. 19). Given Custer's interest in writing and literary culture, his use of the book metaphor as a way to describe Indian life is notable. The book metaphor suggests that Indians are an object to be read, studied, and analyzed; in comparing Indians to an object, Custer further dehumanizes Indians. The passage also suggests that Indian life is exotic—in noting the "mysteries" of Indian life, Custer reveals how he perceives Indian life as substantially different from his own cultural practices as a white American. In many ways, Custer situates himself as an ethnographer with firsthand experience of Indians and Indian culture that he then relays to readers throughout his memoir. In addition to the passage quoted above, in which Custer expresses that he more closely identifies with Indians "adhered to the free open plains", Custer frequently reflects on, describes, and arguably commiserates with Indians throughout his book in ways that seem to contradict the simplistic, colonialist ideology underlying Westward expansion. As Cozzens (2016) argues, oversimplifications of complex historical circumstances have come to define how many citizens and academics understand the Indian Wars and Westward expansion more broadly. While Custer's memoir consistently reflects racist and colonialist ideology, oversimplifying Custer's perspectives compromises the pursuit of a comprehensive understanding of both history and narrative. As Utley and Washburn write, accounts of the Indian Wars that aim to document the Indian perspective sometimes produce unbalanced accounts that assume a simplistic division between whites as "exploitative conquerors" (Utley and Washburn [1977] 2002, p. vi) and Indians as "romantic, innocent victims" (p. vi). Paradoxically, Custer both participates in the displacement of Indian culture while simultaneously documenting what he terms the "wonderful and peculiar powers of the Indian" (Custer [1874] 1976). Analyzing Custer's mixed and often contradictory descriptions of his "enemy" is therefore an important aspect of understanding historical events and reflects how "the government's response to the 'Indian problem' was inconsistent" (Cozzens 2016, p. 8).

Much of the Custer's content regarding Indian life engages in "thick description" (Mueller 2017) typical of ethnography. Like an ethnographer, Custer regularly documents his observations of Indian life as a way to provide readers with insight into Indian culture. Many of these descriptions focus on elements of Indian culture, including warfare and battle strategies, burial practices, oratorical skills, horsemanship, and dress. For example, Custer describes the contents of an empty Indian lodge that "the Indians had fled before the arrival of the cavalry" (Custer [1874] 1976, p. 40). Throughout this passage, Custer employs a seemingly objective tone in documenting the contents of the lodge, describing the contents as "the usual adornments and articles which constitute the household effects of an Indian family" (Custer [1874] 1976, p. 40). In describing the contents of the lodge, Custer makes clear that the scene is essentially "undisturbed" and provides a glimpse into the everyday domestic practices of Indians. Custer observes buffalo robes, doormats, rawhide ropes, paint bags, and "the decaying embers of a small fire built in the center" (Custer [1874] 1976, p. 40). Custer is not alone in exploring the lodge and describes entering the lodge with a doctor from the cavalry. A camp kettle hangs over the fire, and Custer details the doctor's interest in the contents of the kettle: "The doctor, ever on the alert to discover additional items of knowledge, whether pertaining to history or science, snuffed the savory odors which arose from the dark recesses of the mysterious kettle" (Custer [1874] 1976, p. 40). Custer's language situates the doctor as a curious investigator with an interest in Indian life. Custer describes the doctor using a horn spoon to sample the contents of the kettle and notes that the doctor's reaction was one of disgust upon realizing the food in the kettle is dog meat (Custer [1874] 1976, p. 41). The passage also reveals a theme present throughout the memoir: Indian life is consistently depicted as mysterious and ultimately unknowable. Early in the memoir, Custer shares his belief that Indian life is "unknowable" to the white man: "I know that all tribes with which I have been brought in contact carry with them a mysterious something which is regarded with the utmost sacredness and veneration, and upon which the eye of no white man at least is ever permitted to rest" (Custer [1874] 1976, p. 17).

On the surface, these passages seem to reveal Custer's genuine curiosity and interest in Indian life. However, curiosity and interest in the culture of the "other"—even if that interest is genuine—are difficult to separate from the broader forces of colonialism. While Custer configures himself and the doctor as participant-observers, the act of entering the lodge symbolizes the dynamic of colonial conquest underlying Custer's work. In entering and describing the lodge, Custer and the doctor express interest in Indian life while simultaneously invading and occupying an Indian domicile. Custer's interest in Indian life cannot be separated from colonialism. In fact, as Loomba (2005) explains, learning about indigenous peoples and gathering knowledge about their ways of life is an element of colonialism: "No branch of learning was left untouched by the colonial experience. A crucial aspect of this process was the gathering and ordering of information about the lands and peoples visited by, and later subject to, the colonial powers" (p. 53). Many narratives of "first contact" and colonialism present stories about indigenous cultures relayed through the perspective of the colonizer. Curiosity and interest in Indian life is therefore not a departure from the colonial mindset but rather a central means through which colonizers craft and control constructions of the "other" (Loomba 2005, pp. 53–56).

Constructions of Indians as "other" stem not only from Custer's perceptions of Indian life and culture but also from his contextualization of colonialism as warfare. In many ways, Custer imagines the Indian Wars as a kind of theatrical performance of warfare where an "other"—the enemy—is critical. As mentioned above, Custer is simultaneously aware of the inevitable defeat of hostile Indians yet engaged in a fantasy of warfare within which Indians must function as a formidable foe. Custer aestheticizes warfare, regularly describing military engagements in terms of beauty. In one passage, Custer describes forming a circle of troops around an Indian village, explaining that the elements of the scene "all combined to produce an artistic effect, as beautiful as it was interesting" (Custer [1874] 1976, p. 38). For Custer, warfare and the dynamic between the military and its enemy present dramatic scenes not unlike those Custer enjoyed when frequenting the theater in New York City. In one passage, Custer describes an Indian battle line as "one of the finest and most imposing military displays ... which it has ever been my lot to behold" (Custer [1874] 1976, p. 32). In describing the weapons displayed by the Indians, Custer goes on to note, with sarcasm, the "strong love of fair play which prevails in the Indian Department" and the "wonderful liberality of our government, which not only is able to furnish its soldiers with the latest improved style of breechloaders to defend it and themselves, but is equally able and willing to give the same pattern of arms to their common foe" (p. 33). Tinged with sarcasm, this passage reveals "fair play" as a kind of fantasy contributing to the justification of colonialism. For example, the 1890 Wounded Knee Massacre was initially labeled a "battle," despite the fact that the disarmed Lakota were essentially defenseless with many women and children gunned down as they tried to flee to safety (Dunbar-Ortiz 2014, p. 155). Imagining an unfair conflict as an epic military battle is typical of Eurocentric historical narratives, and Custer's ambivalent attitude toward genuine justice reflects an awareness of the theatrical narrative typically used to justify colonialism.

Indian warriors undoubtedly possessed strength, ability, and determination, as evidenced by Custer's defeat at the Battle of the Little Bighorn. However, Custer's characterization of Indians as "hostile enemies" who posed a legitimate threat to the inevitable settling of the American West is problematic. As Brown explains in *Bury My Heart at Wounded Knee: An Indian History of the American West*, the United States federal government used the doctrine of Manifest Destiny to justify the total domination of Indians and their lands. Brown writes of Europeans, "They were the dominant race and therefore responsible for the Indians—along with their lands, their forests, and their mineral wealth" (Brown [1970] 2007, p. 8). While Custer's memoir reflects how Eurocentric and governmental narratives of the Indian Wars attempted to frame colonization as a "battle" between two equal foes, the idea that Indians could prevent or defeat the settlement of the West spurred by Manifest Destiny is inaccurate. Indeed, the arrival of Europeans to the New World brought with it multiple threats that Indians were powerless to counter or influence. These threats included not only disease but also

"European powers pitting one Indigenous nation against another or factions within nations, with European allies aiding one or both sides" (Dunbar-Ortiz 2014, pp. 40–41). Custer describes the "hostile enemy" as not only posing a threat to settlers and the military, but also as threatening those Indians who had resigned themselves to reservation life. In describing the need to ally with reservation Indians, Custer writes,

> The tribes against which we proposed to operate during the approaching campaign had been particularly cruel and relentless in their wanton attacks upon the Osages and Kaws, two tribes living peaceably and contentedly on well-chosen reservations in southwestern Kansas and the northern portion of the Indian Territory. No assistance in fighting the hostile tribes was desired, but it was believed, and correctly too, that in finding the enemy and discovering the location of his winter hiding places, the experience and natural tact and cunning of the Indians would be a powerful auxiliary if we could enlist them in our cause. (Custer [1874] 1976, p. 209)

This passage exemplifies the complexities of Custer's descriptive engagement with Indians as "enemy". While he clearly uses a racist logic when describing Indians as savage and uncivilized, those Indians who have acquiesced to reservation life and by extension Manifest Destiny are imagined as potential allies.

While Custer regularly describes elements of Indian culture, he also recounts key moments where he participates in Indian cultural practices. Most notable is Custer's story about participating in a peace pipe ceremony with a group of Indian chiefs. Custer describes visiting the lodge of Cheyenne chief Medicine Arrows, a relative of Black Kettle, a Cheyenne leader killed by Custer's 7th Cavalry during the Battle of the Washita. Once inside the lodge, Custer observes a medicine man facilitating a ceremony during which he (the medicine man) offers the pipe to Custer. Of being invited to smoke, Custer writes, "A desire to conform as far as practicable to the wishes of the Indians, and a curiosity to study a new and interesting phase of the Indian character, prompted me to obey the direction of the medicine man, and I accordingly began puffing away with as great a degree of nonchalance as a man unaccustomed to smoking could well assume" (Custer [1874] 1976, p. 357). Again, Custer expresses curiosity and a desire to learn about Indian cultural practices. However, this passage also reveals a desire to "conform," to some extent, to the "wishes of the Indians". Custer also yields to "the direction of the medicine man," which indicates a subtle shift in the power dynamic with Custer assuming a subservient role, if only briefly.

Importantly, the peace pipe ceremony is facilitated by the Indian chiefs as a way to broker a peace agreement with Custer. Custer explains that following the peace pipe ceremony, he agrees to a kind of peace pact with the chiefs: "I became for the time being an ardent advocate of peace measures, and informed the chiefs that such was my purpose at the time" (Custer [1874] 1976, p. 358). Custer's use of "for the time being" reflects that his interest in peace was temporary and likely disingenuous. However, Custer's memoir fails to mention a key element of the peace pipe ceremony as remembered from the Cheyenne perspective. Stiles (2016) describes the peace pipe ceremony as follows: "A ritual pipe was prepared, given to Custer to smoke, then passed around; a Cheyenne report claims that the ashes were dumped out on Custer's boots to curse him" (p. 322). Although it remains impossible to confirm every detail surrounding the peace pipe ceremony, these conflicting stories serve as a reminder that Custer's memoir is incapable of achieving a historical record that reflects the Indian perspective.

The peace pipe ceremony emerges as an opportunity for commiseration where Custer ultimately falls short. Following what Stiles (2016) calls "complicated negotiations" (323) regarding the desired release of two white women being held captive by the Cheyenne, Custer captures three Cheyenne leaders and threatens their lives. Stiles (2016) explains, "He [Custer] showed them the tree where he would hang them, so there would be no misunderstanding. After he executed them, he planned to assault the village" (p. 323). Custer's mission to convince the Cheyennes to surrender to the army lasts for several months, ultimately culminating as "Maj. Eugene Carr led the 5th Cavalry and a detachment of Pawnee scouts in a surprise attack on their [the Cheyennes and allies] camp near

Summit Springs in the Colorado Territory. They killed the famous Tall Bull along with scores of men, women, and children" (Stiles 2016, p. 323). During the peace pipe ritual, Custer performs an act of commiseration as part of an overarching colonial strategy. Custer is willing to act peaceably and sympathetically toward Indians who comply with his demands, such as reservation Indians. Those Indians who continue to resist, or who fail to meet Custer's demands, remain squarely in the position of an enemy that must be destroyed in the pursuit of settlement.

Arguably, one passage in *My Life on the Plains* reveals a moment of clear commiseration. This passage appears following Custer's discussion of the Indians' impressive horsemanship skills. Throughout out the memoir, Custer documents his impressions of Indian horsemanship, writing, "Surely no race of men, not even the famous Cossacks, could display more wonderful skills in feats of horsemanship than the Indian warrior on his native plains" (Custer [1874] 1976, p. 199). Custer goes on to describe an Indian warrior thrown from his pony who seemed fated to capture by the cavalry. Custer describes how "comrades of the fallen Indian" (Custer [1874] 1976, p. 201) rushed to his aid with the group of Indians ultimately escaping the cavalry's pursuit. Custer further expresses relief at the Indian's escape:

> Although chagrined at the failure of the pursuing party to accomplish the capture of the Indians, I could not wholly suppress a feeling of satisfaction, if not gladness, that for once the Indian had eluded the white man. I need not add that any temporary tenderness of feeling toward the two Indians was prompted by their individual daring and the heroic display of comradeship in the successful attempt to render assistance to a friend in need. (Custer [1874] 1976, p. 201)

In this passage, perhaps more than any other in his memoir, Custer expresses a sense of happiness at seeing Indians escape the cavalry. In writing that he "could not wholly suppress" this sense of happiness, Custer suggests a lack of control over his own feelings. He seems to experience a genuine, instinctual sense of kinship with the Indians, as he admires their bravery and comradeship—certainly, these are shared values among tribal warriors and the United States Army. However, Custer remains distanced from the Indian warriors. He admires their bravery within a battle scene, of sorts, but he does not reveal any awareness of the Indians as complex humans with whom he might want to learn from or forge a relationship. Custer's language is also careful to emphasize the rarity and transience of his feelings of commiseration toward Indians. In describing his tenderness as "temporary", and in using the language "for once", Custer emphasizes that his feelings are fleeting and that the Indian's escape is an exception rather than the rule. At no point does Custer feel truly threatened by the prospect of a grand-scale defeat by the Indians. Arguably, this hubris contributed significantly to Custer's fall at the Battle of the Little Bighorn.

Ultimately, what Custer's memoir is missing is a sense of genuine justice or mercy. Although he consistently expresses interest in and even respect for various elements of Indian life, the destruction of Indian life remains, in Custer's narrative, inevitable. Of course, as a military officer, he is directly involved in the destruction of Indian life necessitated by Westward expansion and settler colonialism, and he remains, throughout the book and until the day of his ultimate defeat, a willing participant in the destruction of Indian life. While Custer often ruminates on how Indians should be "managed" and expresses a desire for some measure of justice for Indians who have accepted the reservation system, these concerns are extended to only those Indians who have stopped resisting colonization. Custer dedicates an entire chapter of the memoir to an analysis of the Indian Bureau and notes many problems with corrupt agents. Still, in calling for the Indian Bureau to be transferred to the War Department as a way to address corruption, Custer only further reveals his support for state-sponsored assimilation. Custer writes, "At war the Indians are under the control of the military, at peace under the control of the civil officers" (Custer [1874] 1976, p. 174). Any sense of justice or mercy toward Indians remains contingent upon the Indians acquiescing to this control.

The final lines of *My Life on the Plains* capture the significance of the book from a literary and historical perspective. On the brink of a new expedition that would take him to the sacred Black Hills,

Custer directly addresses his readers: "Bidding adieu to civilization for the next few months, I also now take leave of my readers, who I trust, in accompanying me through my retrospect, have been enabled to gain a true insight into a cavalryman's 'Life on the Plains'" (Custer [1874] 1976, p. 381). The value in Custer's memoir ultimately lies not in what it purports to reveal about Indian life, but rather in what it reveals about Custer as a cavalryman and aspiring writer. Indeed, *My Life on the Plains* demonstrates the relationship between war and narrative in that the stories crafted in service of establishing an enemy are often tinged with injustice and an overarching political agenda. Just as Custer's memoir is severely flawed in attempting to depict Indian life from the perspective of the conqueror, dominant historical narratives are often complicit in the same way.

Additionally, *My Life on the Plains* humanizes Custer—often depicted in popular literature and film as a cartoonish, egomaniacal, knight-errant—as a real and complex individual. Many scholars find Custer a difficult subject to write about, largely due to his status as an agent of colonialism. However, as Cozzens (2016) and Utley and Washburn [1977] (2002) argue, dismissing Custer's perspectives because he was aligned with the conquering forces of colonialism does not contribute to a balanced or comprehensive historical narrative. Stiles (2016) understands Custer as a man of contradictions, and indeed, contradictions are evident in Custer's descriptions of Indians. Stiles explains, "By binding Indians' positive attributes to their savage, hostile state, he preserved his racial scheme—and superiority—without denying the truth of his experiences" (369). Surely, Custer was guilty of countless wrongs and injustices, and his memoir does not counter or mitigate those injustices. Nevertheless, the memoir remains an account from someone who was there, reflecting on and facilitating historical forces whose implications continue to shape American life today. As Mueller (2017) argues, "historical figures should be more than one-dimensional caricatures for modern Americans to use as emotional punching bags." Custer's identity as a military icon ultimately rested on the presence of an enemy from which he needed to distance himself in order for the logic of colonialism to take shape. Yet, Custer was face-to-face with that "enemy" in intimate ways that piqued his curiosity as both soldier and writer; the fact that Custer was an agent of colonialism does not mean that his interest in Indian life was disingenuous. Even within a war narrative clearly rooted in colonial ideology, the simplistic divisions between protagonist and antagonist, hero and enemy, are often unstable. Scholars and students can find value in Custer's memoir not for what it purports to reveal about Indian life, but rather in how it reveals the powerful role of narrative as a defining characteristic of war.

Funding: This research received no external funding.

Conflicts of Interest: The author declares no conflict of interest.

References

Brown, Dee. 2007. *Bury My Heart at Wounded Knee: An Indian History of the American West*. With a new foreward by Hampton Sides. New York: St. Martin's. First published 1970.

Callahan, Kathe, Melvin J. Dubnick, and Dorothy Olshfski. 2006. War Narratives: Framing Our Understanding of the War on Terror. *Public Administration Review* 66: 554–68. [CrossRef]

Cox, Alicia. 2017. "Settler Colonialism". *Oxford Bibliographies*. Available online: http://www.oxfordbibliographies.com/view/document/obo-9780190221911/obo-9780190221911-0029.xml (accessed on 6 February 2019).

Cozzens, Peter. 2016. *The Earth is Weeping: The Epic Story of the Indian Wars for the AmericanWest*. New York: Alfred A. Knopf.

Custer, George Armstrong. 1976. *My Life on the Plains, or, Personal Experiences with Indians*. Introduction by Edgar I. Stewart. Norman: University of Oklahoma Press. First published 1874.

Dunbar-Ortiz, Roxanne. 2014. *An Indigenous Peoples' History of the United States*. Boston: Beacon Press.

Kreyche, Gerald F. 1994. The Two Faces of George Armstrong Custer. *USA Today* 122: 2588.

Loomba, Ania. 2005. *Colonialism/Postcolonialism*. New York: Routledge.

Mueller, James E. 2017. Muller on 'A True Insight into a Cavalryman's Life': George Armstrong Custer as Literary Journalist. *American Journalism Historians Association*. Available online: https://ajha.wildapricot.org/Intelligencer/5288325 (accessed on 6 February 2019).

Stiles, T. J. 2016. *Custer's Trials: A Life on the Frontier of a New America*. New York: Penguin Random House.

Utley, Robert M., and Wilcomb E. Washburn. 2002. *Indian Wars*. New York: American Heritage Press. First published 1977.

© 2019 by the author. Licensee MDPI, Basel, Switzerland. This article is an open access article distributed under the terms and conditions of the Creative Commons Attribution (CC BY) license (http://creativecommons.org/licenses/by/4.0/).

Article

Meeting the Enemy in World War I Poetry: Cognitive Dissonance as a Vehicle for Theme

David Poynor

English Department, United States Naval Academy, Annapolis, MD 21402, USA; davidpoynor@gmail.com

Received: 28 January 2019; Accepted: 13 February 2019; Published: 19 February 2019

Abstract: Some World War I poems show an enemy soldier up close. This choice usually proves very effective for expressing the general irony of war, to be sure. However, I submit that showing interaction with the enemy also allows the speaker space to wrestle with internal conflict, guilt, or cognitive dissonance, and that it allows—or even forces—readers to participate in that struggle along with the speaker. While the poets' writings no doubt had therapeutic effects for the poets themselves, I focus more on the literary effects, specifically arguing that the poems are powerful to us readers since they heighten the personal exposure of the poets' psyches and since they make us share the dissonance as readers. I consider poems by Siegfried Sassoon, Wilfred Owen, Robert Graves, Ford Madox Ford, Herbert Read, and Robert Service.

Keywords: World War I; war poetry; cognitive dissonance; enemies; encounters; Siegfried Sassoon; Wilfred Owen; Robert Graves; Ford Madox Ford; Herbert Read; Robert Service

---

The canon of Great War English-language poetry, taken as a whole, is often said to reflect the absurdity and horror and all-encompassing haunting nature of war, and a rather salient theme is the common humanity and victimhood of those on both sides. Certainly there are some poems that speak nationalistically or otherwise derogatorily towards the German aggressors (Kipling 1914, "For All We Have and Are"; 1918, "Justice"; Hardy 1915, "The Pity of It"). But these poems typically refer to the enemy at a rather abstract level. Overall the role of the enemy in World War I poetry—especially by the poets who directly participated in combat—seems to be that of co-victim of a grander evil that afflicts both sides.

In some poems the poets have chosen to show an enemy soldier up close. This choice proves to be particularly effective for expressing the general irony of war, to be sure. But I submit that this approach also allows the speaker space to wrestle with internal conflict, guilt, or cognitive dissonance. Furthermore, the heightened personal exposure—the rawness or vulnerability or authenticity—of the poets' psyches is likely what gives the poems their power, since it demands that the reader participate in the struggle.

The gist of the concept of cognitive dissonance is that when people hold one belief, but find themselves behaving contrarily to that belief, they are in a state of internal discord as to which is true: their belief they said they held, or the behavior they seem to be actually doing. The theory, originally posited by Festinger in the late 1950s (Festinger 1957; Festinger and Carlsmith 1959), suggests that people must come up with some way to resolve the internal dissonance, so they tell themselves either that they did not actually believe so strongly what they had said they believed, or that they did not actually do [much of] what they seemed to be doing, or some other psychological ploy.[1,2] Though much has been made of the scientific testability of Festinger's ideas (See Krause 1972, for example), the essence of Festinger's original conception is that cognitive dissonance causes psychological discomfort and therefore is "a fundamentally motivational state" (Elliot and Devine 1994). This is the sense with which I am most concerned. I am focusing on the idea of internal discord and its effects—which might include madness if it is not mitigated, or telling a story in a way that eases the internal discomfort, or specifically discussing serious mental illness as a way to assure oneself that one is not so far gone.

Frontline soldiers would seem to be particularly susceptible to unresolved cognitive dissonance due to the extreme nature of what they are asked to do and see. For example, perhaps they have been told to be courageous, and they likely consider themselves to be so; but in a battle they find themselves cowering in a shell crater rather than advancing toward the enemy. The soldier could decide he is actually a coward after all (thus his initial belief was wrong), or he could decide the behavior was not cowardice but perfectly natural (thus his behavior was not what it seemed). The first option, identifying oneself as a coward, has a host of other social and internal drawbacks. But the second option may not satisfy either since it is somewhat dishonest to oneself. Such is the dilemma.[3]

Daniel Hipp's book *The Poetry of Shell Shock* (2005) discusses Great War poets Wilfred Owen, Ivor Gurney, and Siegfried Sassoon, putting their creative output in the context of their psychological injuries and recoveries, and arguing that the poems were deliberate and effective therapy (Hipp 2005, pp. 15–43, 44–107). Hipp also traces the developments in the understanding and treatment of "shell shock" in general and points out several theories of the time (ibid. pp. 15–43, 44–107)[4] Hipp's discussions highlight the therapeutic effects of the poets' writings for the poets themselves, but I will focus more on the literary effects, specifically arguing that the poems are powerful to us readers since we are made to share in the dissonance.

Michael Sarnowski, in a recent article in this journal, argues that the most salient and poignant war poems that speak of encounters with the enemy are those that "[shorten] the distance between the realities of ... War and the reader" (Sarnowski 2018, p. 7). For the World War I poets who experienced physical contact with the enemy, Sarnowski suggests, the tangible closeness of the two combatants contributes to the shocking effect, whereas World War II poet-soldiers who did their killing from a distance had to express this same humanization of the enemy in somewhat different ways. Sarnowski's

---

[1] See Festinger 1957, in which he lays out his theory. And the watershed experiment is that of Festinger and Carlsmith 1959, in which subjects were asked to do a task they all thought to be boring (the belief) but to tell the next person that it was fun (the inconsistent action). They were paid either $1 or $20 to do so. In the $20 condition the money explained the seeming discrepancy between the original belief and the inconsistent action, and these subjects showed little cognitive dissonance. The subjects in the $1 condition, though, could not say that the money was the reason for their behavior, so they had increased dissonance; and they sought to resolve it by changing their original attitudes to match their behavior.

[2] The original concept as posited by Festinger and his colleagues is usually spoken of in the context of people changing their minds about something. But more recently the concept has been broadened a good deal. For a good accessible summary of the concept, see McLeod 2018.
McLeod offers this critique: "Is it a perception (as 'cognitive' suggests), or a feeling, or a feeling about a perception? Aronson's revision of the idea of dissonance as an inconsistency between a person's self-concept and a cognition about their behavior makes it seem likely that dissonance is really nothing more than guilt" (McLeod 2018, p. 5). For the purposes of this paper, this reinterpretation will suffice.

[3] Indeed the concept of cognitive dissonance has been applied repeatedly in the context of war. As a single recent example, see Wayne Klug et al. 2011.

[4] Hipp paraphrases MacCurdy's (1918) treatise *War Neuroses* which suggests that because of the nature of trench warfare, "The First World War denied the soldier's acting in accordance with either a peace or war mentality—he could be neither compassionate nor aggressive toward the enemy. Instead, the instinct for survival became foremost in the soldier's mind" (Hipp 2005, p. 22) and again, "The soldier was forced into a prolonged state of waiting, unable to act in any manner other than a defensive posture" (Hipp 2005, p. 22). Freud, of course, would seem to factor in here as well. Freud's explanation was that "The conflict takes place between the old ego of peace time and the new war-ego of the soldier" (quoted in Hipp 2005, p. 26). Indeed, the War brought legitimacy to a Freudian understanding of war neurosis as "a flight from an intolerable, destructive reality through illness" (Leed 1979, quoted in Hipp 2005, p. 25).
For the purposes of this paper, I am not concerned with differentiating Festinger's "cognitive dissonance" from Freud's concept of an internal "ego-conflict" or from MacCurdy's idea of a struggle between conflicting "mentalities," and I even use the terms somewhat interchangeably, since they express the same essential idea.

argument focuses on distance—especially the difference between the combatants' distance in the two Wars' poetry. He suggests that the close distance "makes readers complicit in the actions of war ... [and exposes] readers to the battlefield experience and the degrees of inner turmoil of soldiers" (Sarnowski 2018, p. 7). With regard to the World War I poets, Sarnowski's point is well-taken; there is something exceptionally powerful about the poems that deal with direct interaction with the dead, especially the enemy dead. His discussion of Owen's "Strange Meeting" is also particularly helpful. It is at the end of his paper that Sarnowski briefly touches on the speaker's "inner turmoil" and the importance of that being shared by the reader. This shared internal dissonance is where I want to focus my attention.

Jahan Ramazani's 2016 article in *Modernism/modernity* also discusses how various Great War poets have used the trope of interaction with the enemy in one form or another to conceive of the enemy as "one's kin or mirror image," to "[break] down the narcissism of minor differences and [rhyme] soldiers across national lines," and to "dissolve any notion of one nation's higher claim to honor, freedom, justice, righteousness, and poetry by showing the opposing soldiers to be, in Service's words, 'just the same'"(Ramazani 2016, p. 871). Ramazani's paper is focused on the Great War, and it provides excellent discussion of examples of Great War poems that further a grand theme of "cosmopolitan sympathies," a phrase Ramazani borrows from Isaac Rosenberg's poem "Break of Day in the Trenches".[5]

Ramazani and Sarnowski both show that this theme of common humanity is conveyed especially powerfully in poems that depict a soldier seeing his enemy face-to-face. I submit that one reason this trope is so effective is that it allows—or even forces—readers to vicariously participate in the speaker's internal dissonance.

1. Scope and Method

There are not very many poems in the entire canon that actually show a direct face-to-face encounter with an enemy soldier. For this study I examined the entire contents of Tim Kendall's (2013), Candace Ward's (1997), and Jon Silkin's (1996) excellent anthologies and also the entire collection of Sassoon's war poetry as collected by Rupert Hart-Davis (Sassoon 1983), and Owen's war poetry as collected by C. Day Lewis (Owen 1964) and Jon Stallworthy (1974). Many of the poems convey the horrors of the War, and some of them mention dead soldiers, but only a few poems deal with encountering an enemy, alive or dead, up close.

My initial approach was to categorize Sassoon's war poems (Sassoon 1983) into four groups. There are poems with a specific depiction of enemies, usually dead, of which there are only possibly four. In a second group are poems that specifically and concretely depict a dead fellow English soldier, known or unknown, of which I count 11 for sure and four more that likely fit here best, so 15 in total. A third category is of poems that deal with or mention death or the dead in a less specific or more abstract way, not directly describing the event; in this category I put 38 or 40 poems. The final category is poems that do not deal with death at all (though they may deal with the abysmal fighting conditions or maybe with abstract sadness or longing). In this category are 46 poems written before 1920 and five written after.

A similar catalog for Wilfred Owen's war poems (Owen 1964) yields a similar pattern. Poems in which the speaker directly meets the enemy are very few, only one ("Strange Meeting") or at most three, depending on how they are interpreted. Poems in which the speaker describes dead English fellow soldiers count 10 or 12. Poems that deal with the dead in a less direct way count 19. Poems that do not specifically mention death at all number 21.

---

[5] Ramazani offers this important qualifier: "Of course the poetic cosmopolitanism I've been tracing isn't without its limitations. These cross-national solidarities may have global reverberations but are still largely enacted within a European and North American sphere. None of these poems aspire to solidarities with, say, a Turkish soldier in the Ottoman army. Despite the African, Middle Eastern, South Asian, and other non-European involvements with the war, our published poetic archive is largely European" (Ramazani 2016, p. 869).

Finally, beyond Sassoon and Owen, I count only four that mention encountering the enemy, and which I will discuss in this paper: "Only a Boche" by Robert Service, "That Exploit of Yours" by Ford Madox Ford, "A Dead Boche" by Robert Graves, and "The Happy Warrior" by Herbert Read.

But even among those poems that seem to mention an enemy, there are different levels of intimacy and interaction. Therefore, in this paper I have organized the poems according to the following three categories: poems that depict conversation or intimate interaction with an enemy, poems that depict only the seeing or touching of an enemy, and poems that are unclear about whether the encounter is with an enemy or not. Within those categories I have kept Sassoon's together and Owen's together but without regard to dates.

Whereas other scholars have so capably put the various poets' works into the context of the poets' lives and personal development (see Hibberd 1986, 2003; Stallworthy 1974; Campbell 1999), I have chosen to address the works more as individual pieces of art that all share a common focal point and possibly common themes and techniques. Where necessary I have considered the particular history or situation of the poet, but overall I wanted to examine the poems by type. I will not provide a complete explication for each poem, but will focus on the aspects that are germane to the discussion.

So, let us consider those few poems—four by Siegfried Sassoon, three by Wilfred Owen, one each by Robert Graves, Robert Service, Ford Madox Ford, and Herbert Read—in which the enemy soldier is an actor or foregrounded presence.

2. Poems Depicting Intimate Interaction or Conversation with the Enemy

2.1. "Only a Boche" by Robert Service (1916)

The first poem I want to consider is Robert Service's "Only a Boche" (Service 1916).[6] This poem portrays one of the most extended dealings with a direct face-to-face encounter with the enemy. In this poem the enemy soldier is alive—though barely—at least for a while. The poem's speaker is presumably Service himself (who was an ambulance driver) or someone like him serving in a medical capacity, not as a combatant. This noncombatant speaker marks an important difference from all the others under consideration. Nevertheless, the poet-speaker makes it clear that he is on one side and the Boche is on the other. In the poem, the medical team take in a gravely injured German soldier who apparently dies despite their best efforts, and who lies on his pitiful deathbed in a room where the ambulance-men play cards.

Throughout the poem, the speaker refers to the enemy soldier in a cold, even insulting way: "Only a Boche" (title, lines 24, 47), "What's the use of risking one's skin for a tyke that's going to die?" (line 2), "the cursed foe" (line 16), "confound him" (line 31), and "One foe the less" (line 49). But it is clear those words are bluster, or else they are an ego defense mechanism for dealing with cognitive dissonance, for the speaker's behavior belies his bravado. Despite the Boche's status as an enemy, the speaker takes him in and treats him (lines 1–12), admires his toughness (line 7), and even "carrie[s] him in like our own" (line 8). The dying man is allowed to stay in the presence of the card-players (lines 9–18), and in a break in the card game the speaker goes to the man and observes him closely. During this perusal, Service's speaker notices that "The dying Boche on the stretcher there has a queer resemblance to me" (line 24). This is the central theme of the poem. The speaker goes on:

> It gives one kind of a turn, you know, to come on a thing like that.
> It's just as if I were lying there, with a turban of blood for a hat,
> Lying there in a coat grey-green instead of a coat grey-blue,
> With one of my eyes all shot away, and my brain half tumbling through; (lines 25–28)

---

[6] See Ramazani's (2016) excellent discussion of this poem. Ramazani says, "Although Service has received less literary critical attention than other war poets, 'Only a Boche' and 'A Song of the Sandbags' are vivid dramatizations of a soldier's tentative breakthrough to the shared humanity of the enemy other" (p. 864). I do not discuss "A Song of the Sandbags" in this paper; while it certainly speaks about the men's shared humanity, it does not involve actual meeting of an enemy.

>   -   -   -   -   -   -
>
> And confound him, too! He wears like me on his finger a wedding ring,
> And around his neck, as around my own, by a greasy bit of string,
> A locket hangs with a woman's face, and I turn it about to see:
> Just as I thought . . . on the other side the faces of children three; (lines 31–34)
>
>   -   -   -   -   -   -
>
> 'Zut!' I say. 'He has beaten me; for me, I have only two,'
> And I push the locket beneath his shirt, feeling a little blue. (lines 37–38)

The speaker mentions the contrasts between himself and the German: they wear different color coats and have a different number of children, for example. But ironically, the dying German is noteworthy primarily for his similarity to the speaker himself. The close contact with the dying man has taught a lesson to the speaker and the reader about the common humanity of those on both sides. The speaker knows that the German man's family, so similar to his own, will experience the same anguish as any other family would. The idea that is "kind of spoiling [his] play" (line 45) is that the dying German is so similar to himself.

But the poem is powerful for another reason as well: the speaker reveals an interesting bit of soldierly ego defense, a coping mechanism to which many have resorted when faced with such internal dissonance. After a reverie of sympathy in the fifth to eighth stanzas, he reverts to bravado and the logic of war. He tells himself "War is war, and he's only a Boche, and we all of us take our chance" (line 47). And, perhaps ironically self-congratulatory for his chosen job as a healer and not a killer, he justifies himself when he admits, "I'm heartily glad I'm not/The man who gave him his broken head, the sniper who fired the shot" (lines 49–50). The speaker's response to the horror he has seen is to deny his responsibility for it, but this denial implies that there is something he feels the need to deny. Even before the turn in the ninth stanza, there are hints at the speaker's internal dissonance. His curse "And confound him, too!" (line 31), which might be commonly directed at an enemy soldier, is here uttered only upon recognition of their common humanity. The speaker curses the German, as if to remind himself that the Boche is a dangerous enemy; but actually the enemy has proved the more ordinary and domestic and familial, and thus he has touched the speaker's sense of guilt. Contact with the dying German has left the speaker nonplussed to say the least, and the poem is about the speaker's exposing his inner conflict and his flailing efforts at justifying or at resolving the inner turmoil of what he has got himself into. This uncomfortable wrestling, this raw revelation of his own struggle, is what makes this poem so compelling.

2.2. "Strange Meeting" by Wilfred Owen (1918)

Owen's most poignant example of direct conversation with the enemy is the poem "Strange Meeting" (Owen 1918a), in which the British speaker converses with the German he killed, when both dead men meet in hell.[7] Sarnowski (2018) has done an admirable job explicating the poem, so I will not go to great length here. The gist of Sarnowski's discussion is that the speaker is humanizing his enemy, as the German speaks of his dreams, virtues, passions, and overall hopelessness—all of which are assumed to be the same as the British Tommy feels. I agree that the common victimhood of the two opponents is a salient theme. But one thing I will add is that it is possible that Owen is here voicing and empowering the enemy not just as a way to give some dignity to the German, but also as a way to expiate his (or his speaker's) guilt, much as Service's speaker tried to resolve his cognitive dissonance in "Only a Boche."

---

[7] Dominic Hibberd (2003) writes: "Among the thousands of poems written during the Great War, there are very few about the poet-soldier meeting his dead victim, fewer still in which the two men talk to each other, and perhaps none except "Strange Meeting" in which the killer stands his ground, accepting the truth of what he has done" (Hibberd 2003, p. 311).

The irony and absurdity of war and the common humanity of the enemies are all conveyed without need of the last few lines of the poem. But those lines add something important: "I am the enemy you killed, my friend. / I knew you in this dark; for so you frowned / Yesterday through me as you jabbed and killed" (lines 40–42). This revelation is particularly jarring, for with these violent words "jabbed and killed" we are jolted from our reverie. It was not a distant "thump[ing]" gun that killed these men. No, the speaker cannot fully escape his culpability. But he has strategically recalled his personal guilt only at the end, while foregrounding the corporate guilt which he is more ready to acknowledge.[8]

Another coping strategy is that Owen has made some greater meaning from the whole experience, which he shares with us. The German soldier's speech bemoans his inability to tell the truths of war, now that he is dead. He regrets that now " . . . something had been left / Which must die now. I mean the truth untold" (lines 23–24) and further prophesies, "Now men will go content with what we spoiled, / Or discontent, boil bloody, and be spilled" (lines 26–27). That is, future countrymen will not understand what these speakers have learned. The speech certainly has a mood of sadness and frustration. Those who are best qualified to voice the hell of war are the voiceless dead. But Owen is in fact using the German's would-be speech to tell that very "truth untold," thus deriving at least some meaning from the absurdity, and, importantly, mitigating if not entirely removing his own guilt.

Finally, in this poem, we the readers share in the British soldier-poet's dissonance, for we must ourselves decide what to make of him who on the one hand was a killer but on the other hand is wiser for it. Is the abstracted wisdom worth the very concrete lives of these young men?

2.3. "That Exploit of Yours" by Ford Madox Ford (1918)

According to Peter Robinson 2010, Ford wrote this poem "without knowledge of Owen's 'Strange Meeting'" (Robinson 2010, p. 109), but the similarity is remarkable. In this poem (Ford 1918) a first-person speaker finds himself in hell and speaks directly to the enemy who killed him. As in Owen's poem (Owen 1918a), the realm of the dead is depicted as unthreatening rather than terrible. And as with Owen, there is a mood of resignation. But Owen foregrounds the enemy—whom the speaker has killed—and allows him the largest share of lines in the poem. In Ford's poem, the speaker has been killed by his enemy, he only addresses his enemy at the end, the killer's words are imagined but not directly quoted, and it is not clear that the killer is even in the same place or dead at all.

Before addressing his killer, Ford's speaker observes two other soldiers, one English and one German, who are also meeting and who tell each other—and themselves—the same thing, "Exclaim[ing] always in identical tones: / 'I at least have done my duty to Society and the Fatherland!'" (lines 10–11). The speaker mocks their self-important statement by calling it a "cliché" (line 12) and accusing his killer of probably saying the same thing. But the irony goes even further: the two patriots observed by the speaker are actually not noble at all. The British soldier "Was stuck by a pitchfork, / Climbing a wall to steal apples" (lines 3–4), and the German "died from the fall of his horse on some tram-lines/In Dortmund" (lines 6–7). Indeed these two are not even enemy combatants who faced each other; they died in different places under different non-combat circumstances. They are just as dead as other, more noble, victims, however, and they tell themselves what most of us might tell ourselves about the war dead: that their sacrifice was noble and meaningful. The speaker's derision of

---

[8] Hibberd (1986, 2003) suggests that Owen's poems of this period might be an effort to deal with guilt or dissonance, but from other sources: "his failure to live up to his own standards" (Hibberd 1986, p. 76) as an officer, and his wrestling with the specter of possibly being a coward. After a stressful battle in which Owen encountered physical and emotional injury—but "may have been helpless with shock" (Ibid., p. 75)—his incoming commanding officer hinted if not directly stated that Owen was a malingerer. Says Hibberd, "Owen would have felt himself disgraced . . . . It helps to explain his return to the front in 1918 and the heavy weight of guilt that loads his finest writings" (Ibid., p. 77). Hibberd also summarizes Owen's general conflicted-ness about the war: "A soldier had to ignore [Christ's] commandment [of passivity] because Prussian militarism could only be extinguished by military means" (Hibberd 2003, p. 248).

the "cliché" implies that such a platitude does not ring true. He calls it "strange" (line 12), revealing that he himself is conflicted and unsure how to make sense of his death.

The poet's depictions of the foolish enemies who forever "exclaim" their "cliché" is thematically powerful on its own. But the end—when the speaker confronts his enemy directly—adds something important. We readers may find ourselves conflicted too, since these soldiers are silly while the context of the situation is inherently sad and absurd. But we become even more uncomfortable when, at the end of the poem, Ford has his speaker directly address his own killer:

> "For I will bet my hat that you who sent me here to Hell
> Are saying the selfsame words at this very moment
> Concerning that exploit of yours" (lines 13–15)

Ford's speaker considers that his own death is likely also counted as nothing more than a rousing "exploit" on the part of his enemy. Here again we see some differences from Owen's poem (Owen 1918a) which had the speaker and his enemy share in the wisdom of the grave. In Ford's poem, the speaker is different from his enemy. The enemy is probably saying the same hollow maxims, while the speaker has learned that such statements are foolish. But the poem is inherently frustrating, since—as with Owen's discussion of what might have been—the speaker is in no position to change things beyond uttering what he has observed. Furthermore, having debunked our platitudes, Ford leaves us no axiom to help us make sense of what we have just read.

After all, there is ambiguity in the phrase "you who sent me here to Hell" (line 13). I have been suggesting that this refers to an enemy soldier, but it is hard to ignore the possible double meaning, that we the society, we the readers, are the ones who have condemned him. Regardless of whom he is addressing, we feel the sting when the speaker here calls us out for thinking we understand.

3. Poems Depicting only the Seeing or Touching of an Enemy

3.1. "A Dead Boche" by Robert Graves (1916)

Robert Graves' poem "A Dead Boche" (Graves 1916) shows a meeting with the enemy. But in this poem, the enemy is dead, and the speaker does not interact with him beyond just observing his decaying body. In the second stanza, the poet shows us the dead man. The last lines run thus:

> ... a dead Boche; he scowled and stunk
> With clothes and face a sodden green,
> Big-bellied, spectacled, crop-haired,
> Dribbling black blood from nose and beard. (lines 9–12)

The poet's descriptions are unflinching and disgusting, but they are mostly sensory descriptions only, as a photograph would be. That is, though we see the "dribbling black blood" and the "face a sodden green," these do not carry any implication that the man is an enemy or otherwise to be censured. The body could be that of anyone, foe or friend, as the belly, spectacles, hair, blood, nose, and beard could all belong to anyone. The poet does show that the corpse is repugnant, using words like "mess" (line 8), "unclean" (line 8), the mildly disrespectful "Boche" (line 9), and the clause "he scowled and stunk" (line 9), but those are the closest thing to insult or disrespect in the poem, and they only serve to show that the corpse was a horrible thing. In fact, these most insulting words happen early in the description; as the stanza goes on, the connotations become even more mild and neutral, until we are left only with the perfectly neutral words "spectacled," "crop-haired," and "nose and beard." The poet proceeds in this manner to bring us readers with him. Note that the speaker is well aware of his audience, that we are reading his poems looking for "blood and fame" (line 2). The title, and the first reference to the "Boche" in line 9 have set us up to expect something—that there is something particularly important about the dead man's "Boche" identity, his "enemy-ness." But when we finish the description, we find that he is disgusting only because he is dead, and he could have been anyone. There is nothing particularly enemy-like or hateful about him. Our partisanship has tempered into general pity. But we shouldn't be surprised; the speaker has told us to expect "A certain cure for lust of blood" (line 6).

This poem shows a change of perspective on the part of the poet-speaker. We could call this a case of dissonance, for the speaker, it seems, had crafted a narrative for himself that no longer serves. (See Canary 1980). He himself probably had wanted to "hear of blood and fame," which would at least go some way toward redeeming the horrible experience of war. But he has come to find that such a telling is not ringing true. He feels guilty that he has told such "songs of War" that might lead his readers to expect the same, and he seeks to warn us against his mistake. He warns us, though, just by showing us a picture, and leaves us to wrestle with our own "blood and fame" narratives as he has had to do.[9]

3.2. "The Happy Warrior" by Herbert Read (1919)

Herbert Read's poem "The Happy Warrior" (Read 1919) shows an obvious connection to Wordsworth's poem of a similar name, "Character of the Happy Warrior" (1806) and indeed should be interpreted in light of that connection. Wordsworth asks his reader "Who is the happy warrior? Who is he / That every man in arms should wish to be?" (lines 1–2) and goes on to answer his question by suggesting the happy warrior is a generous and noble spirit, who among other things is described thus:

> . . . if he be called upon to face
> Some awful moment to which Heaven has joined
> Great issues, good or bad for human kind,
> Is happy as a Lover; and attired
> With sudden brightness, like a Man inspired;
> And, through the heat of conflict, keeps the law
> In calmness made, and sees what he foresaw; (Wordsworth 1806, lines 48–54)

In Read's poem, Wordsworth's question is alluded to in the title and in last two lines. But otherwise the poem is starkly different. Read describes the soldier's "painful sobs," (line 1) "strain'd hands," (line 2) "aching jaws," (line 3) "hot parch'd tongue," (line 3) and "Bloody saliva," (line 6). In lines 8–10, the speaker says, "I saw him stab / and stab again / a well-killed Boche." The next two lines are the end: "This is the happy warrior, / this is he . . . " (lines 11–12).

The poem admits none of the values which would seem to be particularly important to a poet. There is no honor, no nobility—the warrior is sobbing and drooling, probably a victim of shell shock based on his crazed appearance. There is not even consciousness or communication—the warrior is "search[ing] unconsciously" (line 4), he is biting his tongue (line 3), and "He cannot shriek" (line 5). In the place of honor, nobility, consciousness, and communication, there is only savage violence.

Thus the poem stands in sharp contrast to Wordsworth's original thematically. This contrast is underscored by the poet's obvious homage to the original, not just in the direct quotation (title, lines 11–12) but also in the jarring manipulation of the original poem's catalog structure. Wordsworth's poem features lines that are on the whole rather abstract. For example, the selection above contains not a single concrete image, the closest things being the dubious phrases "happy as a Lover" (line 51) and "attired / With sudden brightness" (lines 51–52). Read's poem, though, contains terse, disturbing, concrete images in every line but the last two. In the midst of this perverse third-person catalog,

---

[9] Canary (1980) points out that Graves himself objected to the overly-psychological approach to poetry analyses, insisting that each poem "says exactly what it means" (Graves, quoted in Canary 1980, p. 20). But Canary goes on to point out that Graves also placed "stress on the private source of the conflicts held in tension in the poems" (Canary 1980, p. 23) and that he believed poems stem best from "unforeseen fusion in [the poet's] mind of apparently contradictory emotional ideas" (Graves, quoted in Canary 1980, p. 22). Canary suggests these contradictions include various identities of the poet-speaker, and the act of writing imposes order by reconciling the poet's contradictions (Canary 1980, pp. 22–23).

the speaker further corrupts Wordsworth's Romantic template by injecting a short first-person account that tells of the warrior's encounter with the enemy: "I saw him stab / and stab again / a well-killed Boche" (lines 8–10). As if the third-person depiction of the warrior is not disturbing enough, the blunt, unadorned first-person account adds to and confirms the truth of the story.

It is unclear if Read himself actually witnessed this behavior, although it is certainly possible. It might not even seem that the speaker himself seems to feel any particular internal dissonance, but I suggest that the matter-of-fact tone shows the speaker's desensitization to such behavior or is an ego defense such as denial or rationalization. Regardless, the poem seems both to express a general dissonance on the part of society as a whole, and to elicit dissonance on the part of all of us readers when we see that the noble young men we send off to fight are rendered helpless and brutish. The reference to the very popular poem of the very British Wordsworth implies that we readers are also supposed to make that connection and to see the difference between the reality on display and the Romantic renderings so prevalent in the culture. And while the sheer contrasts between the Romantic abstraction and the eyewitness concrete description are powerful in themselves, the injection of the stabbing scene—the treatment of the enemy—is important. It is not just the pitiable ruin of a young man that stirs us so; it is the added detail of his crazed, blinded, fruitless brutality that really brings the point home.

3.3. "Remorse" by Siegfried Sassoon (1918)

Siegfried Sassoon's "Remorse" (Sassoon 1918) is a poem wherein internal conflict is brought out via an encounter with the enemy, in this case still alive. The poem highlights the guilt and horror of what one does to one's enemies. It is not clear that the character himself touched the Germans or participated quite the same as his comrades did, but he is horrified nonetheless. In this poem the character recollects:

> Remembering how he saw those Germans run,
> Screaming for mercy among the stumps of trees:
> Green-faced, they dodged and darted: there was one
> Livid with terror, clutching at his knees . . .
> Our chaps were sticking 'em like pigs . . . 'O hell!'
> He thought—'there's things in war one dare not tell'. (lines 7–12)

The poet here conveys the graphic horrors of war. The words are concrete and active: "run" (line 7), "Screaming" (line 8), "dodged and darted" (line 9) "clutching" (line 10), "sticking 'em" (line 11). The tone is appropriately frenetic and terrible: "Screaming for mercy" (line 8), "Livid with terror" (line 10), "'O hell!'" (line 11). And the poet seems to be showing how the terrible violence of war has impacts beyond its stated aims: not only has it hurt the Germans, but it has hurt the environment which is now "swamp"(line 1) and "pit" (line 1) and "stumps" (line 8), and it has hurt the British soldier himself.

The character is obviously moved by what he has witnessed, and we the readers share in the horror. There is a general sympathy toward the German victims, which we the readers also share. But in this poem it is the brutality of the action—brutality displayed by his own men, even, with all the accompanying guilt and cognitive dissonance that brings—that seems harder to bear than just the horrible ubiquity of death. We the readers share in this brutality too. The speaker ironically tells us exactly that which "one dare not tell," so we now are in on the secret, complicit. But not only do we share the guilt and horror, we watch the character wrestle internally as he decides not to tell what he's seen. Campbell (1999) suggests that the speaker decides to "bottle up the nightmare memories and the sense of guilt that goes with them" (Campbell 1999, p. 179). The brutal action itself is one thing, telling the truth about it is another, and deciding not to tell that truth is yet another. We the readers have experienced all three, because we have watched the poet and his characters do their internal wrestling right in front of us.

3.4. "A Night Attack" by Siegfried Sassoon (1916, Published 1970)

In Sassoon's poem "A Night Attack" (Sassoon 1916), the speaker is safe at an aid or R & R station behind the lines, and yet he says, "I remember things I'd best forget," (line 2) and goes on to describe a traumatic incident. Stanza two starts with the speaker unable to fully forget the war: "To-night I smell the battle, miles away" (line 9), and in stanza four the speaker fully flashes back to the battle itself when he encountered a dead German soldier. He says:

> Then I remembered someone that I'd seen
> Dead in a squalid, miserable ditch,
> Heedless of toiling feet that trod him down.
> He was a Prussian with a decent face,
> Young, fresh, and pleasant, so I dare to say.
> No doubt he loathed the war and longed for peace,
> And cursed our souls because we'd killed his friends. (lines 28–34)

The speaker goes on to imagine what the German was probably doing at the time of his death—likely watching his friends shoveling and otherwise ignoring the British onslaught as best he could, (in the same way the British would have acted on their side). Then in stanza 6 the speaker's identification with the dead Prussian becomes even more pronounced: "Then the damned English loomed in scrambling haste / Out of the dark and struggled through the wire" (lines 46-47). Here the British speaker is able so to see from the German perspective that he can even curse his own side, not just assuming what the man must have thought as in line 34, but actually speaking from the German point-of-view. The last lines of the poem describe the body of the enemy:

> I found him there
> In the gray morning when the place was held.
> His face was in the mud; one arm flung out
> As when he crumpled up; his sturdy legs
> Were bent beneath his trunk; heels to the sky. (lines 53–57)

The "decent face, / Young, fresh, and pleasant" is now "in the mud;" his "sturdy legs" bent awkwardly, or even in a position of kneeling and abject humiliation. The implication is that it is not just the horror of encountering a dead man that has rendered our speaker so emotionally ragged, but that it is the guilt and immorality of witnessing the ruin of a would-be decent fellow person. The speaker has said that he is remembering "things [he'd] best forget" (line 2); his ego no doubt demands that he should forget or try to forget, but he is unsuccessful in this attempt. Rather, his answer to the inner conflict between his duty to fight for England and his revulsion at how he has ruined another man is to entertain a "reassessment of the patriotic ethic" (Campbell 1999, p. 111).[10]

3.5. "Enemies" by Siegfried Sassoon (1917)

A final poem of this type is Sassoon's poem "Enemies" (Sassoon 1917a) in which the speaker mentions the "hulking Germans that I shot" trying to protect a comrade. The setting of the vision is "some queer sunless place / Where Armageddon ends" (line 1–2), which suggests the same realm as Owen would later describe in his "Strange Meeting" (Owen 1918a) and Ford in "That Exploit of Yours" (Ford 1918). The place is "queer" and "sunless" but hardly infernal. Indeed the only thing described as "hot" is the speaker's own "brooding rage" (line 6).

The second stanza shows the friend and the Germans together in the realm of the dead:

---

[10] That the poet is conflicted might also reflected by Sassoon's refusal to publish the poem, likely concerned that "its embryonic pacifist sentiments and the Prussian soldier's view of "damned English" might be altogether too contentious" (Campbell 1999, p. 110).

> He stared at them, half-wondering; and then
> They told him how I'd killed them for his sake—
> Those patient, stupid, sullen ghosts of men;
> And still there seemed no answer he could make.
> At last he turned and smiled. One took his hand
> Because his face could make them understand.

While the speaker seems to have seen the Germans die, there is no gory detail about their bodies. Indeed these Germans are now ghosts who understand their fate and gently gather and take the hand of the dead English friend. There is no horror here, indeed not even much of a sense of guilt. Taken together with the setting, the words "untroubled" (line 4), "patient," (line 9) and "smiled," (line 11) and the clauses "One took his hand," (line 11) and "his face could make them understand" (line 12), establish a tone that is resigned at worst, perhaps even beatific.

The speaker knows he bears some responsibility. He knows he is the one who shot the Germans (line 5) and that he did so in a heated rage (line 6). But this guilt is not nearly as salient as the overall mood of quietness and acceptance. The speaker is quite likely justifying himself: the killing of the enemies is not so bad because they are now in a better place among a brotherhood of the dead. This could be another case of turning a horror into a beauty, as we will see Owen do in "Has Your Soul Sipped?" (Owen 1918b). The situation must have been intense and dire indeed: watching his friend in danger and dying, being unable to help except from a distance, rendering his help by bringing gross death to the friend's assailants, only to have his friend die after all. On recollecting, the speaker's horror is softened into something of a dream to convince himself that he is an agent of something bigger than himself. This dream makes his own guilt less salient, but that comes at the cost of self-deception; he must construct an alternative to the waste he has seen. The dead thus are said to share something beautiful which the rest of us have yet to achieve. The poem is poignant, and its power comes not just from the paradoxical rendering of a horrible scene into a beautiful one, but also from our sense that we have just watched the poet-speaker wrestle with those demons. We are as powerless to stop his self-deception as he was to stop his friend's death.

4. Poems Depicting a Dead Soldier Whose Identity as an Enemy is Uncertain

4.1. "The Rear-Guard" by Siegfried Sassoon (1917)

Sassoon's "The Rear-Guard" (Sassoon 1917b) may be about direct contact with an enemy soldier. In this piece, the soldier's tour of a fetid dugout becomes dramatically hellish when the soldier discovers the man he's been trying to awaken is in fact dead:

> Savage, he kicked a soft, unanswering heap,
> And flashed his beam across the livid face
> Terribly glaring up, whose eyes yet wore
> Agony dying hard ten days before;
> And fists of fingers clutched a blackening wound". (lines 14–18)

The character is horrified and runs out of the dugout, "Unloading hell behind him step by step" (line 25).

"The Rear-Guard" is less obviously about an enemy. In fact, no mention is made of the nationality of either the dugout or the dead man. Tim Kendall's note on this poem indicates that there was an actual incident that precipitated this poem, when either Sassoon or his Company Commander asked directions of a dead man, and in that incident the deceased was German (Kendall 2013, p. 254). The poem's title and the soldier's confusion would seem to imply that the soldier is in the enemy's trench, so taken together we may infer that the dead man is German.

But while this is a harrowing brush with a dead enemy soldier, there is no reflection, no lesson learned, no voice given to the dead. The dead man is horrible, but only because he is dead; shaking a dead Englishman would likely have yielded the same response. This poem certainly is a powerful poem, but its theme is the overall hell of war rather than a particular lesson learned from encountering the enemy.

Nevertheless, the act of encountering the dead man has been impactful. The soldier has been shocked or awakened by and to the horrors around him. The poem is told in third-person, unlike all but one of the other examples; presumably the speaker (whether the same as the soldier or not) is creating distance, telling the poem in third person as a way of easing his troubled mind. The act of writing the poem itself could also be considered an act of "Unloading hell behind him" (line 25), and in fact Hipp (2005) has rendered a very good reading of this poem in these terms. Hipp points out that the character in the poem flees, "Climb[ing] through darkness to the twilight air" (line 24), ironically considering the "twilight" of the violent battlefield to be "rosy" (line 7), better than the "unwholesome air" (line 3) of the safer trench which to him is hell (Hipp 2005, pp. 158–59). Hipp suggests this poetic irony is reflective of Sassoon's wounded and conflicted state, wherein "returning to the war was the only means of achieving inner peace" (Hipp 2005, p. 159; see also Campbell 1999, p. 142).

4.2. *"Has Your Soul Sipped?" by Wilfred Owen (1918)*

Another Wilfred Owen piece that might involve contact with the enemy is "Has Your Soul Sipped?" (Owen 1918b) which mentions a dead boy. It is unclear if this boy is an enemy, a fellow British soldier, purely a poetic construction, or a composite of wounded and dying youth of both sides. Possibly the poem could imply that Owen himself had participated in the killing of an enemy at close range, as is likely based on the stories of his gallantry that won him the Military Cross.[11] Or it could even be that he had seen or participated in the murder of a prisoner (presumably German, but possibly British)—although it should be noted that this is a conjecture for which neither Hibberd nor other biographers give any indication. Alternatively, it may be about a young man under Owen's command, since the metaphor shows a "martyr / Smiling at God," (lines 33–34) and Owen says, "To me was that smile," (line 35) implying an analogous relationship. This is consistent with Hibberd's statement about Owen's anxiety for his perceived failings as an officer (Hibberd 1986, pp. 71–78). I discuss the poem here because it may be about a close encounter with the enemy—though admittedly it may be about some other poor lad. If it is about a fellow British soldier, it still reflects the cognitive dissonance we have seen in the other works under discussion. If it is in fact about an enemy, the argument is so much the stronger.

In the poem, the speaker discusses a strange beauty he found in war. He asks, "Has your soul sipped / Of the sweetness of all sweets?" (lines 1–2) and, starting in the second stanza, he provides his own answer:

> I have been witness
> Of a strange sweetness,
> All fancy surpassing
> Past all supposing.

From here, the poet describes this "strange sweetness" as "sweeter than nocturnes / Of the wild nightingale" (lines 15–16) and "sweeter than odours / Of lifting leaves" (lines 19–20). Then the poem gradually turns away from nature imagery and towards words more associated with war, as the sweetness is now said to be "Sweeter than death" (line 23) "Or the proud wound / The victor wears" (lines 27–28). Finally, the speaker says the sweetness is sweeter than all these things . . .

---

[11] Hibberd (2003) includes the text of the citation accompanying Owen's Military Cross: "On the Company Commander becoming a casualty, he assumed command and shewed fine leadership and resisted a heavy counter attack. He personally manipulated a captured enemy M.G. from an isolated position and inflicted considerable losses on the enemy. / Throughout he behaved most gallantly" (p. 376).
Interestingly, Owen's brother Harold has a different version which paints Wilfred as less violent; it reads "He personally captured an enemy Machine Gun in an isolated position and took a number of prisoners." Hibberd discusses the efforts of Harold and other writers to protect Wilfred's reputation after his death (ibid., pp. 367–76).

> Or the sweet murder
> After long guard
> Unto the martyr
> Smiling at God;
> To me was that smile,
> Faint as a wan, worn myth,
> Faint and exceeding small,
> On a boy's murdered mouth.

The poem exhibits the use of pararhyme or "consonantal rhyme" as Lewis calls it (Owen 1964, p. 113), which strikes me as creating a haunting and suspenseful mood. The pararhyme leads to a pervasive sense that the clusters of images in the poem are less than solidly connected, that the poet-speaker is knowingly linking things that do not quite go together as neatly as he implies.

This poem is troubling, partly because the horrible is so close to—even identical to—the sweet. We can perhaps appreciate that there must be some beauty in the relief that an imprisoned martyr must feel when long-anticipated death finally comes, but it is less clear how the death of a murdered boy fits the same beauty. Regardless of the incident itself that gave rise to the poem, Owen's point seems to be that in war there is a reordering of values, an acceptance of the surreal, and a desire to affix meaning to the meaningless. Owen is dealing with cognitive dissonance by celebrating an ugliness as if it were beauty.

George Johnson (2010) suggests that part of Owen's dissonance has to do with his homosexuality, and Johnson interprets "Has Your Soul Sipped" in this light, suggesting that the crux is that the speaker of the poem is enraptured with the smile of the dead boy. Borrowing from and extrapolating Johnson's reading, I suggest that the somewhat surprising ending to the poem—"All his life's sweetness / Bled into a smile" (lines 45–46)—is multi-layered and ironic in many ways: not only is the speaker daringly expressing his ironic attraction to that which is dead, finding beauty in the hell around him, but he also is expressing another great secret: that the boy's mouth itself is what is attractive. At another level, the paradox of finding beauty amid the war might be rather starkly poignant, but ultimately it could be acceptable to readers as something raw and authentic from a young man struggling to understand the hell he has been forced into; but the paradox of the bard's homoerotic attraction to the boy would likely not be acceptable at all, and yet it may be the more deeply-seeded. Finally, it is noteworthy that both conflicts in a sense are forced onto him: he is a victim of the war, of the society that caused the war, of his desires, and of the society of readers who want to hear what he has to say and yet simultaneously do not. I do not doubt that such socio-sexual conflicts as Johnson describes are indeed part of Owen's motivation. Regardless, such conflicts would surely augment the already-tangible cognitive dissonance any soldier would face.

4.3. "Mental Cases" by Wilfred Owen (1918)

"Mental Cases" is another poem of Owen's that describes encountering dead soldiers (Owen 1918c). In this case, again, it is unclear if the dead are enemies or comrades. This anonymity is probably part of Owen's point, though. The "Multitudinous murders they once witnessed" (line 12), the "blood from lungs that had loved laughter" (line 14), the "shatter of flying muscles" (line 16), and "Carnage incomparable" (line17) are witnessed just the same, whether done to enemies' bodies or to comrades'. Perhaps that is why Owen does not specify the victims. Rather, the horror is shared, by those who died and by those who killed, by those who went insane and by those who did not, by all of us.

The poem opens with the question "Who are these?" (line 1) and describes the mental cases as "purgatorial shadows" (line 2), "Baring teeth that leer like skulls' teeth wicked" (line 4). At the end of the first stanza the speaker asks again: "Surely we have perished / Sleeping, and walk hell; but who these hellish?" (line 8–9). The speaker is establishing a contrast here between "we" and "they," stating that "we" are among those who "walk hell"—thus, probably soldiers. But the distinction between "we" and "they" is cleverly undercut later when the word "us" is used in a more inclusive and poignant sense.

In the last few lines, the mental cases are:

> ... plucking at each other;
> Picking at the rope-knouts of their scourging;
> Snatching after us who smote them, brother,
> Pawing us who dealt them war and madness. (lines 25–28)

The trauma, the horror, the understandable collapse into insanity which these men face is the fault of "us," not them. Combatants and non-combatants alike, we are all guilty of their ruin.

But there is a psychological element too, across several layers. The speaker refers to the mental cases as "them," creating some distance between them and himself (and us). But it is clear that he sympathizes with them, that he understands and sides with them, even against "us" and himself. This identification with the stricken but also as a commentator could be a means of ego defense as well. Clearly, the "mental cases" themselves are not to blame, but what allows the speaker to have escaped their fate? Blaming "us who dealt them war and madness" could be Owen spreading the blame, which is much too heavy for a single soul. Arthur Lane (1972) says, "Owen is unambiguous in assigning the greater guilt, the guilt of complicity in evil, to the reader and to himself" (Lane 1972, p. 155). Indeed Owen was an officer, and thus he shares some of the responsibility of "dealing" the madness, but he shares the blame with all officers, and with those senior statesmen, and with his entire nation, and with us the readers.[12]

5. Discussion and Conclusions

We know the poets themselves did experience internal dissonance. Silkin (1996) discusses in a philosophical way the conflicting roles of the poet who is not just a mouthpiece but also an artist, and he illustrates this conflict with quotes from one of Owen's letters: "'Thus you see how pure Christianity will not fit in with pure patriotism,'" (p. 21) and again, "'And am I not myself a conscientious objector with a very seared conscience?'" (p. 21). These dissonances—Christian versus patriot, conscientious objector versus confirmed killer, even poet versus participant—provide the power for much of the greatest poetry from Owen and his fellow soldier-poets. Indeed, Silkin suggests the stark dissonance has actually contributed to the poets' output: "This is the nub of Owen's poetry, from which the compassion flows. Compassion is the blood that issues from the wound, and the wound is caused by our soldiering" (p. 21).

Owen was torn with such internal dissonance. Sassoon was Mad Jack the war hero but also an outspoken critic of the war, not just through his famous renunciation, but also through his satiric and barbed poems obviously intended to strike a nerve. Graves's interposition on Sassoon's behalf—arranging for Siegfried to be sent to Craiglockhart instead of being cashiered or worse—was also an act that would have elicited dissonance, since Graves found himself having to work within the objectionable system in order to save his friend from that same system. Robert Service found himself doing his bit, hoping his non-combatant role would spare his conscience perhaps, but nonetheless seared by what he saw.

Since the dissonance was such a salient experience to all of these poets, and so central to their very themes, they likely sought to express that as many ways as they could. Poems about the enemy are one effective means for that expression. We have considered poems in which the speaker directly converses with an enemy, poems in which the speaker only sees or touches a dead enemy, and poems which could be about an enemy but do not make it clear. In all of these, the idea of cognitive dissonance has yielded meaningful readings. I suggest this is because the poets are allowing us to observe their

---

[12] Lane (1972) also points out other inner conflict revealed in the poem. He points out what others have noted—that there is a borrowing from Dante and from the book of Revelation (See also Hipp 2005, p. 72; Kendall 2013, p. 279)—but also notes that "Though the poem's images may echo traditional religious conceptions, the world within which it moves is unremittingly secular; the tension between the two factors is an indication of Owen's tortured speculation about a hell which men have designed, and in which men are condemned to suffer" (Lane 1972, p. 154).

internal dissonance, at no time more prominent than when in contact with the enemy, since such personal exposure elicits powerful reactions in us as readers.

Of course, beyond these three types of enemy-encounter poems, there are other powerful poems from the Great War which do not involve contact with the enemy at all. While we have seen how these enemy-encounter poems are conducive to expressing the poet's cognitive dissonance, these poems are the not only ones that convey inner turmoil, to be sure. However, I submit these poems about the enemy convey the dissonance in particularly powerful ways.

Interestingly, I am not sure that the poems featuring direct intimate interaction were necessarily the most moving type of the three. All three of my categories seemed capable of showing internal dissonance and of eliciting the same in the reader, even those that were unclear as to the dead man's identity. Perhaps a key is that, whether in an extended conversation or in a very brief horrific glimpse, the encounter with the dead (especially a dead enemy) does bring the two fighters into close contact. The power of this contact is consistent with Sarnowski's idea that distance matters (2018). Indeed, it may be that dissonance and distance are loci of power, and exposure to the dead—of either side—is another. This is a topic that would be worth exploring in future research.

Further research would also do well to consider the differences between poems by combatants like Graves, Sassoon, and Owen, and poems by non-combatants like Service, John McCrae, May Wedderburn Canaan, and Mary Borden. After all, of all the poems considered for this paper, it was a poem by Robert Service of the ambulance corps that was the only one to portray direct physical contact with a living enemy soldier, and with profound results. This too seems to be rich ground for further exploration.

Indeed, the poets are full of the wisdom of war—the first principle of which is that we and our enemies share a common susceptibility to death. But a darker wisdom might be that even gaining this understanding often involves trauma to the soul. We as readers cannot, perhaps, experience the poets' turmoil as our own, not fully. But we can learn vicariously what they had to learn traumatically. Thus, on some occasions, the poets let us see their own internal dissonance, and their vulnerability and honesty are what gives their poems such power.

Funding: This research received no external funding.

Conflicts of Interest: The author declares no conflict of interest.

References

Campbell, Patrick. 1999. *Siegfried Sassoon: A Study of the War Poetry*. Jefferson: McFarland and Co.

Canary, Robert H. 1980. The Lyric Poet. In *Robert Graves*. Twayne's English Authors Series 279. Boston: Twayne Publishers, pp. 15–29. Available online: http://link.galegroup.com/apps/doc/CX1897700011/GVRL?u=anna82201&sid=GVRL&xid=93a962f5 (accessed on 25 January 2019).

Elliot, Andrew J., and Patricia G. Devine. 1994. On the Motivational Nature of Cognitive Dissonance: Dissonance as Psychological Discomfort. *Journal of Personality and Social Psychology* 67: 382–94. [CrossRef]

Festinger, Leon. 1957. *A Theory of Cognitive Dissonance*. Stanford: Stanford University Press.

Festinger, Leon, and James M. Carlsmith. 1959. Cognitive Consequences of Forced Compliance. *The Journal of Abnormal and Social Psychology* 58: 203. [CrossRef]

Ford, Ford Madox. 1918. That Exploit of Yours. In *The Penguin Book of First World War Poetry*. Edited by Jon Silkin. London: Penguin.

Graves, Robert. 1916. A Dead Boche. In *Poetry of the First World War: An Anthology*. Edited by Tim Kendall. Oxford: Oxford World Classics.

Hardy, Thomas. 1915. The Pity of It. In *Poetry of the First World War: An Anthology*. Edited by Tim Kendall. Oxford: Oxford World Classics.

Hibberd, Dominic. 1986. *Owen the Poet*. Athens: University of Georgia Press, pp. 71–82.

Hibberd, Dominic. 2003. *Wilfred Owen: A New Biography*. Chicago: Ivan R. Dee, pp. 243–304.

Hipp, Daniel. 2005. *The Poetry of Shell Shock: Wartime Trauma and Healing in Wilfred Owen, Ivor Gurney, and Siegfried Sassoon*. Jefferson: McFarland and Co.

Johnson, George M. 2010. 'Purgatorial Passions': 'The Ghost' (a.k.a. Wilfred Owen) in Owen's Poetry. *The Midwest Quarterly* 58: 152. Available online: http://link.galegroup.com/apps/doc/A217772403/ITOF?u=anna82201&sid=ITOF&xid=88c15348 (accessed on 8 January 2019).

Kendall, Tim. 2013. *Poetry of the First World War: An Anthology*. Oxford: Oxford World Classics.

Kipling, Rudyard. 1914. For All We Have and Are. In *Poetry of the First World War: An Anthology*. Edited by Tim Kendall. Oxford: Oxford World Classics.

Kipling, Rudyard. 1918. Justice. In *Poetry of the First World War: An Anthology*. Edited by Tim Kendall. Oxford: Oxford World Classics.

Klug, Wayne, Anne O'Dwyer, Deirdre Barry, Leah Dillard, Haili Polo-Neil, and Megan Warriner. 2011. The Burden of Combat: Cognitive Dissonance in Iraq War Veterans. In *Treating Young Veterans: Promoting Resilience through Practice and Advocacy*. Edited by Diann Cameron Kelly, Sydney Howe-Barksdale and David Gitelson. New York: Springer Publishing Co., pp. 33–79.

Krause, Merton S. 1972. An Analysis of Festinger's Cognitive Dissonance Theory. *Philosophy of Science* 39: 32–50. [CrossRef]

Lane, Arthur E. 1972. *An Adequate Response: The War Poetry of Wilfred Owen and Siegfried Sassoon*. Detroit: Wayne State University Press.

MacCurdy, John. 1918. War Neuroses. In *The Poetry of Shell Shock: Wartime Trauma and Healing in Wilfred Owen, Ivor Gurney, and Siegfried Sassoon*. Jefferson: McFarland and Co.

McLeod, Saul A. 2018. Cognitive Dissonance. Available online: https://www.simplypsychology.org/cognitive-dissonance.html (accessed on 9 January 2019).

Owen, Wilfred. 1918a. Strange Meeting. In *Poetry of the First World War: An Anthology*. Edited by Tim Kendall. Oxford: Oxford World Classics.

Owen, Wilfred. 1918b. Has Your Soul Sipped. In *The Collected Poems of Wilfred Owen*. Edited by C. Day Lewis. New York: New Directions.

Owen, Wilfred. 1918c. Mental Cases. In *Poetry of the First World War: An Anthology*. Edited by Tim Kendall. Oxford: Oxford World Classics.

Owen, Wilfred. 1964. *The Collected Poems of Wilfred Owen*. Edited by C. Day Lewis. New York: New Directions.

Ramazani, Jahan. 2016. 'Cosmopolitan Sympathies': Poetry of the First Global War. *Modernism/Modernity* 23: 855–74. [CrossRef]

Read, Herbert. 1919. The Happy Warrior. In *The Penguin Book of First World War Poetry*. Edited by Jon Silkin. London: Penguin.

Robinson, Peter. 2010. 'Written at least as well as prose': Ford, Pound, and Poetry. In *Ford Madox Ford: Modernist Magazines and Editing*. Edited by Jason Harding. International Ford Madox Ford Studies 9. General editor Max Saunders. The Ford Madox Ford Society. New York: Rodopi, pp. 99–114. Available online: https://epdf.tips/ford-madox-ford-modernist-magazines-and-editing-international-ford-madox-ford-st.html (accessed on 11 February 2019).

Sarnowski, Michael. 2018. Enemy Encounters in the War Poetry of Wilfred Owen, Keith Douglas, and Randall Jarrell. *Humanities* 7: 89. [CrossRef]

Sassoon, Siegfried. 1916. A Night Attack. In *Poetry of the First World War: An Anthology*. Edited by Tim Kendall. Oxford: Oxford World Classics.

Sassoon, Siegfried. 1917a. Enemies. In *The War Poems of Siegfried Sassoon*. Arranged and Introduced by Rupert Hart-Davis. London: Faber and Faber.

Sassoon, Siegfried. 1917b. The Rear Guard. In *Poetry of the First World War: An Anthology*. Edited by Tim Kendall. Oxford: Oxford World Classics.

Sassoon, Siegfried. 1918. Remorse. In *The War Poems of Siegfried Sassoon*. Arranged and Introduced by Rupert Hart-Davis. London: Faber and Faber.

Sassoon, Siegfried. 1983. *The War Poems of Siegfried Sassoon*. Arranged and Introduced by Rupert Hart-Davis. London: Faber and Faber.

Service, Robert. 1916. Only a Boche. In *Poetry of the First World War: An Anthology*. Edited by Tim Kendall. Oxford: Oxford World Classics.

Silkin, Jon. 1996. Introduction. In *The Penguin Book of First World War Poetry*. Edited by Jon Silkin. London: Penguin, pp. 16–77.

Stallworthy, Jon. 1974. *Wilfred Owen*. London: Oxford University Press, London: Chatto & Windus.

Ward, Candace, ed. 1997. *World War One British Poets: Brooke, Owen, Sassoon, Rosenberg and Others*. Mineola: Dover.

Wordsworth, William. 1806. Character of the Happy Warrior. In *The Poetical Works of William Wordsworth*. Edited by William Knight. London: MacMillan, Vol. IV, Available online: http://www.gutenberg.org/files/32459/32459-h/32459-.htm#CHARACTER_OF_THE_HAPPY_WARRIOR (accessed on 11 February 2019).

© 2019 by the author. Licensee MDPI, Basel, Switzerland. This article is an open access article distributed under the terms and conditions of the Creative Commons Attribution (CC BY) license (http://creativecommons.org/licenses/by/4.0/).

Article

Enemy Encounters in the War Poetry of Wilfred Owen, Keith Douglas, and Randall Jarrell

Michael Sarnowski

Department of English, Liverpool Hope University, Taggart Ave, Liverpool L16 9JD, UK; michaelsarnowski@gmail.com

Received: 30 August 2018; Accepted: 11 September 2018; Published: 14 September 2018

Abstract: While some war poets amplify the concept of anonymity for enemy soldiers, projecting an "us vs. them" mentality, other defining voices of war counter this militaristic impulse to dehumanize the enemy. This pivot toward describing the World Wars more like humanitarian crises than an epic of good and evil is most notable in poems that chronicle both real and imagined close-range encounters between combatants. The poem "Strange Meeting" by British First World War soldier Wilfred Owen uses the vision of two enemy soldiers meeting in hell to reinforce his famous notion that war is something to be pitied. As a result of technological advancements in the Second World War and the increasing distance of combat, the poems "Vergissmeinnicht" and "How to Kill" by British Second World War soldier Keith Douglas wrestle with dehumanizing the enemy and acknowledging their humanity. "Protocols" by American Second World War soldier Randall Jarrell is an imagined view of civilian victims, and is a reckoning with the horrors human beings are capable of committing.

Keywords: First World War; Second World War; Wilfred Owen; Keith Douglas; Randall Jarrell; war poetry; distance; soldiers; enemies; encounters

---

Carrying waning traditions forward, such as presenting the enemy as anonymous, monstrous figures, as Robert Graves does in his elegiac "Goliath and David," is a trope that faded over the course of the First World War (Fussell 1975, p. 78). With the enemy presented as an overwhelming Goliath, Graves positions a "calm and brave" (Graves 1918, "Goliath and David" 37) fellow soldier as a pure-of-heart underdog whose "Scorn blazes in the Giant's eye" (Graves 1918, "Goliath and David" 27). While some major poets of the First World War such as Robert Graves amplified the concept of anonymity for enemy soldiers, projecting an "us vs. them" mentality, other defining voices of World War poetry countered this militaristic impulse to dehumanize the enemy. This pivot toward describing the war more as a humanitarian crisis than an epic of good and evil is most notable in poems that chronicle close-range encounters between combatants. The poem "Strange Meeting" by British First World War soldier Wilfred Owen uses the vision of two enemy soldiers meeting in hell to reinforce his famous notion that war is something to be pitied. As a result of technological advancements in the Second World War and the increasing distance of combat, the poems "Vergissmeinnicht" and "How to Kill" by British Second World War soldier Keith Douglas wrestle with dehumanizing the enemy and acknowledging their humanity. "Protocols" by American Second World War soldier Randall Jarrell is an imagined view of civilian victims that forces readers to reckon with the horrors human beings are capable of committing.

Taking influence and encouragement from meeting Siegfried Sassoon while they were both on medical leave from the Western Front, Wilfred Owen utilized the experience of other soldiers in his poetry as a mode of war commentary. Differing from Sassoon's portraits of life in the trenches for his fellow soldiers by recognizing the shared humanity of an enemy soldier, Owen's 1918 poem "Strange Meeting" is an example of compassion which begins with a movement mimicking Dante's journey into the depths of hell in *Inferno*. Owen's speaker escapes battle through a tunnel (by dying we can presume, though actual tunnel systems were used to support the trenches through troop and supply movement) where he comes across the body of a dead enemy soldier and realizes "we stood in hell" (Owen 1986, "Strange Meeting" 10). To console the dead soldier, the speaker says "Here is no cause to mourn," a consolation which sets the stage for the dead soldier's response to carry the remainder of the poem (Owen 1986, "Strange Meeting" 14). Just as the literal warning sign Dante passes upon his entry to hell reading "abandon all hope, ye who enter here," the dead soldier challenges the speaker by arguing for what has been lost as a consequence of war (Alighieri 1999, "Canto III" 7). For it is "the undone years [...] Whatever hope is yours" and the hunt for "the wildest beauty in the world" which has been lost in the eyes of the enemy soldier (Owen 1986, "Strange Meeting" 15–16, 18). Sassoon attempted to inject impartiality by distancing himself and writing of the plight of other soldiers, while Owen uses the enemy soldier as a conduit to express the same message that threads through many of his most recognized poems: the loss of youth and "the pity of war" (Owen 1986, "Strange Meeting" 25). The irony of this moment is that the similarities recognized between Owen's speaker and this enemy combatant are only learned when they meet face to face in death. "Strange Meeting" reflects trench warfare, a mode of combat in which oppositional sides remained tucked away from one another in dug out channels, because in both the poem and fighting from trenches the oppositional soldiers typically only saw one another when one side charged over the top of the trenches to try and advance position, a time which ultimately was the moment of death for hundreds of thousands of soldiers. To confront one another in close combat, soldiers are reminded that the opposition is human and the violence committed is done with a degree of intimacy. According to the dead enemy soldier in "Strange Meeting," they are mourning "the pity war distilled," a statement which rightfully personifies war as a damaging force that the two figures of the poem have learned the brunt of first hand (Owen 1986, "Strange Meeting" 25).

Most of "Strange Meeting" is portioned out to the opposition, giving voice to the usually anonymously depicted enemy soldier, an act of compassion and humanity by Owen that is rarely displayed in First World War poetry. It is easier to train soldiers to carry out orders when they have absolved themselves of individualism and view themselves as part of a collective, or in other words, "the Army's high command to imposing an institutionally-sanctioned collective identity upon the mass of soldiers" (Lukasik 2008, p. 197). The same anonymization happens when soldiers view the enemy as a collective evil rather than an army of individuals with their own thoughts, histories, and aspirations. Regardless of the inspiration for Owen to write about this meeting—either literal and drawn from the experience of encountering a dead enemy soldier, or figurative as an imagined encounter of two deceased soldiers meeting in hell—he is cultivating a sense of empathy for the enemy and contextualizing the nature of the conflict within geopolitical aims and not personal motivations. More notable to Owen than their differences in nationality is the fact that they share and embody a history of warfare that leaves mankind either "content with what we spoiled" (Owen 1986, "Strange Meeting" 26) or they will be "discontent, boil bloody, and be spilled," suggesting that they are either complicit with the human and emotional costs of war or are at risk of being killed by a complicit opposition (Owen 1986, "Strange Meeting" 27). The final stanza conveys the heightened moments of closeness when we learn that the second speaker is not only an enemy soldier, but one who was killed by the first speaker, and recalls the reaction of the first speaker in the act of killing: "I am the enemy you killed, my friend./I knew you in this dark for so you frowned/Yesterday through me as you jabbed and killed" (Owen 1986, "Strange Meeting"40–42). This possible description of a bayoneting, an act that brings two combatants close enough to touch, is a stark difference from the distance of bullets and shells fired from one trench to another. Owen establishes a parallel between the closeness of combat and the oft-ignored similarities of combatants. Owen is not suggesting that they share political aims or personal goals, but that they are one-in-the-same, both cogs in the bloodied wheels of warfare throughout history, an image he presents with the archaic description of "when blood had clogged their chariot-wheels/I would go up and wash them from the sweet wells," implying that his role as a soldier is to keep the wheels of war moving (Owen 1986, "Strange Meeting" 34–35). By intentionally referencing the use of a chariot, Owen is speaking about war in the twentieth century as if it is no different from the battles fought by the Roman Empire. Despite technological advancements from the chariot wheel to the continuous track of tank wheels, Owen is making the case that war is still war, and the killing of others that it entails is all the more harrowing when conducted at a range close enough to console someone.

The brutal legacy of the close combat of trench warfare in the First World War is a strategy that is largely abandoned in the Second World War. Not only are the Battle of the Somme and Verdun reminders of catastrophic casualties from failed strategies, but the technological advancements that are made in the interwar period drastically change the way war is conducted. This shift toward the heavy utilization of air attacks, while still fighting on land and sea, produced a change in mindset for combatants. As explained by Diederik Oostdijk, "The mechanized, industrialized nature of modern warfare had eroded the possibility of heroic dueling, and according to the World War II poets, heroic agency thus belonged to the past" (Oostdijk 2011, pp. 30–31). For this reason, there are fewer Second World War poems that capture the same close-range observations between combatants such as those made by Owen and Sassoon. Nonetheless, there are poets who chronicle the transition of warfare between close range and far distances. Keith Douglas was a member of the British tank corps who primarily served in the North Africa campaign and died in the invasion of Normandy. Douglas' poem "Vergissmeinnicht" follows in the tradition of Owen's "Strange Meeting" in that it personalizes and humanizes the enemy by acknowledging their loved ones.

Coming close enough to the dead enemy soldier to rummage through his personal belongings, Douglas' speaker finds "the dishonoured picture of his girl/who has put: Steffi. Vergissmeinnicht," which translates as "forget me not" (Douglas 2011, "Vergissmeinnicht" 10–11). Though Douglas jeers the dead soldier for the rigor mortis that has set into his "equipment," the poem exhibits sympathy for the loved ones who will experience the loss of this soldier (Douglas 2011, "Vergissmeinnicht" 15). This recognition of the service and emotional weight of non-combatants is relatable for many soldiers, but until the Second World War this had not been a thoroughly explored topic in war poetry by soldier-poets themselves. There is a case to be made that non-combatants who wrote during the First World War addressed war from the perspective of life away from the front lines, including war nurses like Vera Brittain and Mary Borden who tend not to receive the same attention or acclaim as male poets, including civilians like Rudyard Kipling, Thomas Hardy, and D.H. Lawrence. While many First World War soldier-poets allude to the ignorance of non-combatants and describe their naivety toward the realities of war, the poetry of combatants during the Second World War is a historically underrepresented field compared to that of civilians. In "Vergissmeinnicht," Douglas draws our attention to the dead enemy soldier's lover Steffi, contrasting her loss with the soldier's undignified death, remarking "she would weep to see today/how on his skin the swart flies move" (Douglas 2011, "Vergissmeinnicht" 17–18). Though the enemy soldier has been killed, it is his lover Steffi who will undergo "mortal hurt" (Douglas 2011, "Vergissmeinnicht" 24). Douglas struggles to humanize the enemy, but he recognizes the humanity of the loss as experienced by the loved ones of combatants. However, this compassion only comes to fruition because of the intimate interaction of sifting through enemy soldier's valuables, and being forced to recognize the enemy as human by learning of their life outside of the war.

More characteristic of Second World War poetry, Douglas' "How to Kill" is a poem which offers the distanced perspective of a tank officer scouting an enemy soldier through a tank periscope. It is through the angled sight that the speaker zeroes in on his soon-to-be victim, remarking "Now in my dial of glass appears/the soldier who is going to die" (Douglas 2011, "How to Kill" 7–8). Similar to "Vergissmeinnicht," "How to Kill" is an invasion of privacy where the enemy soldier is unaware he is being watched as "he smiles, and moves about in ways/his mother knows, habits of his" (Douglas 2011, "How to Kill" 9–10). Again, the focus momentarily shifts from the battlefield to the home front, as the enemy soldier is described by the absence he has left in the home life of his family. When the speaker orders the shot to be taken, the enemy soldier's absence from the ranks of the living is described in simplistic terms: "Death . . . has made a man of dust/of a man of flesh" (Douglas 2011, "How to Kill" 12–14). Sympathy for the family of the soldier evaporates just as quickly, as the extinguishing of life is self-congratulatory, referred to as "sorcery" and an act that causes the speaker to feel "amused/to see the centre of love diffused/and the wave of love travel into vacancy" (Douglas 2011, "How to Kill" 14, 15–17). In amazement, the speaker acknowledges "How easy it is to make a ghost" (Douglas 2011, "How to Kill" 18) and describes the act of killing as where "man and shadow meet" (Douglas 2011, "How to Kill" 22). The cumulative effect of this commentary on executing an enemy soldier is how distance influences one's response to culpability and guilt. In contrast to the sustained recognition of loved ones left behind in "Vergissmeinnicht," the undercurrent of "How to Kill" lies in the fascination with the ease of killing, while the distance between killer and victim in turn keeps emotions at a distance.

Furthermore, Douglas's emotional void is conveyed without any mention of the weaponry itself. The only technological tool mentioned in "How to Kill" is the periscope, and it shortens the distance between the speaker and the enemy soldier without feeling the level of human connection found in "Vergissmeinnicht." "How to Kill" is an impersonal poem about killing, and it is the heightened mechanization of war that makes this possible. Soldiers in the Second World War learned to deal with advancements in weaponry that made killing from great distances possible, while maintaining minimal risk for the perpetrator. For this reason, as Peter Lowe suggests in his analysis of Keith Douglas, "modern war poetry often seeks out the dissonance between Homer's text and the near-mechanised slaughter of the Western Front" and that twentieth-century war poets possess a "distrust of anything that seeks to make war sound more elevated than it is" (Lowe 2014, p. 301). Similar to this characterization of Douglas, Siegfried Sassoon also defended against this elevated view of war, challenging the opinions of non-combatants, about whom he writes in "How to Die":

> You'd think, to hear some people talk,
>
> That lads go West with sobs and curses,
>
> And sullen faces white as chalk,
>
> Hankering for wreaths and tombs and hearses. (Sassoon 1984, "How to Die" 9–12)

Sassoon refutes the idea that soldiers were eager to ship off to war and die for their country. Lorrie Goldensohn suggests that Douglas' "'How to Kill' is the successor of Siegfried Sassoon's 'How to Die,'" a parallel that acknowledges that the movements of action and repercussion swing in both directions (Goldensohn 2003, p. 128). In the tradition of Owen and Sassoon, Douglas chronicled his Second World War experience with simplicity and directness. As implied in its title alone, "How to Kill" is a commentary devoid of a sense of glory. By making the reader complicit in the act by describing the mindset and action taken, neutrality is removed. Effectively, war poems that chronicle death in detail force readers to accept a broader view of the war; to support the war is to support the acts of brutality it fosters, and one cannot reap victory without consenting to the death of others. Though Goldensohn describes "How to Kill" as being written with a "sober decency" for its plain speech when compared to the grotesque details of Sassoon's poetry, "How to Kill" is proof of an emotionally callused speaker (Goldensohn 2003, p. 128). The speaker in "How to Kill" is detached from the act not only by distance, but in the acknowledgement of how little effort is necessary to kill. In the poem's closing lines, "A shadow is a man/when the mosquito death approaches," Douglas intentionally uses a blood sucking insect to convey his idea that such a seemingly insignificant thing—an insect bite, like a trigger pull—can cause the transition from life to death (Douglas 2011, "How to Kill" 23–24). Rather than depicting a typical heroic act of defence, "How to Kill" is a matter-of-fact, proactive, procedural retelling of the ease of killing from the point of view of the aggressor. Douglas uses distance as a barrier between the speaker and feelings of guilt, remorse, or shame, and instead capitalizes on the absence of these feelings that result from being compliant in the murder of a soldier from afar.

Since "How to Kill" is a direct poem, it seems unlikely that Douglas is using distance as a coping mechanism to dissociate his feelings from his actions, and more probable that he is grappling with the unexpected speed and relative technological ease with which war is now fought. With models in Owen and Sassoon writing First World War poems that captured the pressure and relentlessness of trench warfare, Douglas seems caught off guard by how little engagement is necessary to accomplish the goal of killing the enemy. This stunned response to the literal distance between combatants and the figurative distancing that occurs when the enhanced mechanization of war challenges the conventional relationship and emotional engagement of soldiers during combat, a concern shared by the American Second World War poet Randall Jarrell.

Despite being one of the most recognizable American poets of the Second World War, Randall Jarrell did not see first-hand action, a circumstance that would shape his writing. As a celestial navigator and flight instructor in the US Army Air Force, Jarrell's poetry resisted Auden's suggestion that a war poet "can only deal with events of which he has first-hand knowledge" (Oostdijk 2011, p. 110). Jarrell used his distance from Second World War battles as an asset and took a creative approach to his subjects, including drawing his attention to soldiers away from battle (either seeing the war from above or from training grounds in the US), to women and children civilians, and to Holocaust victims, oftentimes speaking on behalf of "those who cannot testify for themselves" (Gubar 2006, p. 23). By presenting thoughts from this unique perspective of both participant and outsider—balancing the closeness to troops, machinery, and strategy with the distance from battle—Jarrell's poems speak to war mechanization and distance by focusing on the machinery of the State, that of both allies and enemies. Similar to the concept that the soldier is a pawn acted upon by the State, as Jarrell's "The Death of the Ball Turret Gunner" accomplishes in the transition from birth to death and armed service to sacrifice, Jarrell's assembly-line descriptions of the path from enlistment to death paint the duty of soldiers as a submissive act, marionettes whose strings are controlled by the State. As a result, enemy soldiers are largely absent from Jarrell's poems, and therefore his encounter with the enemy is through the imagined experience of those who were their victims, such as the children and families being taken to a concentration camp in "Protocols."

Though consistently critical of the State and military of which he was a part, Randall Jarrell was not averse to defining the Second World War as a conflict that needed to be fought. Jarrell's greatest justification and support for the defence against the Axis Powers come in the form of empathic poems on the civilians victimized by war. Jarrell's poem "Protocols" is an example of the compassion he held for others by giving voice to child victims of the Holocaust and, having appeared in a 1945 issue of *Poetry*, may be the first American poem published on the topic of the Holocaust (Flanzbaum 1998, p. 260). "Protocols" vacillates between the voices of two children taken by train from Odessa to a concentration camp. There is no judgment, only recollection, as the children's observations exude innocence and the unknowable horror they are about to encounter. The two voices are denoted as one in plain text and the other italicized. Here is the poem in its entirety:

We went there on the train. *They had big barges that they towed,*

We stood up, there were so many I was squashed.

There was a smoke-stack, then they made me wash.

It was a factory, I think. *My mother held me up*

And I could see the ship that made the smoke.

When I was tired my mother carried me.

She said, "Don't be afraid." But I was only tired.

Where we went there is no more Odessa.

They had water in a pipe–like rain, but hot;

The water there is deeper than the world

And I was tired and fell in my sleep

And the water drank me. That is what I think.

And I said to my mother, "Now I'm washed and dried,"

My mother hugged me, and it smelled like hay

And that is how you die. And that is how you die. (Jarrell 1981, "Protocols")

The regimented form of three quintet stanzas in which slant rhymes between the children's voices such as *"squashed"*/"wash," *"towed"*/"smoke," and *"dried"*/*"die"* ricochet off of one another to create a sense of cohesion and order that mirrors the movement of Holocaust victims. This imagined memory of the children depicts the systematic operation of The Final Solution in plain, simple speech. "We went there on the train" (Jarrell 1981, "Protocols" 1) one child says at the outset of the poem, to which the other child adds *"there were so many I was squashed"* referring to the overcrowded trains shipping Jews to the camps (Jarrell 1981, "Protocols" 2). Upon arrival at the camps, the first child notices a smoke-stack, "It was a factory, I think," the awful irony being that the child is right to associate the image of a smoke-stack with a factory, unaware that they are the raw material and the end product is death (Jarrell 1981, "Protocols" 4). The first speaker recalls that "they made me wash," also unaware that the lie of the shower was the precursor to death in the gas chambers, a misdirection sustained until the last moments of life, just as the cruelty of faux-inspirational signs such as "Arbeit macht frei" (work sets you free) were placed at the entry of many concentration camps (Jarrell 1981, "Protocols" 3). The double meaning of this act of cleansing, literal and ethnic, makes the pending betrayal all the more appalling. All the while, the children in "Protocols" tell us of the efforts made by their parents to free them from fear, as one child is held up by their mother so they *"could see the ship that made the smoke"* (Jarrell 1981, "Protocols" 5) while the other is told "Don't be afraid" (Jarrell 1981, "Protocols" 7).

To understand the power of this historical moment is to recognize the ease with which image association paints a scene of dread so quickly. In the first stanza, by learning that the speakers are on a "train," *"squashed"* with people, and their destination is a factory-like area with a "smoke-stack," like a game of word association, many would leap to visions of the Holocaust. However, Jarrell does not say it himself, nor does he mention the war, the year, or any biographical detail other than *"Where we went there is no more Odessa,"* a reference which could be absorbed as a definitive detail to confirm the poem's subject (Jarrell 1981, "Protocols" 8). Jarrell embodies the voices of children he never met to bring the darkest acts of the war to his readers, and in doing so eliminates the buffer between safe citizens and victims. By removing the literal distance between reader and victim, mimicking that closeness with the claustrophobic descriptions of Jews overcrowded in train cars, Jarrell transfigures distance to document the industrialized destruction of people. Just as soon as these puzzle pieces begin to reveal the true nature of the children's testimonials, the poem concludes with naivety, tenderness, and admission. The children go into the showers with their families and feel consumed by the water, *"The water there is deeper than the world . . . the water drank me"* (Jarrell 1981, "Protocols" 10, 12). The first child follows orders, says "Now I'm washed and dried" and is hugged by their mother (Jarrell 1981, "Protocols" 13). In the harrowing final step of the eradication of the children, both voices say "And that is how you die," a haunting echo that simultaneously brings mass suffering down to the level of the individual while the repetition of the line ensures we do not forget that this is a story that happened over and over (Jarrell 1981, "Protocols" 15). In contrast to Owen's "Strange Meeting" and Douglas's "Vergissmeinnicht" and "How to Kill," Jarrell's "Protocols" is a poem in which soldiers are absent altogether. Jarrell recognizes the importance of seeing these events through the eyes of child victims, defenceless against the Nazi apparatus. This concept is heightened by the subsequent absence of weaponry, as the civilians being transported to their deaths are not armed from a distance in a tank like the speaker in "How to Kill," nor are they armed like the soldiers in "Strange Meeting" had been with their guns and bayonets. As much as this immense horror tells us about the innocence and naivety of the children who voice "Protocols," it levies equally damning criticism of the unseen, unheard enemy perpetrators. Those capable of genocide—whether the Nazi hierarchy or varied ranks of officers, guards, and ordinary executioners—are portrayed not by their presence in "Protocols," but by their ominous omission.

To mechanize the murder of civilian populations in wartime, the Nazi regime instituted protocols to structure their attempt to eradicate the Jewish people. The contrast created by having a poem titled "Protocols," defined as "the official procedure or system of rules governing affairs of state or diplomatic occasions" ("Protocol" n.d.), and having this systematic procedure shown through the eyes of innocent children highlights the inhumanity of the process being described. As outsiders, the closeness that Jarrell brings us to this horrible reality is described by Lorrie Goldensohn, who suggests that "parts of the reader-writer contract ask that we, altogether too safe outside the text, not be made voyeurs of pain and that we not turn too expeditiously away from the children to examine ourselves" (Goldensohn 2003, p. 216). Though any document on the Holocaust will be emotionally impactful, Goldensohn is arguing that the importance of Jarrell's "Protocols" is that it strikes a balance between drawing our attention to the suffering of others, while showing caution not to veer so hard in the direction of the grotesque and thereby push readers away from viewing the speaking children as if they could be their own. Particularly when considering the 1945 publication date, "Protocols" has deep emotional potential when one considers how awareness of the depravity of the Holocaust was spreading, though the full scope would take years and lifetimes to learn and process.

Randall Jarrell's poem "Protocols" speaks to the overarching order of war, though it is seemingly antithetical to describe war as orderly when all impulses point to it being a chaotic agent of change. Nonetheless, the mechanization of weaponry, strategy, and the systematic control of soldiers and civilians that occurred with the onset of the World Wars is undeniable. In "Protocols", Jarrell is shortening the distance between the realities of the Second World War and the reader, and does so by invoking comprehensible details and the observations of children forced to a concentration camp. In doing so, Jarrell breaks down the Second World War into details that uninvolved readers can understand, and which will allow them to emotionally connect to the suffering of others. Ultimately, the development of empathy is key to the resonance of these poems, just as identified in Wilfred Owen's "Strange Meeting" and Keith Douglas' "Vergissmeinnicht" and "How to Kill." In Owen's "Strange Meeting," the close proximity of trench warfare is a catalyst for a thoughtful encounter between deceased enemy combatants. In Douglas' "Vergissmeinnicht," similar to "Strange Meeting," a British soldier comes upon a deceased enemy soldier, and upon going through his personal belongings becomes cognizant of the loved ones who will feel the brunt of his death. The same detached sense of empathy is conveyed in "How to Kill," where the speaker is more so in disbelief over how easy it is to take a life than he is concerned with killing his enemy, and how that human fragility will be felt by the enemy soldier's mother.

Each of these poems humanize others and bring the fragility of human life to a closeness that makes it impossible to avoid, regardless of nationality or cause. Utilizing as fluid a concept as distance in war poetry and extending the focal point beyond the suffering of soldiers is a more encompassing approach to analysing the complexities of war. By manipulating the way distance is used, the traditions of war poetry are disrupted because it makes readers complicit in the actions of war. This shift towards exposing readers to the battlefield experience and the degrees of inner turmoil of soldiers was particularly notable in First World War poetry because of the way war was fought at close range and in trench-laced fields. With the further change in Second World War combat, where greater damage could be done from greater distance and population centres became military targets, the importance of maintaining a sense of intimacy in war poetry is heightened because such irrevocable and divisive behaviour leaves less room for blind patriotism. Following the groundwork laid by Wilfred Owen, Keith Douglas and Randall Jarrell use empathy and varying levels of distance to remind non-combatants of the true cost of war, and to show that permissiveness of nations to conduct war comes at a moral price.

Funding: This research was funded by a Vice-Chancellor's PhD Scholarship at Liverpool Hope University.

Conflicts of Interest: The author declares no conflict of interest. The founding sponsors had no role in the design of the study; in the collection, analyses, or interpretation of data; in the writing of the manuscript, and in the decision to publish the results.

References

Alighieri, Dante. 1999. Canto III. In *The Inferno of Dante: A New Verse Translation*. Translated by Robert Pinsky. New York: Noonday.
Douglas, Keith. 2011. How to Kill, Vergissmeinnicht. In *The Complete Poems*. London: Faber and Faber.
Flanzbaum, Hilene. 1998. The Imaginary Jew and the American Poet. *ELH* 65: 259–75. [CrossRef]
Fussell, Paul. 1975. *The Great War and Modern Memory*. New York: Oxford University Press.
Goldensohn, Lorrie. 2003. *Dismantling Glory: Twentieth-Century Soldier Poetry*. New York: Columbia University Press.
Graves, Robert. 1918. Goliath and David. In *Fairies and Fusilliers*. New York: Alfred A. Knopf.
Gubar, Susan. 2006. *Poetry After Auschwitz: Remembering What One Never Knew*. Bloomington and Indianapolis: Indiana University Press.
Jarrell, Randall. 1981. Protocols. In *The Complete Poems*. New York: Farrar, Straus & Giroux.
Lowe, Peter. 2014. Stripped Bodies and Looted Goods: Keith Douglas's Iliad. *The Cambridge Quarterly* 43: 301–24. [CrossRef]
Lukasik, Sebastian Hubert. 2008. Military Service, Combat, and American Identity in the Progressive Era. Ph.D. dissertation, Duke University, Durham, NC, USA, September 29.
Oostdijk, Diederik. 2011. *Among the Nightmare Fighters: American Poets of World War II*. Columbia: University of South Carolina.
Owen, Wilfred. 1986. Strange Meeting. In *The Poems of Wilfred Owen*. Edited by Jon Stallworthy. New York: W. W. Norton.
"Protocol". n.d. *Oxford English Dictionary*. Available online: https://en.oxforddictionaries.com/definition/protocol (accessed on 1 April 2018).
Sassoon, Siegfried. 1984. How to Die. In *Collected Poems, 1908–1956*. London: Faber and Faber.

© 2018 by the author. Licensee MDPI, Basel, Switzerland. This article is an open access article distributed under the terms and conditions of the Creative Commons Attribution (CC BY) license (http://creativecommons.org/licenses/by/4.0/).

Article

Enemy and Officers in Emilio Lussu's *Un anno sull'Altipiano*

Dario Marcucci

Department of Comparative Literature, The Graduate Center, CUNY, New York, NY 10016, USA; dmarcucci@gradcenter.cuny.edu

Received: 17 December 2018; Accepted: 1 February 2019; Published: 6 February 2019

Abstract: This essay explores the concept of enemy in Emilio Lussu's WWI memoir *Un anno sull'Altipiano* (A Soldier on the Southern Front, 1938). The memoir portrays the conflict on the oft-forgotten Alpine Front, where Italian and Austro-Hungarian armies clashed from 1915 to 1918 in a series of battles fought at high altitudes. I argue that two crucial dynamics of modern warfare shape the concept of enemy in WWI literature: the impossibility of close-range encounters, which was due to the superiority of defensive firepower, and hatred for one's own officers, which stemmed from the corrosive environment of the trenches, where the aggressive attitude of high-ranking officers often led hundreds of thousands to pointless death. I show how, in Lussu's memoir, these dynamics subvert the traditional image of the enemy as imposed by military propaganda, and finally elicit feelings of empathy.

Keywords: World War I; Italian Front; memoir; Emilio Lussu; trench warfare

---

WWI mechanized warfare deeply transformed key military concepts such as combat, battlefield, and enemy. Two groundbreaking studies from the 1970s, Paul Fussell's *The Great War and Modern Memory* (1975) and Eric Leed's *No Man's Land. Combat and Identity in World War I* (1979), address these transformations by focusing on their consequences on soldiers' mindset and perception of the war. In this article, I examine the concept of enemy in Emilio Lussu's WWI memoir *Un anno sull'Altipiano*, (A Soldier on the Southern Front, 1938), and I frame my analysis with Fussell and Leed's observations on the subject. I argue that the two dynamics of modern warfare that Fussell and Leed relate to the concept of enemy are particularly evident in Lussu's memoir, and strongly characterize the narration. These dynamics are hatred for one's own officers (Fussell 1975, p. 83) and the invisibility of the enemy (Leed 1979, p. 124).

The former refers to the widespread internal conflict provoked by the aggressive attitude of high-ranking officers, who generally considered their troops cannon fodder. On all the fronts, Staff officers, who conducted the operations from behind the lines, ignored the change in warfare that made offensive tactics bloody and worthless. Except for rare cases, and especially during the early stages of the conflict, the officers' strategy (or lack of it) consisted of hurling men against fortified trenches powerfully defended by machine guns. The distance between the troops who lived and died in the trenches, and the officers who conducted the operations from safe positions, resulted in suspiciousness and, often, in hatred (Fussell 1975, p. 84). These feelings shaped the combatants' perception of the enemy.

The latter refers to the drastic change in warfare that occurred in September 1914, when, after the first battles on the Western Front, the incontrovertible superiority of defensive firepower led to a general stalemate. Soon, the stalemate resulted in unprecedented trench warfare, and the battlefields turned into what Germans called "menschenleere" ('unpopulated'). Leed relates this expression to the dreariness and solitude of the landscape at the Front, and the invisibility of the enemy, entrenched somewhere beyond no-man's-land (Leed 1979, pp. 19–20).

On the Italian Front—where Lussu fought as a lieutenant in the Italian army—both the dynamics I have described were particularly evident. Indeed, along with modern warfare, it was the very geography of the Front—stretching over 400 miles across the Alps, at the border between Italy and the Austro-Hungarian Empire—that made the enemy a not tangible entity. Furthermore, in the Italian army, the harshness of the officers and the iron discipline they demanded were perhaps unmatched, and often resulted in a conflict within the conflict. In Lussu's memoir, the combined pressure of the disappearance of the enemy and brutality of the officers finally elicits feelings of commiseration with the enemy. For the author, such feelings pivot on the awareness that the Austrians were making the same pointless sacrifice, led by equally blind and ruthless officers.

Considering the context in which Lussu wrote his memoir, during the Fascist Regime, more than twenty years after the events took place, this representation is politically significant. Lussu, who after serving in WWI became a committed antifascist, exposed the actual dynamics that regulated human interactions at the Front. In so doing, his work took a clear stand against the Regime, which, since its formation in the early 1920s, imposed itself as the "only legitimate heir" of the conflict (Janz 2002, p. 627), and manipulated the memory thereof by authorizing only an idyllic picture of the army. *Un anno sull'Altipiano* completely rejects the picture imposed by the political propaganda. Lussu depicts daily life in the high-mountain trenches, the struggles and the fights endured by the soldiers in a hostile environment, and the ambivalent feelings for the enemies beyond the front line and those who commanded from behind.

The narration opens in June 1916, during the Austro-Hungarian offensive known as *Strafexpedition*, which aimed to encircle the Italian army by breaking through the Asiago Plateau, in the Venetian Pre-Alps. To reinforce the line, the Italian Command sent the infantry division to which the author belonged—Sassari Brigade—to counter the attack. Lussu's memoir chronicles the year the brigade spent on the Plateau, from June 1916 to July 1917. The author, who experienced fighting first-hand, recounts in first person events and people, never indulging in digressions but prioritizing facts. Yet, these facts are emblematic, as they exemplify crucial dynamics of modern warfare. The first passage that engages with the concept of enemy is a description of trench warfare in chapter VII. This description illustrates the dynamic historians define as "live and let live" (Heyman 2002, p. 52):

> "Opposite the enemy trenches, at varying distances between fifty and three hundred meters, following the lay of the land and the edge of the forest, we set about building our own trenches. They were our homes, which the Austrians, now on the defensive, surely didn't think of attacking." (Lussu 2014, p. 84)

Here, the unnerving proximity between contrasting units that characterizes trench warfare results in rejecting any offensive drive, therefore in "days of calm" (Lussu 2014, p. 84). Among frontline soldiers, days of calm such as those were quite common; the live and let live attitude—namely the tendency of avoiding useless fighting through unofficial agreements—caused long cease-fires, especially during pauses between major battles. Tacit pacts generally included not shooting during prearranged times, allowing the enemy to venture into no-man's-land to recover bodies, and even to use the latrine without risking their life. Live and let live could be a reaction to the ferocity of commanders, whose offensive spirit often led hundreds of thousands to pointless death; or a reaction to weather conditions, especially on the Alps, where fighting was frequently impossible because of snow storms, avalanches, hard rain, and fog. More accurately, live and let live was a reaction to trench warfare overall, and to the treacherous paradox it entailed: the enemy was close and invisible at the same time.

This paradox triggered a radical transformation in the combatants' mindset. Leed refers to German military historian and officer Wilhelm Von Schramm's theory. Von Schramm, who fought both on the western and eastern fronts, maintains that the invisibility of the enemy, combined with the hardship of life in trenches, and the defensive nature of the war, weakened the aggressive spirit of the soldiers (Leed 1979, p. 111). In his 1990 study *A War Imagined*, Samuel Hynes comments on a review of Robert Nichols' *Ardours and Endurance* by British writer and essayist Edmund Gosse. Gosse stresses that, in Nichols' poems, there is "no anger against the enemy. There is no mention of the Germans from beginning to end; the poet does not seem to know of their existence." (Hynes 1991, p. 190). Despite the propaganda aimed at dehumanizing the enemy, modern warfare itself and its specific dynamics prepared the logistic and psychological conditions that led to limitations on fighting and to feelings of indifference for the enemy.

For the first soldiers who experienced it, the invisibility of the enemy triggered a psychological shock, the intensity of which depended on their complete unawareness of modern conflict, and on their early attitude toward it. Throughout Europe, among the first wave of volunteers, the predominant feelings at the outbreak of the conflict were exaltation and enthusiasm. In analyzing the cultural roots of these feelings, German historian George L. Mosse emphasizes the role of artistic and intellectual movements that dominated the cultural atmosphere of the mobilizing nations (Mosse 1991, p. 54). Interventionist avant-gardists and intellectuals were able to sense the needs of this generation of young men, and played a decisive role in shaping their fighting mindset.

For instance, in Italy, the Futurists welcomed the war as the epochal event that projected the nation into modernity. For them, the spectacular display of technology that was changing the face of the countryside at the Belgium–France border epitomized the archetype of a new aesthetic experience grounded on the interaction between modernity and violence, two sides of the same coin. The Futurist picture of the war mirrored the manners and aims of the military propaganda and had its fundamental principle in the individual aggressive spirit.

Yet, such an aggressive spirit, along with the Futurist ideals of movements and aggression, soon clashed with a reality made of deadlock, "menschenleere", and invisibility of the enemy. This clash was the turning point of modern warfare, and it triggered the psychological shock that transformed the approach to the fight. Like a counteraction to the aggressive posture of August 1914, this shock could result in the live and let live attitude described by Lussu, or in the indifference towards the enemy found by Gosse in Nichols' poems. More importantly, this psychological shock was the first, necessary step toward more solid feelings of commiseration, that is, the repudiation of the concept of otherness imposed by political propaganda, and the ultimate acknowledgment of the enemy's humanity.

Trench warfare's paradox fostered indifference but precluded commiseration as an invisible enemy is impossible to hate, but also impossible to empathize with. In the early chapters of Lussu's memoir, all references to the Austrians attest to the impossibility of humanizing an enemy without identity. To humanize the fight, it is necessary to abandon trench warfare, which allows close-range encounters only during the deadly assaults that took place in no-man's-land. The chance occurs when the Sassari Brigade is sent to resist the *Strafexpedition* on the Asiago Plateau. For Lussu and his comrades, the event, welcomed as a relief, marks the beginning of mountain and maneuver warfare:

> We would finally be liberated from that miserable life, lived fifty or a hundred yards from the enemy trenches, in that ferocious promiscuity […]. We would stop killing each other, every day, without hate. The war of maneuver would be something else. A successful maneuver, two hundred thousand, three hundred thousand prisoners, just like that, in a single day, without that horrific, generalized slaughter; just the success of an ingenious strategic encirclement. (Lussu 2014, p. 10)

What stands out in this passage is the desire to defeat the enemy without shedding their blood. To achieve this goal, Lussu evokes a type of warfare in which close-range encounters were human and bloodless; a type of warfare that modernity made outdated and impossible. Lussu's idealization of the maneuver tactic mirrors the feeling that, at the outbreak of the war, misled thousands of young middle-class men from all the mobilizing nations into volunteering. Joining a war that everyone, on every side, thought would be brief and victorious; the first volunteers who reached the fronts clung to a romanticized idea of fighting, and were totally unprepared for what modern warfare turned out to be. The ultimate expression of this idealization was the myth of the duel, a fight one on one that fostered individual values and skills. These myths and misconceptions died only a few weeks after the declarations of war, when the armies built the first trenches. Dueling demands actual encounters, which allows one to acknowledge the antagonist's humanity. Lussu's attempt to overcome the enemy's invisibility epitomizes the attempt to overcome modern warfare's dehumanization.

In *Un anno sull'Altipiano*, the construction of a mindset predisposed to commiseration revolves around the necessity of establishing visual contact with the Austrians. Yet, the very geography of the front frustrates such a necessity as mountain warfare destabilizes the traditional structure of the battlefield. In chapter III, as soon as the brigade reached the Asiago Plateau, the author notices the great confusion that reigns on that sector of the front:

> On the edge of the plateau, at thirty-five hundred feet, it was pure chaos. We'd arrived there on June 5 via Val Frenzela from Valstagna, under the tightest security measures, because it wasn't clear where our guys were and where the Austrians were. (Lussu 2014, p. 17)

The "pure chaos" of mountain battlefields affects the emotional state of the soldiers, whose first tasks are to control, organize, and map the space. Despite any optimistic prevision, mountain warfare exacerbates the invisibility of the enemy as it deprives the troops not only of the sight of the enemy, but also of the knowledge of their position. On the plateau, Lussu meets a Lieutenant-Colonel commanding a battalion stationed there. The dialogue between the two soldiers explores this aspect:

> It's more than a year now that I've been fighting in this war, on just about every front, and I've yet to look a single Austrian in the face. Yet we go on killing each other every day. Killing each other without even knowing each other, without even seeing each other! It's horrible! That's why we're all drunk all the time, on one side and the other. (Lussu 2014, p. 35)

The Lieutenant-Colonel's speech emphasizes the lack of human factor that typifies the fights of WWI; there is no hate or empathy between antagonists as modern warfare prevents actual encounters. The Lieutenant-Colonel asks:

> "Have you ever killed anyone? You, personally, I mean, with your own hands?"
>
> "I hope not."
>
> "Me, nobody. I mean, not anyone I've seen." (Lussu 2014, p. 35)

Modern warfare made fighting and killing mechanized acts that turned men into cogs of a machine that they could not control. The Lieutenant-Colonel's remark—"with your hands"—conveys the tragedy of a generation of soldiers who lost their identity as fighters, stuck in a limbo where both hatred and empathy were impossible.

The invisible enemy signifies invisible danger. In Lussu's memoir, the first invisible danger is artillery, which in WWI "dictated those laws that regulated life and death" (Leed 1979, p. 97). The piece of artillery most commonly used by the Austro-Hungarian army was the mountain howitzer Skoda 75 mm Model 15, which had a maximum range of more than 9000 yards. For the troops, for whom a considerable part of life consisted in huddling in narrow dugouts while undetectable weapons fired from miles away, facing such distant and invisible threats was psychologically draining. Disorientation and a sense of impotence were fundamental factors of attrition warfare, and revolved around the impossibility of controlling the surrounding space. The confusion that reigned on the battlefield frequently led to episodes of friendly fire. Extremely common on the Italian Front, friendly fire was another decisive element in shaping the combatants' psychology, and consequently in defining the notion of enemy. Lussu and the Lieutenant-Colonel touch upon the theme:

> "Quite often, our own artillery pounds us into the ground, shelling us instead of the enemy."
> "The Austrians artillery fires on its infantry all the time, too." (Lussu 2014, p. 35)

The danger of being bombed by one's own artillery creates a bond between Italian and Austrian troops; both face an invisible enemy that is not on the battlefield, but somewhere in the rear lines.

The rear line is a particular space of warfare; it does not participate in the atrocity of the battlefield; therefore, it does not belong to the front-soldiers' reality. The "sharp division between Staff and troops" that Paul Fussell points out (Fussell 1975, p. 83) is fundamentally a spatial one. In war, what makes the greatest difference is being or not being at the frontlines. The presence of someone who supervised the action from safe positions, namely high-ranking Staff officers, unavoidably affects the interaction between soldiers of opposing sides. Lussu portrays an environment in which, for soldiers who live and die in the trenches, it is easier to empathize with those who are experiencing the same conditions than with their own commanders, whose main role is to send troops to die in no-man's-land. Proximity to death bonds more than uniforms divide. In discussing the famous truce of December 1914, Modris Eksteins stresses how "trench conditions spurred the development of a friendly feeling between the warring parties, but the deteriorating relationship between officers and men" (Eksteins 1989, p. 106). Then, in an investigation on the psychological conditions of those who experienced the Great War, a distinction between troops and Staff officers appears to be more significant than a distinction between contrasting troops.

The history of the Italian Front proves that often commanding officers were, for their own soldiers, more dangerous than the enemy. Until he was in charge, Italian Chief of Staff Luigi Cadorna based his strategy on his military treatise *Frontal Attack and Tactical Training*. Issued only a few months before Italy's mobilization and feared by the troops, who nicknamed it after the cover "libretto rosso" (little red book), the treatise promoted suicidal aggressive spirit as the first requirement to win the war. Despite countless reports on the nature of modern warfare and the dangers it entailed, Cadorna—like many generals of all the belligerent armies—waged the war through a blind offensive strategy, which resulted in frequent and fruitless mass slaughter. Deeply convinced of the indolence of his army, Cadorna imposed hard disciplinary methods that included arbitrary executions and the ancient, cruel practice of decimation. Informed by such mentality, Cadorna's subordinates, both Staff and frontlines officers, were as harsh as their Chief. In the attempt to please Cadorna, they imitated his methods zealously, and generally had little concern for their men, whose difference in social class made them even more distant. Cadorna's favorite motto was "the superior is always right, especially when he is wrong" (Schindler 2001, p. 109), and this principle regulated the relationship between men and officers on the Italian Front during the conflict.

Such a corrosive polarity reached a breaking point during the Twelfth Battle of the Isonzo, better known as the Battle of Caporetto. On October 1917, heavily reinforced by German units, the Austro-Hungarian army was able to break through on the eastern sector of the front, conquering miles of ground and pushing back the Italians. While the High-Command experienced the defeat as a mutiny, some Italian intellectuals interpreted it as a general strike from work that nobody wanted to do; work imposed by the ruling class. Writer and soldier Ardengo Soffici, for instance, titled a famous article about Caporetto *The Strike of the Peasant-Soldiers* (Lo sciopero dei contadini soldati, 1934). Military historian John Keegan emphasizes the importance of Cadorna's harsh discipline and of the social distance between men and officers in the Italian army's collapse at Caporetto (Keegan 1999, pp. 343–50). Additionally, Italian historian Mario Isnenghi underlines how one of the causes of the defeat was the ultimate failure of propaganda aimed at creating an enemy that the troops did not perceive as such (Isnenghi 1967, p. 14). In the confusion of the retreat, the notion of enemy blurred. Reportedly, Italian soldiers welcomed the defeat by shouting "viva l'Austria!" (long live Austria), and fraternized with German and Austrian troops; for those made prisoners, the war was over. In contrast, Italian officers reacted to what they perceived as mass desertion by harshly punishing their own troops. In *A Farewell to Arms*, Ernest Hemingway gave a memorable account of those chaotic days, recounting the summary executions endured by the troops. At Caporetto, for those who faced a firing squad, the perception that the real enemy was behind the lines was undoubtedly strong.

Lussu illustrates the officers' practice of using firing squads against their troops in Chapter XVIII of his memoir. This sequence describes a bombardment in preparation for an attack. When a company of Italian soldiers leaves their position pummeled by friendly fire, a Major, "overwhelmed by a surge of rage" (Lussu 2014, p. 240), orders the executions of twenty of them for mutiny in the face of the enemy. Yet, the firing squad deliberately misses the targets. Then the Major decides to punish the soldiers himself and starts shooting, but the firing squad kill him immediately. The bitterness of the setting—the deafening artillery barrage before an assault—mirrors and underlines the officer's frenzy, which turns into madness when the firing squad refuses to obey. In this passage, Lussu portrays the obsession for discipline and the carelessness for human life that dominated soldiers' life at the Front; in representing the Major as "enraptured and unable to pay attention to anything but his own voice" (Lussu 2014, p. 242), the author stresses the unbridgeable distance between officers and troops.

Such a theme peaked with the memorable character of General Leone, inspired by the actual General Giacinto Ferrero. Leone is a frontline officer, who operates in the trenches in close contact with troops and commands the infantry division stationed on the plateau. Having an officer such as him in their own trenches signifies, for the Sassari Brigade, having an enemy in their own home. With his fanatic, harsh, sadistic, and pointlessly daring temperament, he perfectly embodies the prototype of the Italian Army's high-ranking officer. Since his first appearance, General Leone terrorizes his men with disdain and carelessness for life. One episode of Chapter VII stands out as significant. While inspecting the trenches, Leone climbs upon a pile of rocks to look at the enemy lines with his binoculars, and, voluntarily, exposes himself uncovered from chest to head. Austrian snipers start shooting, but surprised by the exceptionality of the event, miss the target. After a few seconds, Leone comes down, composed and untouched, and turns to one of the several soldiers who witnessed such an exhibition of arrogance:

> "If you're not afraid," he said, turning to the corporal, "do what your general just did." "Yes, sir", the corporal replied. And leaning his rifle against the trench wall, he climbed up on the pile of rocks. Instinctively, I grabbed the corporal by the arm and made him come down. "The Austrians have been alerted now," I said, "and they certainly won't miss on the next shot." With a chilling glance, the general reminded me of the difference in rank that separated me from him. I let go of the corporal's arm and didn't say another word. (Lussu 2014, p. 55)

Naturally, when the corporal exposes himself out of the trenches, Austrian snipers do not miss. What role does the enemy play in this sequence? They do not have an identity, yet they are merely the invisible executor of a deterministic reaction: if a soldier exposes himself outside of a trench, he triggers a mechanism that unavoidably kills him. The process does not involve a direct human factor.

A deeper and more significant human involvement between the opposing troops can be found in the description of a failed offensive, in Chapter XV. What Lussu depicts in this famous sequence is a typical WWI assault: as the Italian infantry advance into no-man's-land, Austrian machine guns shoot at point blank, mowing down the defenseless men. It is a situation seen countless times on the battlefields of the Great War; but this time something different happens:

> Suddenly, the Austrians stopped shooting. I saw the ones who were in front of us, their eyes thrust open with a terrified look, almost as though it were they and not us who were under fire. One of them, who didn't have a rifle, cried out in Italian, "*Basta! Basta!*" "*Basta!*" the others repeated from the parapets. The one who was unarmed looked like a chaplain. "Enough, brave soldiers, don't get yourselves killed like this!" We came to a halt for an instant. We weren't shooting, they weren't shooting. The one who seemed to be a chaplain was leaning out so close to us that if I had reached out my arm I could have touched him. He had his eyes fixed on us, and I looked back at him. From our trench a harsh voice cried out, "Forward! Men of my glorious division, forward! Forward against the enemy!" It was General Leone. (Lussu 2014, p. 123)

For the first time, human interaction occurs. Finally, the enemy is not an invisible entity, manifesting itself only as mere executor of warfare mechanics; they have a voice—incredibly speaking their opponents' language—and they are so close that they can be touched and looked at in the eyes. The sudden and unexpected proximity leads to an exceptional event: commiseration arises, and the Austrians cease fire. Meanwhile, from his safe position behind the parapet, General Leone commands his men forward, against the machine guns. This sequence is emblematic as it epitomizes the dynamic shaping the notion of enemy: when those beyond the lines cease to be an invisible entity referred to as "the enemy", the war mechanisms jam. By overcoming the enemy's invisibility, a close-range encounter between combatants allows identification, and paves the way for empathy.

Chapter XIX illustrates the ultimate stage of this dynamic by chronicling an Italian expedition in no-man's-land. After the failure of the maneuvers, on the Asiago Plateau, trench warfare has started again. In preparation of the imminent assault, an Italian squad leaves the trench to observe the Austrian emplacements. Assisted by darkness, Lussu and one comrade find a good observation post from which they can look safely into the Austrian trenches. After a whole night spent on the spot, at dawn, they see the enemies.

> The Austrians were right there, up close, almost at arm's length, calm and unawareness, like so many passersby on a city sidewalk. A strange feeling came over me. Not wanting to talk, I squeezed the arm of the corporal, who was on my right, to communicate my amazement to him. He, too was intent and surprised, and I could feel the trembling that came over him from holding his breath for so long. An unknown life was suddenly showing itself to our eyes. Those indomitable trenches, against which we had launched so many futile attacks, had nevertheless ended up seeming inanimate, like dismal empty structure, uninhabited by living beings, a refuge for mysterious and terrible ghosts. Now they were showing themselves to us, in their actual lived life. The enemy, the enemy, the Austrians, the Austrians! There is the enemy and there are the Austrians. Men and soldiers like us, in uniform like us, who were now moving, talking, making themselves coffee. (Lussu 2014, p. 159)

In *The Uncanny*, Nicholas Royle posits that the feeling we call uncanny "can take the form of something familiar unexpectedly arising in a strange and unfamiliar context" (Royle 2003, p. 1). There is nothing more ghostly and unfamiliar, in the battlefields of the Great War, than the enemy trenches; they represent the ultimate boundary before the "paradoxical otherness of enemy terrain" (Fussell 1975, p. 76). Yet, in this utterly unfamiliar dimension, something familiar arises: men making themselves coffee. Lussu is astonished.

> Bizarre! So why shouldn't they be making themselves coffee? Why in the world did it seem so extraordinary to me that they should make themselves coffee? And, around ten or eleven, they would have their rations, exactly like us. (Lussu 2014, p. 160)

The revelation of the enemy's humanity exposes the mystifications of military propaganda, which nourishes the conflict by imposing the "us versus the others" mindset. Having such a mindset is necessary to bear the devastating slaughter of modern warfare; the encounter between Lussu and the nameless Austrian soldier challenges the essence of war itself.

As in the passage previously reported—where the Austrians cease fire because they look at the Italians "as though it were they who were under fire"—the key concept of this sequence is identification. In *Group Psychology and the Analysis of the Ego* (1922), Sigmund Freud terms identification as "the earliest form of an emotional tie with another person" (Freud 1989, p. 46). These emotional ties hold members of social groups or mass movements together; therefore, the very existence of social groups hinges on the identification among its members. An army is a particular type of social group; Freud defines it as "artificial group" as its integrity is not spontaneous but requires human intervention in the person of the Commander-in-Chief. By directing his men's emotive impulses to the right targets, namely hatred to the enemy and dedication to the officers, the Commander-in-Chief promotes identification and protects the integrity of his army.

The unprecedented size and complex structure of WWI modern mass armies complicated the process of identification, especially for a young nation such as Italy. In the Italian army, the linguistic and social segmentation interfered with the construction of a solid artificial group (Isnenghi and Rochat 2018, pp. 148–49). In such a problematic context—where individual impulses were strong and potentially dangerous for the integrity of the group—the military propaganda reacted by attempting to trigger what Freud calls "suggestion" (Freud 1989, p. 26). The suggestion is a deep emotive alteration of the members of a group, who, guided by the authoritative figure who leads them, end up feeling the same emotion, like a contagion. One of the most effective forms of suggestion at hand of military propaganda is the denial of enemy's humanity, which leads to the construction of that "us versus them" mentality that fosters the fight. Yet, modern warfare itself triggers counter-suggestions: dynamics such as identification with the enemy and hatred for one's own officer destabilize the ethical structure of the army and make commiseration possible.

Bewildered by the sudden appearance of the enemy and the revelation of his humanity, the soldier is faced with an internal struggle. Yet, it is not a struggle between empathy and sense of duty, but a struggle between empathy and suggestion. In mechanized warfare, suggestion triggers automation, which overcomes sense of duty; fighting means merely reacting to mechanisms that cannot be controlled and understood. As soon as he sees the enemy, the soldier reacts mechanically and starts taking aim.

> I had all the time I wanted to take aim. I planted my elbows firmly on the ground and started to aim. The Austrian officer lit a cigarette. Now he was smoking. That cigarette suddenly created a relationship between us [...] In an instant, my act of taking aim, which had been automatic, became deliberate. I became aware that I was aiming, and that I was aiming at someone. [...] I had a man in front of me. A man! (Lussu 2014, p. 162)

The cigarette triggers a dramatic change in Lussu's mindset, for it disintegrates the sense of otherness intrinsic to the concept of enemy, that is, the suggestion that ties him to the artificial group he belongs to. In the middle of the mechanized hell of WWI, everyday objects such as a cup of coffee or a cigarette are emotional signifiers that remind the author of his own and his enemy's humanity. Finally, the uncanny stemmed from the presence of familiar elements within an unfamiliar context turns into commiseration.

> "you know ... like this ... one man alone ... I can't shoot. You, do you want to?"
> "Me neither." (Lussu 2014, p. 164)

Both Lussu and his comrade refuse to murder the Austrian soldier, who keeps on smoking his cigarette, unaware of the danger. Italian soldier poet Fausto Maria Martini recounts a similar episode that occurred to him at Pal Grande, on the eastern sector of the front, on 17 November 1916. The poem describing the event is titled *Perché non t'uccisi* (Why I did not kill you, 1917), and its last lines illustrate synthetically the process of identification experienced by Lussu:

> I did not kill you,
>
> Unknown sad-eyed enemy,
>
> For I was afraid of dying with you. (Martini 1969, p. 205)

The three episodes of the memoir addressed in this essay—General Leone commanding a soldier to expose himself to enemy fire, the failed assault, and the final sighting of the Austrians—represent the enemy's progressive acquisition of voice and human essence. In the first sequence, the enemy is the invisible executor of a mechanical reaction; in the second, they are bodily men, able to perceive the atrocity of war and empathize with their opponents; in the third, the enemy is finally an individual, whose humanity is conveyed through everyday actions and objects. Peaking with the soldier's refusal to kill, this progression gradually disintegrates the fundamental trait of mechanized warfare, the disappearance of the enemy, and finally resolves the paradox of a system where fighting does not involve hate. Additionally, these episodes illustrate how trench warfare's dynamics direct hate to the wrong target: the officer. In *Un anno sull'Altipiano*, the officers are the first source of danger for their own troops; therefore, they are represented as the real enemy.

By defining all these forces at work, Lussu exposes what Mosse calls the "Myth of the War Experience" (Mosse 1991, p. 7), that is an ideological approach to the memory of the conflict, promoted after the war by German and Italian propaganda especially. This approach aimed at purging the remembrance of the conflict of any dissonant antimilitaristic impulse, thus constructing a legacy of positive memories that the arising totalitarianisms could exploit to establish their position in the society.

Although in his memoir's foreword Lussu claims he merely depicted life and death at the front without any ideological filter—"the war as we actually lived it" (Lussu 2014, p. vii)—his depiction takes a clear political stance, and contrasts Fascist ideology by standing as the Anti-Myth of Italian WWI literature. In their 1991 monograph *1916–1917, mito e antimito: Un anno sull'Altipiano con Emilio Lussu e la Brigata Sassari*, Italian scholars Paolo Pozzato and Giovanni Nicolli question the historicity of Lussu's work, and state its hybrid nature between novel and history. Yet, what makes *Un anno sull'Altipiano* one of the most realistic literary depictions of the Alpine Front is its dry and essential portrayal of modern warfare dynamics, which, by transforming the mindset and personalities of those who fought, convey the complexity of the psychological experience of WWI.

Funding: This research was funded by a Provost's Pre-Dissertation Research Fellowship at The Graduate Center, CUNY.

Conflicts of Interest: The author declares no conflict of interest. The funders had no role in the design of the study; in the collection, analyses, or interpretation of data; in the writing of the manuscript, or in the decision to publish the results.

References

Eksteins, Modris. 1989. *Rites of Spring*. Boston: Houghton Mifflin.
Freud, Sigmund. 1989. *Group Psychology and the Analysis of the Ego*. New York: Norton & Company.
Fussell, Paul. 1975. *The Great War and Modern Memory*. New York: Oxford University Press.
Heyman, Neil. 2002. *Daily Life during World War I*. Westport: Greenwood Press.
Hynes, Samuel. 1991. *A War Imagined*. New York: Atheneum/Macmillan.
Isnenghi, Mario. 1967. *I vinti di Caporetto nella letteratura di guerra*. Venice: Marsilio.
Isnenghi, Mario, and Giorgio Rochat. 2018. *La Grande Guerra*. Bologna: Il Mulino.
Janz, Oliver. 2002. Grande Guerra, memoria della. In *Dizionario del Fascismo*. Edited by Victoria De Grazia and Sergio Luzzatto. Torino: Einaudi.
Keegan, John. 1999. *The First World War*. New York: Knopf.
Leed, Eric. 1979. *No Man's Land. Combat & Identity in World War I*. London: Cambridge University Press.
Lussu, Emilio. 2014. *A Soldier on the Southern Front*. Translated by Gregory Conti. New York: Rizzoli.
Martini, Fausto Maria. 1969. *Tutte le poesie*. Milano: Edizioni IPL.
Mosse, George. 1991. *Fallen Soldiers: Reshaping the Memory of the World Wars*. New York: Oxford University Press.
Royle, Nicholas. 2003. *The Uncanny*. New York: Routledge.
Schindler, John. 2001. *Isonzo: The Forgotten Sacrifice of the Great War*. Westport: Praeger.

© 2019 by the author. Licensee MDPI, Basel, Switzerland. This article is an open access article distributed under the terms and conditions of the Creative Commons Attribution (CC BY) license (http://creativecommons.org/licenses/by/4.0/).

Article

Two 1916s: Sebastian Barry's *A Long Long Way*

Allison Haas

Department of Liberal Arts and Education, The University of Minnesota Crookston, Crookston, MN 56716, USA; haasx085@crk.umn.edu

Received: 11 February 2019; Accepted: 21 March 2019; Published: 23 March 2019

Abstract: As Paul Fussell has shown, the First World War was a watershed moment for 20th century British history and culture. While the role of the 36th (Ulster) Division in the Battle of the Somme has become a part of unionist iconography in what is now Northern Ireland, the experience of southern or nationalist Irish soldiers in the war remains underrepresented. Sebastian Barry's 2005 novel, *A Long Long Way* is one attempt to correct this historical imbalance. This article will examine how Barry represents the relationship between the First World War and the 1916 Easter Rising through the eyes of his politically-conflicted protagonist, Willie Dunne. While the novel at first seems to present a common war experience as a means of healing political divisions between Ireland and Britain, this solution ultimately proves untenable. By the end of the novel, Willie's hybrid English–Irish identity makes him an outcast in both places, even as he increasingly begins to identify with the Irish nationalist cause. Unlike some of Barry's other novels, *A Long Long Way* does not present a disillusioned version of the early 20th century Irish nationalism. Instead, Willie sympathizes with the rebels, and Barry ultimately argues for a more inclusive Irish national identity.

Keywords: *A Long Long Way*; Sebastian Barry; contemporary Irish fiction; 1916 Easter Rising; Ireland; World War One

---

1. Introduction

More than 8.5 million soldiers died in the First World War, and almost 50,000 of them were Irish (Ferriter 2004, p. 388). The scale and slaughter of the war, the American literary and cultural historian Paul Fussell has argued, shattered British Victorian notions of history and "reversed the Idea of Progress" (Fussell 1975, p. 8). In Ireland, as Irish historian R. F. Foster explains, the war had profound political consequences: "it temporarily defused the Ulster situation; it put Home Rule on ice; it altered the conditions of military crisis in Ireland at a stroke; and it created the rationale for an IRB rebellion" (Foster 1988, p. 471). For these reasons, Foster (1988) argues, "the First World War should be seen as one of the most decisive events in modern Irish history" (p. 471). But what Foster terms an "IRB rebellion"—better known as the 1916 Easter Rising—has largely eclipsed the Irish experience of the Great War in Irish historical narratives, even though Ireland contributed roughly 210,000 men to the war effort.[1]

In April of 1916, just a few months before the Somme, a coalition of rebels led by Padraig Pearse and James Connolly (among others), staged a coup in Dublin, taking over several important administrative buildings and issuing a "Proclamation of an Irish Republic." The disorganized, slipshod rebellion provoked a harsh response from British authorities, who executed 15 of its leaders over a 10-day period and, in the process, turned a formerly apathetic public's sympathies towards the rebels

---

[1] This number comes from Fitzpatrick (1996), who retrieves it from Ireland's 1923 memorial records. As fellow historian Ferriter (2004) notes "the exact definition of 'Irish' remain[s] uncertain" (p. 388) for reasons that will become clear over the course of this article.

(Beckett 1966, p. 441). William Butler Yeats (2000) famously summarized the effect of the so-called Easter Rising in the refrain of his poem "Easter 1916": "All changed, changed utterly / A terrible beauty is born."

The convergence of these two events was not an accident. The First World War came at a time when divisions that had been festering between Ireland and Britain over the long 19th century were finally coming to a head. An Irish Home Rule bill had been approved by the British Parliament in 1914, despite significant opposition from unionist Protestants. The outbreak of the war in 1914, however, delayed its implementation. The Easter Rising was, in part, a reaction to this delay that put the 19th century axiom "England's difficulty is Ireland's opportunity" into practice.

The Easter Rising became a foundational event in most histories of Ireland, but the significance of the First World War to 20th century Irish history is frequently overlooked. In his preface to the Trinity History Workshop's collection *Ireland and the First World War* (1986), David Fitzpatrick laments the frequency with which works of Irish history "treat the war as an external factor which did little more than modify the terms of political debate and redefine political alignments in Ireland [and] reduce a social catastrophe, which left few people untouched, to the status of a minor if unfortunate disturbance" (viii). The same is true of Irish literature. Declan Kiberd's nationalist literary history of Ireland, *Inventing Ireland* (1995), a 695-page tome, devotes nine pages to the theme of "The Great War and Irish Memory," and most of these discuss the war only in relation to the Easter Rising (Kiberd 1995).[2] Even Foster's well-respected *Modern Ireland: 1600–1972* (1988) does not devote much time to the Irishmen who participated in the war, although it does examine at length the war's effect on IRB strategy and the British response to the Rising.

Recent years, though, have seen a shift in the cultural and historical responses to Irish involvement in the First World War. Frank McGuinness's 1985 play *Observe the Sons of Ulster Marching Towards the Somme* was widely praised for its depiction of the Irish unionist soldiers of the 36th (Ulster) Division.[3] The subject of this article, Sebastian Barry's novel *A Long Long Way*, was released to critical acclaim in 2005. On the 100th anniversary of the Battle of the Somme in July 2016, the Republic of Ireland and the Royal British Legion (Republic of Ireland) held a joint Centenary Commemoration Ceremony (Department of the Taoiseach 2018).

2. 'I Will Go Down—If I Go Down at All—As a Bloody British Soldier'

Part of the problem with defining an Irish experience of the First World War is that at the time of the war the island of Ireland was culturally and politically divided.[4] British colonization from the 17th century onwards had created a class of Protestant landowners and industrialists. Members of the "Protestant Ascendancy," as it was known, spoke English and belonged to the Church of Ireland. They both benefited from and contributed to British occupation of the island. Meanwhile, most of the landless and working classes identified as culturally Irish[5] and remained Roman Catholic.

---

[2] To be fair to Kiberd, he does acknowledge the Republic's neglect of the war: "Only a state which was anxious to repudiate its own origins could have failed—after a predictable period of post-independence purism—to evolve a joint ceremony which celebrated the men who served in either army" (Kiberd 1995, p. 240).

[3] This depiction was all the more remarkable for the fact that McGuinness is a Catholic from County Donegal (in the northwest corner of the Republic of Ireland, near the border with the North). In an interview, McGuinness emphasized that "the Battle of the Somme was a key date in Irish history as well as a significant day in Ulster Protestant history . . . in terms of impact, it was as powerful as 1916 was for the nationalists" (McGuinness 2010).

[4] The information in the next few paragraphs will be extremely familiar to anyone with a background in Irish Studies or an understanding of Irish history. I include it here because I believe such a background is a necessary to understand the historical resonance of *A Long Long Way* (and of Barry's work as a whole). The same is true of the many footnotes in this and later sections in which I seek to clarify terms and concepts that are well-worn for those who study Irish history and literature, but less familiar to those outside the field.

[5] Before the 19th century, many of them would also have spoken Irish. However by 1900, the Irish language had almost become extinct due to the Great Famine of the 1840s and a British assimilationist educational policy. The "Gaelic Revival" at the turn of the century included a renewed interest in the Irish language, as well as in Irish pre-Christian mythology, music, and sport.

Generally speaking, it was in the interests of the Protestant classes for Ireland to remain a part of the United Kingdom and they, therefore, mostly identified as unionists.[6] Catholics, on the other hand, were more likely to be Irish nationalists, supporting independence from Britain. These divisions, along with Britain's interest in maintaining a grip on its Irish colony, would lead to successive conflicts from the Easter Rising in 1916 through the Irish War of Independence (1919–1921), the Irish Civil War (1922–1923), and the Northern Irish "Troubles" (1968–1998). The divisions endure to this day.[7]

All this is to explain that while, a great number of Irishmen fought and died in the First World War, the meaning of the term "Irishmen" is debatable. What is certain is that soldiers from the island of Ireland made up a significant portion of the British Army at the outbreak of the war, and that more joined in successive, targeted recruiting campaigns. In total, historian Fitzpatrick (1996) estimates "Ireland's aggregate male contribution to the wartime forces was about 210,000" (p. 388). However, history had conspired so that Protestants/unionists and Catholics/nationalists had wildly different motivations for joining the war effort.

Two groups of "volunteers" were at the center of army recruitment in Ireland, although neither of them had anything to do with the conflict in continental Europe. The introduction of a 1912 Irish Home Rule bill in the British Parliament had angered and frightened unionists—particularly in the north of Ireland, the province known as Ulster.[8] Fearing that Irish Home Rule would make them a cultural and religious minority in the nation, some of them swore to take up arms rather than submit to a Dublin-based parliament. Thus, the Ulster Volunteer Force (UVF)[9] was born (Ferriter 2004, pp. 117–22). Alarmed by the arming of their political opponents, the nationalist Irish Volunteers were formed shortly thereafter (Ferriter 2004, p. 122). At the onset of the war in July 1914, the leaders of *both* groups encouraged their members to enlist and support the war effort. Fitzpatrick (1996) explains:

> The political leaders of both volunteer forces (Sir Edward Carson [UVF] and John Redmond [Irish Volunteers]) found common cause with the Allies in a fight which each expected to bring political benefits. For Redmond ... Irish participation in the war promised the reward of early Home Rule; while Carson saw an opportunity to strengthen Ulster's case for exclusion by demonstrating that Ulster loyalism was more than a rhetorical figment. (p. 386)

If these rationales seem confusing and contradictory, that is because they were. In *A Long Long Way*, the situation is described succinctly as "a veritable tornado of volunteers" (Barry 2005, p. 95).

In hindsight, it is easier to understand the unionist rationale for supporting the war effort, but this historical perspective is shaped by almost a century of political propaganda on both sides. At the time, the leader of the Irish Volunteers, John Redmond, was firm in his beliefs and persuasive in his appeals for Irish Volunteers to join the British Army. His most famous recruiting speech was given in the town of Woodenbridge in September of 1914. In it, Redmond claimed:

---

[6] This is a generalization to which there are many notable exceptions. W. B. Yeats, for example, came from this class and was active in the Irish cultural revival and movements for independence.

[7] The Good Friday Agreement (1998) is generally cited as the end of unionist and nationalist paramilitary violence in Northern Ireland. However, a 2015 study found that "all the main groups operating during the period of the Troubles remain in existence" at the time of the report (Villiers 2015, p. 1). The question of the border between the Republic (an EU member) and Northern Ireland has been a central issue in Brexit negotiations, which are ongoing at the time of this article (Campbell 2018).

[8] The island of Ireland is divided into four provinces: Connaught (west), Leinster (east), Munster (south), and Ulster (north). These are subdivided into 38 counties. The principality of Northern Ireland is made up of the six easternmost counties of the province of Ulster. When Ireland gained independence in 1921, the island was partitioned, with the 32 southern counties becoming the Irish Free State (today the Republic of Ireland) and the six northern counties remaining part of the United Kingdom (Northern Ireland). For the purposes of clarity, this article will use the terms "Ireland" and "Ulster" in their historic senses, to mean, respectively, the island as a whole and the northernmost nine counties. When I make reference to contemporary political divisions, I shall use the official terms "Republic of Ireland" (or simply "Republic") and "Northern Ireland."

[9] The "original" UVF had a brief resurgence in activity after the partition of Ireland in 1923 (Ferriter 2004). In the 1960s, a paramilitary group in Northern Ireland adopted the name and symbols of the UVF. The group was responsible for some of the most brutal atrocities of the Troubles and remained active through (at least) 2013 (McKittrick 2013). Although the later UVF claims to be a direct descendent of the 1913 organization, it is one of several loyalist paramilitary organizations that formed during the Troubles, and there is little to verify this claim (Who are the UVF 2011).

This war is undertaken in the defence [sic] of the highest principles of religion and morality and right, and it would be a disgrace forever to our country, and a reproach to her manhood, and a denial of the lessons of our history, if young Ireland confined her efforts to remaining at home to defend the shores of Ireland from an unlikely invasion and to shrink from the duty of approval on the field of battle of that gallantry and courage which has distinguished our race through its history. (Connell 2014)

Redmond's so-called "Woodenbridge Speech" "led directly to a split between moderate and advanced nationalists in the Volunteer ranks" (Foster 1988, pp. 472–73). As Jackson (2003) notes, Redmond may have been making "a reciprocal gesture" to the British government that would shortly (he believed) grant Home Rule, but he "succeeded only in encouraging thousands of his followers to march to their deaths" (p. 173). But Redmond's stance was, at the time, a popular one. Much more popular, for example than those in favor of open rebellion: "the total number of insurgents (perhaps 1500) [in the Easter Rising] underlines the extent to which militant separatism was a marginal phenomenon in Irish society; there were, by way of contrast, over 150,000 men in the Redmondite National Volunteers" (Jackson 2003, p. 173).

Furthermore, Redmond's call-to-arms was not the only reason that Irish nationalists would have been drawn to the war effort (see Figure 1). Pro-war propaganda framed the conflict as being fought to defend the rights of small nations (particularly Belgium, which was majority Catholic), which made it a natural parallel for the Irish nationalist cause (Peatfield 2018). This point of view was aided by British recruiting campaigns that emphasized atrocities being committed against Belgian civilians (Tierney et al. 1988, p. 49).

Figure 1. Irish First World War recruitment poster. This 1915 recruitment poster personifies Ireland as a woman with a harp. In doing so, it draws on Irish nationalist iconography (Irish WW1 Recruitment Poster 2012). Used under the Creative Commons license.

The organization of the British Army reflected the political divisions of the new Irish recruits, at least to a degree. The 36th (Ulster) Division was made up almost entirely of Ulster Volunteers, while the 16th Division contained a large number of Irish Volunteers (Fitzpatrick 1996, pp. 390–91). These Irish divisions were involved in some of the most famous and bloody battles of the war.

Most notable among these is the Somme, in which the 36th (Ulster) Division lost 2000 men in a single day (Pheonix 2016). The 16th (Irish) Division suffered similarly heavy losses at the related battles of Guillemont and Guinchy (The Somme Association 2019a). In the summer of 1917, the 16th and 36th Divisions fought side-by-side and succeeded in taking the village of Wytschaete. This might be the closest the war came to providing for the hopes of many, including John Redmond, that nationalists and unionists fighting side-by-side might be encouraged to resolve their differences (Callinan 2014). Both divisions suffered such heavy casualties, however, that they were withdrawn and reconstituted in the spring of 1918 and were virtually unrecognizable by the end of the war (The Somme Association 2019b).

As political divisions persisted in 20th-century Ireland, so did the divided legacy of the war. From the unionist perspective, the First World War was fought as a defense of the British Empire and, by extension, of the union between Britain and Ireland. In unionist traditions the war, and particularly the "blood sacrifice" of the 36th Division at the Somme "came to represent . . . a conclusive demonstration of Ulster's unshakeable loyalty to the Union" (First World War 1998, p. 205) and is a popular subject for murals (see Figure 2). In what Foster (1988) calls "a policy of intentional amnesia," however, the First World War is largely absent, from Irish nationalist historiographies. While it is understandable that the Easter Rising and the subsequent War of Independence and Civil War would eclipse the Great War in Irish history, the fact remains that thousands of Irish nationalists fought and died with the British Army and believed that they were doing so for their country. Thomas Kettle, an Irish Volunteer, Member of Parliament (MP), and lieutenant in the British Army, predicted their fate. In the wake of the Easter Rising, he reportedly told a friend: "these men [the 1916 leaders] will go down to history as heroes and martyrs and I will go down—if I go down at all—as a bloody British soldier" (Mulhall 2019). Kettle was killed in action a few months later.

Figure 2. Belfast Unionist Mural (2010). This UVF mural includes a depiction of the charge at the Somme in the top right panel. The red lettering in the center reads "The Peoples [sic] Army 1912–2002—90 Years of Resistance." Used under the Creative Commons liscense.

3. Irish Historical Fiction and Sebastian Barry

In the introduction to his work on contemporary Irish historical fiction, *Haunted Historiographies: the Rhetoric of Ideology in Postcolonial Irish Fiction*, Matthew Schulz quotes a 2008 interview with Sebastian Barry: "The fact is we are missing so many threads of our story that the tapestry of Irish life cannot but fall apart. There is nothing to hold it together" (qtd. in Schultz 2014, p. 5). Schultz (2014) uses this quote to argue that questions of Irish identity, historical and otherwise, have shifted from "a debate about the necessary or unnecessary homogeneity of Irish civilization to a program that establishes ambiguity as one crucial characteristic of Irishness in the twenty-first century" (p. 5). If one accepts Schultz's argument, then Sebastian Barry might be considered the poster boy for a version of Irishness that is defined by ambiguity.

Since he first rose to prominence with his 1995 play, *The Steward of Christendom*, Barry has been known for examining the "forgotten" experiences of 20th-century Irish history in his fiction.

Barry's eight novels and 14 plays draw on his own family's history to tell a series of interlocking stories. *A Long Long Way* is no exception to this pattern. Willie Dunne, the novel's protagonist, is the son of Thomas Dunne, the principal character in *The Steward of Christendom*. Two of Willie's sisters—Annie and Lilly—also feature in their own novels: *Annie Dunne* (2002) and *On Canaan's Side* (2011), respectively. Together, Barry's works of historical fiction create something like an imaginary archive that seeks to fill in holes in his own family history, and—by extension—the history of his country:

> I grew up with people, particularly my father, who weren't interested in history or the sense of the end of history. I mean it was understandable because they'd been through all these wars, even vicariously, in the 20th century, starting with 1916, which his father, my grandfather, had been in. But to me it mattered because there were other things thrown in my way as well, like my other grandfather being in the British army. So there were complications that needed to be worked out. (Heaney 2018)

In "working out" these complications, Barry creates his own version of this history, albeit, one that is based in fiction. The body of his work acts as a kind of meta-version of Suzanne Keen's notion of the "romance of the archive." Keen describes the process this way: "The central romance of the archive ... lies in the recovery or re-discovery of the 'truth,' a quasi-historical truth that makes sense of confusion, resolves mystery, permits satisfying closure, and, most importantly, can be located" (Keen 2001). While most of Barry's body of work does not fall into the exact category of novels that Keen discusses, it is hard not to see his literary project as related, in the sense that his novels seek to fill in the gaps—those "missing threads"—of Irish history.

Barry consistently frames his goal in telling these stories as a personal one but, of course, he cannot avoid the political implications of interpreting history. As Robert Holton (1994) notes:

> History is a story that is not solely concerned with time and events: in its representations of those times and events, it functions as a powerful form of self-representation and self-definition. Indeed, it is through such shared narratives that the social identity of communities is constituted, both positively (by inclusion) and negatively (through exclusion or demonisation, for example). (Holton 1994, p. 246)

For this reason, Holton (1994) argues, the line between narratives of history and historical fiction are not as distinct as some might prefer:

> the similarity of the mediating roles played by concepts such as intentionality and point of view in the discussion of the writing both of history as narrative and of narrative fiction tends to work against the absolute separation of these two genres ... both seek to construct coherent narrative representations of events. (p. 11)

While Barry does not present his novels as historical fact or "truth," by retelling and re-interpreting Irish historical narratives, he is still entering into a longstanding and contentious debate.

To give a painfully reductive summary, Irish historical narratives fall into two broadly-defined camps: nationalist and revisionist. Nationalist historians tend to approach Irish history from a postcolonial perspective. Their work is "nationalist" insofar as it interprets centuries of violence, rebellion, and disaster as leading, ultimately, to the formation of the Irish Free State/Republic of Ireland. While many Irish nationalist historians and critics are skeptical of present-day Irish politics, their approach to Irish history tends to emphasize the radical potential in the fight against British colonial rule. Attempts to articulate an "Irish" national literature means that many contemporary literary critics fall into the nationalist camp. One of the most prominent of these is Declan Kibered, whose seminal book *Inventing Ireland*, traces the development of a literary and historical "Irish" identity from the 16th century onwards.

Many Irish revisionist historians would characterize the nationalist approach as, at best, naïvely poetic and at worst, dangerously sectarian.[10] Revisionists tend to emphasize the incongruities of historically "Irish" identities, and point out that the white, English-speaking, Western European nation of Ireland has little in common with Britain's other former colonies. Revisionists often benefit from meticulous historical research and see their work as driven by facts rather than ideology. However, they are also, in the words of Cullingford (2001), "sometimes less aware of the interests served by their own ostensibly factual narratives" (p. 1).

Barry does not really fit neatly into either side of this debate. His novels riff off major events of the nationalist version of history—especially the 1916 Easter Rising, the Irish War of Independence, and the Civil War. But they also follow characters that are usually ignored or vilified by committed nationalists—loyalist Catholics, apolitical emigrants, soldiers in the British Army. For this reason, some nationalists have taken issue with the viewpoints represented by some of his characters. Kiberd, for example, generally praised *Annie Dunne* in a 2002 review, but also suggested rather tartly that the novel was weakest it attempted to "appeal to that herd of independent minds which believes that it is a holy and wholesome thing to dismantle the narrative of nationalism" (Kiberd 2002). But, in general, Barry's progressive humanist politics and well-crafted literary stylings mean that he is generally embraced by the Irish establishment: so much so, in fact, that in 2018 he was appointed as the Republic of Ireland's second-ever Laureate for Irish Fiction (Doyle 2018).

4. A Long Long Way

With this background in mind, it seems almost inevitable that Barry would take an Irish experience of the First World War as a subject for a novel. In fact, the seeds of *A Long Long Way* were planted early in his canon: Willie Dunne first appears (as a ghost) in *The Steward of Christendom*. *A Long Long Way* itself takes place between 1914 and 1918 and follows Willie Dunne through his experiences as a member of the 16th Irish Division of the British Army. Published in 2005, *A Long Long Way* was well-received by critics and was shortlisted for the prestigious Man Booker Prize. Reviews of the novel tend to either paint the story as a corrective re-telling of the forgotten history of Irish soldiers in the First World War or as a Great War novel with an "Irish" twist. *A Long Long Way* is both these things. It is also, as Badin (2015) writes, one of Barry's most traditional (which is to say, least postmodern) works of historical fiction.

That said, *A Long Long Way* is also one of Barry's most sympathetic treatments of Irish nationalism. While from Willie's perspective the Easter Rising is, in the terms of Briggs (2017), "carnage and confusion," its actual purpose is not disavowed in the text. In fact, however chaotic and ill-conceived it may appear, the Rising is violence in service of a defined goal; therefore, it contrasts starkly with the "carnage and confusion" of the trenches, which is mechanized, anonymous, and serves no clear purpose. Over the course of the novel, Willie is traumatized by both types of violence, but while the violence of the trenches leaves him shell-shocked and numb, the Rising provides the catalyst for something like a political awakening. Finding his Irish–English–Loyalist–Catholic identity untenable and understanding that he is on the wrong side of Irish history, Willie nevertheless ends the novel as a reluctant nationalist. It is the contrast between the violence of the Easter Rising and Willie's experience in the trenches that, in my view, makes *A Long Long Way* Barry's most nuanced take on Irish nation building.

---

[10] If this seems an exaggerated response, it is important to remember that, during the Troubles in the latter half of the 20th century, the stakes of this debate could be literally life and death. Historical narratives were a key part of sectarian identity for both nationalists and unionists in Northern Ireland.

5. Conflicting and Converging Identities

Like many of Barry's protagonists, Willie is born into a family of complex loyalties. The Dunnes are "Castle Catholics";[11] Thomas Dunne, Willie's father, is the chief superintendent of the Dublin Metropolitan Police (DMP). Despite the religious discrimination that he faces—he has "risen as high as a Catholic could go" (Barry 1998, p. 44) in the DMP—Thomas is fiercely loyal to the Victorian ideals of the Protestant Ascendency and, more broadly, the entire British Empire. The contradictions of Thomas's identity are magnified in his son. The seeds of an identity crisis are sown into Willie Dunne's very name. The surname, Dunne, is Irish in origin. It is a derivative of the O'Duinn, a clan which was known to be "hostile to English interest" (Neafsey 2002, p. 6) in the 16th century. Willie's first name, however, comes from "the long-dead Orange King" (Barry 2005, p. 3) William of Orange (William III of England), who cemented England's Protestant rule in the late 17th century.[12] Throughout Willie's short life, events conspire to draw out these conflicting identities. He falls in love with the working-class daughter of one of the strikers his father injured during the DMP's violent dispersal of the 1913 Dublin Lockout.[13] He joins the British Army, but finds himself unable to shoot when fighting the rebels during the Easter Rising. By the end of the book, he is literally branded with the symbols of both England and Ireland: an explosion burns the imprint of a fellow soldier's medal into his chest, leaving a mark in the shape of "a little harp and a little crown" (Barry 2005, p. 276).

At the beginning of the novel, Willie looks up to his father both figuratively and literally and hopes to deal with these conflicting identities in the same way that Thomas does. But Willie is barred from joining the DMP by his height, which will "never reach six feet, the regulation height for a recruit" (Barry 2005, p. 6) and his decision to enlist is motivated by the less-restrictive requirements for the army. Willie signs up at the recruiting office, "his height never in question" and is satisfied to find that "if he could not be a policeman, he could be a soldier" (Barry 2005, p. 15).

Even beyond the more lax height restriction, joining an Irish division of the British Army seems like one possible way for Willie to reconcile his conflicting identities. The outbreak of the war gives Willie the opportunity to be part of a global movement:

> Why, he [Willie] read in the newspaper that men who spoke only Gallic came down to the lowlands of Scotland to enlist, men of the Aran Islands that spoke only their native Irish rowed over to Galway. Public schoolboys from Winchester and Marlborough, boys of the Catholic University School and Belvedere and Blackrock College in Dublin. High-toned critics of Home Rule from the rainy Ulster countries, and Catholic men of the South alarmed for Belgian nun and child. Recruiting sergeants of all the British world wrote down names in a hundred languages, a thousand dialects. Swahili, Urdu, Irish, Bantu, the click languages of the Bushmen, Cantonese, Australian, Arabic. (Barry 2005, p. 14)

At the beginning of the war, the unification of the empire against a common enemy papers over the "deep, dark maze of intentions" (Barry 2005, p. 15) of those who have enlisted. These men also find a unified soldierly identity that, significantly, takes "A Long Way to Tipperary" as its anthem: "every man Jack of them knew 'Tipperary' and sang it as if most of them weren't city-boys but hailed from the verdant fields of that country.[14] Probably every man in the army knew it, whether he was from Aberdeen or Lahore. Even the coolies sang 'Tipperary' while they dug: Willie had heard

---

[11] The phrase, often used pejoratively, referred to Irish Catholics who worked for the colonial British regime, which had its administrative center in Dublin Castle.
[12] William of Orange's victory at the Battle of the Boyne in 1690 is not a distant historical event in Ireland. In unionist communities in Northern Ireland, it is still commemorated each year on July 12 with militaristic marches which often, provocatively, pass through Catholic neighborhoods.
[13] Thomas's role in the Dublin Lockout of 1913 is central to the plot of *The Steward of Christendom*. Although the Lockout was a labor movement, it is closely associated with nationalism. James Connolly, who organized the lockout, was the leader of the Irish Citizen Army and one of those executed after the 1916 Easter Rising.
[14] County Tipperary is in the fertile midlands of Ireland.

them" (Barry 2005, p. 57). For Willie, who is at this point entirely apolitical, blending into this mass of humanity seems like it might allow for a reconciliation of his own polarized identities.

Over the course of the novel, several characters express hope that the war might lead to unity within Ireland as well.[15] Father Buckley is the most vocal proponent of this view. He hopes that "Nationalist and Unionist Irish soldiers fighting side by side might some day foment a greater understanding of each other and bring Ireland in spite of the recent rebellion to a place of balance" (Barry 2005, p. 195). At certain points in the novel, this possibility seems like it might be realized. Barry describes a friendly animosity between unionist and nationalist soldiers, writing that they "liked to trade insults with each other when they passed by chance on the road, or fetched up in billets near each other" (Barry 2005, p. 144). Under the right circumstances, this animosity can turn into something like camaraderie, like it does after the victory at Guinchy. The 16th Irish Division has secured victory at that town, and Christy Moran describes their reception by the 36th Ulster Division: "And those devious Ulster lads from the 36th milling about and calling us wonderful fucking Paddies, that's what they said, and shaking our hands" (Barry 2005, p. 225).

The clearest expression of this uneasy unity, though, comes in an inter-regimental boxing tournament, which pits "a Belfast man called William Beatty" against "a tall bleak-faced hero called Miko Cuddy" (Barry 2005, p. 191). The match takes place sometime in the fall of 1916, and "the recent trouble in Dublin" (Barry 2005, p. 195) is certainly on everyone's mind. However, it is more significant to the proceedings that this "Battle of the Micks" (Barry 2005, p. 191) takes place shortly after the Battle of the Somme. The sectarian competition, which might have been life-or-death in a different context, is termed "unobjectionable" (Barry 2005, p. 191) by Father Buckley: "by which he meant it wasn't an engagement in the field of death and therefore no one would get killed by machine-gun or shrapnel bomb" (Barry 2005, p. 191). Indeed, the fight ends up being (mostly) a fair and even match, with the two competitors treating each other as fellow sportsmen. But the match does nothing to actually solve partisan divisions. Instead, it merely downgrades them to a form of entertainment. The spectators of the boxing match view it as a "great spectacle" (Barry 2005, p. 190) not because it will have any effect on the future of their nation, but because it provides a momentary distraction from the coming winter, which will bring only "suffering in the raw ditches of that world" (Barry 2005, p. 191). The common identity of the men at this point comes from suffering, not idealism. After enduring gas attacks, constant bombings, and utterly random violence perpetrated by an unseen, anonymous enemy, the men find relief in a small-scale, clear-cut conflict between two of their own.

But trauma, Barry will show, is not stable ground on which to build an identity, particularly when there is no clear rationale behind the suffering. Although it is nominally a victory, Willie's experience at the Guinchy and Guillemont is one of his most traumatic: "at least four men of their platoon were gone, and maybe two thirds of the company, and maybe half the battalion was dead, and another third terribly wounded . . . The field hospital couldn't manage the deluge of grief and distress. The world was distressed into a thousand pieces" (Barry 2005, p. 186). Guinchy itself, the village that has been won, is "only a stretch of flattened ground with some light white patches were bricks and mortar of houses had long since been pulverized" (Barry 2005, p. 185). This victory that bonds the soldiers is hollow; its only lasting impact is trauma.

6. Easter, 1916

In contrast to the battle at Guinchy, the Easter Rising was a short-term disaster but a long-term victory. In *A Long Long Way*, Willie witnesses the Easter Rising firsthand, and the personal and political consequences of this experience reverberate throughout the novel. Although Willie witnesses "a

---

[15] These characters echo the sentiments expressed in John Redmond's 1914 speech to the House of Commons in which he expressed hope that nationalist and unionist soldiers fighting side-by-side might be "good for the future welfare and integrity of the Irish nation" (Callinan 2014).

thousand deaths" (Barry 2005, p. 246) over the course of the novel, the Rising is the first time that he connects death with a political purpose.

Willie is in Dublin when the Easter Rising breaks out, on his way back to the front from his first furlough. The violence in his home city is startling and confusing, and Willie thinks at first that the Germans have invaded Ireland. When told to step away from "the enemy" (a man handing out copies of the Proclamation), Willie responds "What enemy?" (Barry 2005, p. 88) and when told that the proclamation is addressed to "the people," he asks "What people?" (Barry 2005, p. 90). A political innocent, Willie has no knowledge of the unrest that has been brewing in his native city, and when the Rising brings it to a head, his world is turned, suddenly and bafflingly, upside down. Familiar household items become tools of war as the company builds a barricade out of furniture from nearby houses. Familiar places, like "the intersection of the canal and the Ballsbridge road" (Barry 2005, p. 91) have suddenly become battlefields. Familiar people have become "the enemy."

In the midst of this turmoil, Willie finds himself face-to-face with a rebel soldier, "a shivering man, a very young shivering man in a Sunday suit and a sort of military hat" (Barry 2005, p. 92). The soldier attempts to take Willie captive, but is fatally injured by a shot from Willie's captain. Unwilling to shoot the man himself, and feeling that "it would be heartless not to attend to the man in some fashion" (Barry 2005, p. 92), Willie kneels beside the rebel as he dies. As Willie watches the man's blood stream across the familiar street, the soldier insists that he is "An Irishman ... fighting for Ireland" (Barry 2005, p. 92) and says his act of contrition. Two full pages of description are devoted to the rebel's death, and Willie will literally carry "the young man's blood to Belgium on his uniform" (Barry 2005, p. 97). This experience is sharply contrasted with his confrontation of another enemy, just a few pages later. Thrown into hand-to-hand combat with a German soldier, Willie sees the man as "a grey monster in a mask" and imagines him as an enemy invader: "He stood over Willie and all Willie could think of were Vikings, wild Vikings sacking an Irish town" (Barry 2005, p. 113). The German is only humanized after his death through the family pictures and trinkets in his pockets, and Willie never wonders at his motivations for coming to the war.

The Rising, on the other hand, is (literally) something to write home about. In a letter to his father, Willie expresses sympathy for the executed 1916 leaders and the young man whom he watched die: *"When I came through Dublin I saw a young lad killed in a doorway, a rebel he was, and I felt pity for him. He was no older than myself. I wish they had not seen fit to shoot the three leaders"* (Barry 2005, p. 139). Thomas sees his son's sympathy for the nationalist cause as a personal affront and when Willie is next home on furlough, he accuses him of betraying the family legacy:

> Now, that they might have killed me at the gates of St. Stephen's Green, that that demon woman Markievicz might have marched up and shot her bullet into my breast and taken this life out of me, before I had to open a bitter letter and read those bitter words and feel the bitter bile loosen in the very centre of my body, so that I was crying in the darkness, crying in the darkness, for a fool and a forsaken father! (Barry 2005, p. 247)

Thomas is particularly enraged because of the death of "one of [his] recruits" (Barry 2005, p. 246), presumably the historical Constable Michael Lahiff, who was shot during the Rising near St. Stephen's Green and later died of his wounds.[16] Willie, however, cannot muster outrage at this act of violence. Within the scene, he is described as "a man of five foot six who had seen a thousand deaths" (Barry 2005, p. 246). Trauma and disillusionment make it impossible for Willie to argue with his father in this instance; he simply turns and goes "back down the worn stairs and out in to the gathering dark" (Barry 2005, p. 248).

---

[16] The question of whether or not Constance Markievicz, who was leading the group of rebels in St. Stephen's Green, was the one who shot the unarmed constable remains unresolved. Firsthand accounts of the incident vary (Arrington n.d.).

The key to Willie's change of heart, however, is not just the Rising. Instead, it is another death that he witnesses at the front, although not in anything like a battle. Jesse Kirwan[17] is an Irish Volunteer who has enlisted in the war effort because of John Redmond's appeals. Jesse has not yet seen the war when Willie meets him in Dublin, both of them on their way to the front, but he is well-versed in Irish politics. It is Jesse who explains the Proclamation of the Irish Republic to Willie, along with the reasons for and implications of the Rising.

Jesse is a tragic figure from the beginning. As the soldiers rally behind their barricade in order to fire on the General Post Office, Jesse huddles with a copy of the Proclamation, "intently weeping" (Barry 2005, p. 90). Later, at the front and after the leaders of the Rising have been executed, Jesse undertakes a silent protest and hunger strike.[18] When Willie is called to his side, he explains his reasoning: "an Irishman can't fight this war now. Not after those lads being executed ... I won't serve in the uniform that lads wore when they shot those others [sic] lads" (Barry 2005, p. 155). He is not eating, he says, "so I can shrink, and not to be touching the cloth of this uniform, you know? I am trying to disappear, I suppose" (Barry 2005, p. 155). The result of the Rising is that Jesse has come to see his own self-concept—as an Irishman fighting in the British Army—as untenable. Ironically, in the midst of so much bloodshed and mayhem, Jesse's desire for self-annihilation represents the ultimate act of treason, and he is court-martialed and executed. Willie manages to be part of the burial detail and the text explains that, ultimately, Jesse got his final wish: "that earth [where Jesse is buried] would be disturbed four or five times in the coming years. Jesse Kirwan would be blown out of his resting-place and scattered across the bombed earth, blown and scattered again, till every morsel of him was entirely atomized and defunct" (Barry 2005, p. 161). At the time, Willie does not understand Jesse's decision, and he wonders "what in the world was the matter with [Jesse] that he refused to obey orders?" (Barry 2005, p. 149).

By the end of the novel, though, Willie is faced with his own marginalization as an Irishman within the British army and as a British soldier in Ireland. Having lost his family, his sweetheart, and any other sense of his identity, Willie finally decides that Jesse may have been on to something after all: "Finally, the words of Jesse Kirwan had penetrated deep into the sap of his brain and he understood them. All sorts of Irelands were no more, and he didn't know what Ireland there was behind him now" (Barry 2005, p. 286). But Willie, knowing the war is almost over, decides he will seek knowledge rather than death: "No, he did not understand Jesse Kirwan entirely, but he would seek to in the coming years, he told himself. At least in the upshot he would try to know that philosophy" (Barry 2005, p. 287). "That philosophy" is, presumably, the nationalism that led Jesse to join the British army in the first place and that, ultimately, led to his death at its hands. But Willie's path to this understanding will not be clear:

> But how would he live and breathe? How would he love and live? How would any of them? ... How could a fella like Willie hold England and Ireland equally in his heart, like this father before him, like his father's father, and his father's fathers' father, when both now would call him a traitor, though his heart was clear and pure, as pure as a heart can be after three years of slaughter. (Barry 2005, p. 287)

The answer, of course, is that Willie cannot "hold England and Ireland equally in his heart," even though he has been branded with the symbols of each nation.

---

[17] The Kirwans are another family in Barry's fictional universe. His play *Prayers of Sherkin* (1997) features Jesse's parents.

[18] Jesse's chosen method of protest is historically feasible: imprisoned British suffragettes had been using hunger strikes as a method of political protest since before the war. But the act of a hunger strike has particular resonance within the later Irish nationalist movement. Most famously, in Northern Ireland during the 1970s and 1980s, imprisoned members of the IRA, including the MP Bobby Sands, used the hunger strike as part of their campaign to be treated as political prisoners (Linehan 2017).

7. An Inclusive Nationalism

Ultimately, *A Long Long Way* represents an argument for a more inclusive Irish national identity. This argument is neither particularly new nor particularly controversial in Irish literary circles, but what is provocative about this novel in particular is the way it locates the possibility of this new identity in *both* the Easter Rising *and* the First World War. The Easter Rising and the Proclamation issued therein is a well-accepted focal point for nationalists arguing against the religious and social conservatism of the Irish Free State. For such scholars, "the execution of James Connolly and the defeat of the anti-Treaty Republicans in the Civil War meant the extinction of the socialist, feminist, and non-sectarian possibilities inherent in the Proclamation of the Republic" (Cullingford 2001, p. 2). Willie's slow acceptance of nationalism hints at the Rising as a source of such possibilities, but the ending of the novel also illustrates the ways in which the war creates an Irish community that crosses social, economic, and political barriers.

While the last few months of Willie's life are filled with bitterness and pain, they do contain a glimpse of what such a nation might look like. Alone on his second furlough, having been exiled from his family, Willie makes his way to the home of his first captain—Captain Pasley. Pasley came from a family of land-owning farmers in County Wicklow, near the place where Willie's father was raised. Willie had regarded Pasley as a good captain, closely connected with the land and well-suited for leadership: "he had an air of confidence, which was a good air when you were all stuck out in foreign fields, and even the birds did not sing the same run of notes" (Barry 2005, p. 32). Pasley respected his men and bonded with them over their shared homesickness, worrying over the work, and particularly the "liming of the fields" (Barry 2005, p. 32) that his father will have to do in his absence. But Pasley's confidence and honor were of no use against the ravages of 20th century warfare. He was killed in the first gas attack on his platoon after he (both nobly and foolishly) insisted on "hold[ing] the fort" (Barry 2005, p. 46) as his men fell back in retreat.

In a world of strict divisions, Willie's religion and class should separate him politically from the Pasleys,[19] but as he moves towards his former captain's estate, he finds these barriers breaking down. He meets the rector of the local Protestant church, who registers that Willie's name is "unlikely to be a Protestant one" (Barry 2005, p. 356) but nonetheless gives him polite directions. Arriving at the house, Willie has "enough sense" (Barry 2005, p. 256) not to go to the grand front door, and instead knocks at the servants' entrance to the kitchen. He first assumes that the woman who answers the door is the cook, but later realizes that it is Mrs. Pasley herself. Even Willie's conceptions of the roles the two of them ought to play in regard to mourning, too, are overturned: "He had come, he had thought, to comfort the captain's parents. How could there be comfort in a fool sitting in the kitchen with his tongue tied and his heart scalded?" (Barry 2005, p. 259). These characters gather together as Ireland is on the cusp of nationhood, united by the shared trauma and grief wrought by an entirely different conflict. They will all, ultimately, be left out of official versions of nationalist history, but this brief moment demonstrates the possibility of a different kind of national community—one that is only made possible by the war.

Barry's protagonists tend to be victims of the process of Irish nation-building. In *On Canaan's Side*, for example, Willie's sister Lilly Dunne spends most of her life fleeing the political consequences of her husband's involvement with the Black and Tans.[20] Thomas Dunne, though more unsympathetic than either Willie or Lilly, eventually goes mad in an Ireland that no longer has a place for him. But *A*

---

[19] Although they are not overly wealthy, the Pasleys are landowning, Protestant farmers, and therefore a part of the colonial Anglo-Irish class. Willie, despite his father's politics, is still Catholic and only marginally middle-class.

[20] Dubbed "Black and Tans" because their hastily-assembled uniforms combined police (black) and army (khaki) items, this newly-created force was brought in to Ireland by the British during the War for Independence to supplement the existing policy and military presence. Black and Tans in particular were notorious for their brutality and lack of discipline. Many were, in fact, veterans of the First World War, who received only a scant few months of training before being sent to Ireland to put down the insurgency. In Ireland and for some Irish Americans, the phrase "black and tan" is still strongly associated with ruthlessness and violence (McKittrick 2006).

Long Long Way does not completely fit this pattern. Willie is a victim of *both* the mass, anonymized violence of the First World War *and* the consolidation of an "Irish" identity around the sacrifice of the 1916 rebels. At the same time, Barry represents new possibilities as inherent in both these disruptions, and so he complicates but does not debunk the founding myth of Irish nationhood. While Willie does die tragically in the last days of the fighting, Barry's representation of his story suggests a new and more complex approach to a painful point in Irish history.

Funding: This research received no external funding.

Acknowledgments: Thanks to Rachel McCoppin for encouraging me to write this article and for listening to my excited chatter about 20th century Irish history. Thanks also to Stacie Varnso for reminding me to rein in the parentheses. Finally, thanks to Sara Brandel for her wise edits and constant friendship.

Conflicts of Interest: The author declares no conflict of interest.

References

Arrington, Lauren. n.d. Did Constance Markievicz Shoot the Policeman? Conference of Irish Historians in Britain. Available online: http://irishhistoriansinbritain.org/?p=18 (accessed on 21 January 2019).

Badin, Donatella A. 2015. "People Mired in History": Sebastian Barry and Cultural Memory in a European Perspective. In *Towards 2016: 1916 and Irish Literature, Culture, and Society*. Edited by Seán Crossen and Werner Huber. Trier: Wissenschaftlicher Verlag Trier, pp. 155–66.

Barry, Sebastian. 1998. *The Steward of Christendom*, Acting ed. New York: Dramatist Play Services, Inc.

Barry, Sebastian. 2005. *A Long Long Way*. New York: Penguin Books.

Beckett, James Camlin. 1966. *The Making of Modern Ireland: 1603–1923*. London: Faber and Faber.

Belfast Unionist Mural. 2010. Wikimedia Commons. Available online: https://commons.wikimedia.org/wiki/File:Belfast_unionist_mural.jpg (accessed on 21 January 2019).

Briggs, Marlene A. 2017. The New Great War Novels: Revisiting the War's Myths through Contemporary Fiction. In *Teaching Representation of the First World War*. Edited by Debra Rae Cohen and Douglass Higbee. New York: The Modern Language Association of America, pp. 265–76.

Callinan, Elaine. 2014. Redmond Pledge that Nationalists and Unionists Would Fight Together in First World War. *The Irish Times*, May 14. Available online: https://www.irishtimes.com/culture/heritage/redmond-pledge-that-nationalists-and-unionists-would-fight-together-in-first-world-war-1.1786617 (accessed on 21 January 2019).

Campbell, John. 2018. Q&A: The Irish Border Brexit Backstop. *BBC*, December 13. Available online: https://www.bbc.com/news/uk-northern-ireland-politics-44615404 (accessed on 21 January 2019).

Connell, Joseph E. A., Jr. 2014. John Redmond's Woodenbridge Speech. *History Ireland*, 22. Available online: https://www.historyireland.com/volume-22/john-redmonds-woodenbridge-speech/ (accessed on 21 January 2019).

Cullingford, Elizabeth Butler. 2001. *Ireland's Others: Gender and Ethnicity in Irish Literature and Popular Culture*. Cork: Cork University Press.

Department of the Taoiseach. 2018. Irish Soldiers and the First World War. Department of the Taoiseach. Available online: https://www.taoiseach.gov.ie/eng/Historical_Information/State_Commemorations/Irish_Soldiers_in_the_First_World_War/ (accessed on 21 January 2019).

Doyle, Martin. 2018. Sebastian Barry Revealed as New Laureate for Irish Fiction. *The Irish Times (Dublin)*, February 8. Available online: https://www.irishtimes.com/culture/books/sebastian-barry-revealed-as-new-laureate-for-irish-fiction-1.3383687 (accessed on 21 January 2019).

Ferriter, Diarmond. 2004. *The Transformation of Ireland*. New York: The Overlook Press.

First World War. 1998. *The Oxford Companion to Irish History*. Edited by S. J. Connolly. New York: Oxford University Press.

Fitzpatrick, David. 1996. Militarism in Ireland, 1900–1922. In *A Military History of Ireland*. Edited by Thomas Bartlett and Keith Jeffry. New York: Cambridge University Press.

Foster, Robert Fitzroy. 1988. *Modern Ireland: 1600–1972*. New York: Penguin Books.

Fussell, Paul. 1975. *The Great War and Modern Memory*. New York: Oxford University Press.

Heaney, Mick. 2018. Sebastian Barry: Part of me when I was Young Would Have Poisoned the Soup of Every Other Writer. *The Irish Times*, February 10. Available online: https://www.irishtimes.com/culture/books/sebastian-barry-part-of-me-when-i-was-young-would-have-poisoned-the-soup-of-every-other-writer-1.3383391 (accessed on 21 January 2019).

Holton, Robert. 1994. *Jarring Witnesses: Modern Fiction and the Representation of History*. Hemel Hempstead: Harvester Wheatsheaf.

Irish WW1 Recruitment Poster. 2012. Wikimedia Commons. Available online: https://commons.wikimedia.org/wiki/File:Irish_WWI_recruitment_poster.jpg (accessed on 21 January 2019).

Jackson, Alvin. 2003. *Home Rule: An Irish History 1800–2000*. New York: Oxford University Press.

Keen, Suzanne. 2001. *Romances of the Archive in Contemporary British Fiction*. Toronto: University of Toronto Press.

Kiberd, Declan. 1995. *Inventing Ireland: The Literature of the Modern Nation*. Cambridge: Harvard University Press.

Kiberd, Declan. 2002. The Perils of Raj Revisionism: Annie Dunne. *The Irish Times*, May 18, p. 59.

Linehan, Hugh. 2017. The Long History of the Irish Hunger Strike. *The Irish Times*, September 21. Available online: https://www.irishtimes.com/culture/heritage/the-long-history-of-the-irish-hunger-strike-1.3228103 (accessed on 21 January 2019).

McGuinness, Frank. 2010. Frank McGuinness Interview: Waiting for the Spark to Come. *AgendaNi*, March 5. Available online: https://www.agendani.com/waiting-for-the-spark-to-come/ (accessed on 21 January 2019).

McKittrick, David. 2006. Ireland's War of Independence: The Chilling Story of the Black and Tans. *The Independent*, April 21. Available online: https://www.independent.co.uk/news/world/europe/irelands-war-of-independence-the-chilling-story-of-the-black-and-tans-5336022.html (accessed on 21 January 2019).

McKittrick, David. 2013. Surge in Belfast Violence Blamed on Resurgent UVF. *Belfast Telegraph*, January 7. Available online: https://www.belfasttelegraph.co.uk/news/northern-ireland/surge-in-belfast-violence-blamed-on-resurgent-uvf-29011837.html (accessed on 21 January 2019).

2019. Tom Kettle's Words of War. RTE. Available online: https://www.rte.ie/centuryireland/index.php/articles/tom-kettles-words-of-war (accessed on 21 January 2019).

Neafsey, Edward. 2002. *The Surnames of Ireland: Origins and Numbers of Selected Irish Surnames*. Kansas City: The Irish Genealogical Foundation.

Peatfield, Lisa. 2018. Why Men of Ireland Volunteered to Fight in the First World War. *The Imperial War Museum*. Available online: https://www.iwm.org.uk/history/why-men-of-ireland-volunteered-to-fight-in-the-first-world-war (accessed on 21 January 2019).

Pheonix, Eamon. 2016. The Somme—20,000 Men Walked Slowly to their Death on the First Day. *The Irish News*, June 30. Available online: http://www.irishnews.com/news/2016/06/30/news/the-somme---ulster-unionism-s-blood-sacrifice-584061/ (accessed on 21 January 2019).

Schultz, Matthew. 2014. *Haunted Historiographies: The Rhetoric of Ideology in Postcolonial Irish Fiction*. Manchester: Manchester University Press.

The Somme Association. 2019a. 16th Irish Division. The Somme Association. Available online: http://www.irishsoldier.org/history/16th-irish-division (accessed on 21 January 2019).

The Somme Association. 2019b. 36th Ulster Division. The Somme Association. Available online: http://www.irishsoldier.org/history/36th-ulster-division-0 (accessed on 21 January 2019).

Tierney, Mark, Paul Bowen, and David Fitzpatrick. 1988. Recruiting Posters. In *Ireland and the First World War*. Edited by David Fitzpatrick. Gigginstown: Lilliput Press.

Villiers, Theresa. 2015. *Assessment on Paramilitary Groups in Northern Ireland*. Belfast: Northern Ireland Office.

Who are the UVF? 2011. *BBC News*, June 22. Available online: https://www.bbc.com/news/uk-northern-ireland-11313364 (accessed on 21 January 2019).

Yeats, William Butler. 2000. Easter 1916. [1916]. In *Yeats's Poetry, Drama, and Prose*. Edited by James Pethica. New York: W.W. Norton & Co., pp. 73–75.

© 2019 by the author. Licensee MDPI, Basel, Switzerland. This article is an open access article distributed under the terms and conditions of the Creative Commons Attribution (CC BY) license (http://creativecommons.org/licenses/by/4.0/).

Article

Demonizing the Enemy, Literally: Tolkien, Orcs, and the Sense of the World Wars

Robert T. Tally Jr.

Department of English, Texas State University, San Marcos, TX 78666, USA; robert.tally@txstate.edu

Received: 17 January 2019; Accepted: 9 March 2019; Published: 12 March 2019

Abstract: A seemingly inescapable feature of war is the demonization of the enemy, who becomes somehow less human and more deserving of death in times of military strife, which unsurprisingly helps to justify the violence against them. This article looks at the development, character, and role of the orcs—creatures that are in some senses, *literally* demonized—in J. R. R. Tolkien's writings in connection with the ideological need to demonize the enemy in World Wars I and II. Yet, in creating an enemy whom the heroes could kill without compunction, Tolkien also betrayed his own sympathy for the devils, perhaps owing to his own experiences as a soldier. This ambiguity pervades Tolkien's writings, even as his demonized orcs are dispatched by the thousands, thus shaping the *sense* of warfare and our experience of it according to the desire to simplify, and make more comprehensible, the martial narrative.

Keywords: J. R. R. Tolkien; fantasy; war; narrative; ideology

1. Introduction

In his powerful study of the First World War, Paul Fussell elaborated upon the logic that seemed to underwrite a soldier's ability or willingness to kill his fellow man. Fussell pointed to what he called "gross dichotomizing," which he identified as "a persisting imaginative habit of modern times, traceable, it would seem, to the actualities of the Great War." As he explained,

> "We" are all here on this side; "the enemy" is over there. "We" are individuals with names and personal identities; "he" is a mere collective identity. We are visible; he is invisible. We are normal; he is grotesque. Our appurtenances are natural; his, bizarre. He is not as good as we are. Indeed, he may be like "the Turk" on the Gallipoli Peninsula, characterized by a staff officer before the British landings there as "an enemy who has never shown himself as good a fighter as the white man." Nevertheless, he threatens us and must be destroyed, or, if not destroyed, contained and disarmed. (Fussell 1975, p. 75)

The racial distinction, of course, is part of the demonization of the enemy as well—Fussell's quotation of the British officer comes from Robert Rhodes James's 1965 book, *Gallipoli* (James 1965, p. 86)—but racial difference explains little about the gross dichotomizing Fussell identifies, particularly as the "sides" in question were equally "white," that is, British and German. (It is well worth recalling that the British Royal Family itself *was* German, and during the war, in June 1917 specifically, King Georg V cannily opted to change the family's ancestral moniker from the rather Teutonic-sounding House of Saxe-Coburg and Gotha [i.e., *Haus Sachsen-Coburg und Gotha*] to a more English-like House of Windsor, owing to quite understandable anti-German sentiment in the United Kingdom at the time.) Fussell goes on to quote British soldiers apparently in awe of the enemy's "monstrous and grotesque" attributes. "Sometimes the shadowy enemy resembled the vilest animals," with enemy soldiers being compared to water-rats scrambling into their holes or earwigs scattering under a rotten tree stump (Fussell 1975, p. 79). Fussell notes that descriptions of the German dead frequently mentioned the bodies' porcine qualities. All of this contributes to the general idea that one's wartime enemy is not entirely human.

At the very moment when these impressions were being felt and expressed by his fellow enlisted men, a young soldier in the Lancashire Fusiliers was working on what he referred to as "my nonsense fairy language" (Tolkien 1981, p. 8), in connection with which he would develop an elaborate series of connected myths, a *legendarium* in which fair but tragic elves and bold but equally tragic men took up arms against an insuperably powerful evil Enemy, one whose "vilest deed," it could be said, was to create the demonic race of orcs (Tolkien 2002, p. 47). (Please note that Tolkien's texts are inconsistent in the capitalization of the word *orc* and those signifying other "races," and I have opted to use lowercase spelling except when quoting directly from texts in which the uppercase appears.) As J. R. R. Tolkien later confessed to his son, while the latter was serving in the Royal Air Force during the *next* World War, part of the urgency with which he wrote these tales emerged from a longing to make sense of the terrible world in which he was living, to express his "*feeling* about good, evil, fair, foul in some way: to rationalize it, and prevent it just festering." Tolkien encouraged his son to write, as a way of dealing with these pains that come with serving as a common soldier in a great war. As he continued, "In my case it generated Morgoth and the History of the Gnomes [i.e., the earliest versions of *The Silmarillion*]. Lots of the early parts of which (and the languages)—discarded or absorbed—were done in grimy canteens, at lectures in cold fogs, in huts full of blasphemy and smut, or by candle light in the bell-tents, even some down in dugouts under shell fire. It did not make for efficiency and present-mindedness, of course, and I was not a good officer" (Tolkien 1981, p. 78).

Tolkien does not here, or really anywhere else in his letters, demonize Britain's or the Allies' wartime enemies. He has too much respect for Germanic cultures—though not for Nazis, whom he blamed for perverting and abusing the majestic Nordic mythologies and folklore to serve their own foul ideological ends (see Tolkien 1981, pp. 55–56)—to imagine the German soldiers as subhuman. John Garth has suggested otherwise, noting that Tolkien during World War I may have connected his idea of goblins (also known as orcs) and trolls to Germans, particularly in his earliest version of "The Fall of Gondolin," but Garth concedes that "Tolkien later insisted there was no parallel between the Goblins he had invented and the Germans he had fought, declaring 'I've never had those sorts of feelings about the Germans. I'm very anti that kind of thing'" (Garth 2003, pp. 218–19). Moreover, as a combat veteran of "the Great War," Tolkien had too much respect for the common soldier one either side of the lines of battle to envision them as inhuman, animal-like, or unworthy of life. Even during and after World War II, Tolkien expressed anger at those in England who called for destroying the Germans, stating that "The Germans have just as much a right to declare the Poles and Jews exterminable vermin, subhuman, as we have to select the Germans: in other words, no right, whatever they have done" (Tolkien 1981, p. 93). If Tolkien's fantasy narratives required the presence of orcs in order to have a distinctively demonized enemy for the heroes to battle, it was certainly not a matter of substituting orcs for Germans or any other real-world enemy of England. Indeed, in one of the few instances among his wartime letters in which he refers to orcs metaphorically, Tolkien does so only to note that "in real life they are on both sides, of course" (p. 82). Janet Brennan Croft has analyzed the manner by which Tolkien's use and characterization of the orcs parallels the demonization of the enemy in wartime, and she specifically connects Fussell's observations with Tolkien's (see Croft 2004, pp. 47–50). However, Croft notes Tolkien's misgivings about the demonization of the enemy, as he revised his ideas about the orcs over the years, often in the attempt to make them less worthy of sympathy by denying their free will and humanity. But still, the stories required enemies to be clearly demarcated as such, and the orcs served that purpose. Tolkien's desire for narrative, as it might be called, is not informed by a need to demonize the enemy, but as a need to make sense of the war and the world in which it is waged.

In this essay I want to discuss these two elements of the wartime narrative impulse in terms of modern fantasy's effectiveness as a means for imagining the world system as whole, but especially in the context of World Wars I and II. The demonization of the enemy is, I believe, a critical element of *Realpolitik*; if it is so useful in wartime, that is in part because of its intensely practical political value, war after all being merely the continuation of politics by other means, as Carl von Clausewitz famously put it. As such, the practice is subject to political critique. But the demonization of the enemy is also a crucial element in formulating incidents, persons, and events into a cognizable narrative, and this narrative impulse in turn shapes the way in which the world and everything in it is understood. Narrative is, in this manner, a sense-making system, and the more readily elements within a narrative can be assimilated into identifiable tropes, themes, categories, and patterns, the more easily the purportedly underlying reality can be given shape and made meaningful.

Demonizing the enemy makes for a pragmatic short-cut for overcoming the genuine apprehension of confusion and complexity by offering a simplistic, straightforward identity, which in turn serves as its own justification for action and reaction. The development, deployment, and legacy of Tolkien's orcs, which function in both *The Hobbit* (where they are referred to as *goblins*) and *The Lord of the Rings* as enemies to be dispatched without the slightest hint of moral compunction, offer a case study in the literal demonization of the enemy, but Tolkien's orcs also suggest ways in which this facile demonization can inspire meaningful critique of the very system they were meant to help make visible. The basic humanity of Tolkien's inhuman creatures, as I have discussed at length elsewhere (see Tally 2010), invites readers to question the racial and moral hierarchies presented in the narratives themselves, and also in the world we live in.

2. Generating Demons

I should state clearly up front that I do not mean to suggest that Tolkien used orcs or other enemies as allegorical counterparts to any "real-world" enemies fighting in the World Wars. As I discuss in the next section, Tolkien was extremely wary of such demonization of the enemy, particularly when connected to race, even though his own racialized rhetoric and descriptions in *The Lord of the Rings* can be problematic at times. The orcs of *The Lord of the Rings* most certainly do not represent German, Russian, or Japanese soldiers, and Tolkien makes clear in his wartime letters to his son Christopher that the orc, if it were to be viewed metaphorically as a violent, boorish, uncivilized person, would be well represented in every country in the world. Yet, in the fantasy writings for which he is most famous, the orc stands out among the various enemies—a category that includes "evil" men, as well as such traditional monsters as dragons, trolls, fell beasts (wolves, for instance), and god-like villains, Morgoth or Sauron—as a special case of demonization.

Contrary to much popular belief, Tolkien did not create the race of orcs, although his writings did more to shape the characteristic images of these creatures in fantasy novels, films, and video games than perhaps any other twentieth-century writer. As Tolkien himself noted, the word *orc* appears in Old English, where it had the apparent meaning of "demon" (see Tolkien 1981, pp. 177–78). Indeed, the word *orcnéas* appears in *Beowulf*, where Tolkien translated it "haunting shapes of hell" (see Tolkien 2014, pp. 161–62). In Tolkien's overall *legendarium*, orcs emerge as the mortal enemies of the primordial elves, later men (although some men fight alongside the orcs), and sometimes dwarves (and, in *The Hobbit*, it is suggested that dwarves conduct trade with orcs or goblins). Their primary narrative function seems limited to the role of cannon fodder for the enemy's war machine, and orcs form the rank-and-file of Morgoth's armies in *The Silmarillion*, and of both Sauron's and Saruman's armies in *The Lord of the Rings*. (Interestingly, whether affiliated with "Bolg of the North" or the goblins of the Misty Mountains, the orcs in *The Hobbit* appear to fight for themselves, not for any "Big Bosses," as two memorable orcs will later refer to them.) As enemy soldiers, the orcs are certainly demonized, but Tolkien's writings concerning the origins and character of the orcs make it clear that he does not view them as literal demons.

Tolkien's published and posthumously released writings give different accounts of the origins of orcs within Middle-earth, but for the most part he did not imagine them to be *demons* in the traditional sense of the word. In order to understand to role of orcs in his writings, one first needs to get a basic understanding of the broader mythological system upon which Tolkien's narratives rest. In Tolkien's mythology, which is ascribed to the beliefs and histories of the elves, there is one god, Eru or Ilúvatar, but from him emanates an infinite number of god-like, or perhaps angelic, beings known as the Ainur. At the beginning of the world, some of these Ainur descended to Arda (i.e., the planet Earth), and the mightiest of them formed the pantheon of Tolkien's myths, the Valar or "powers" of the Earth. Lesser Ainur, but still very powerful god-like beings, also came to Arda, and many of these served the Valar in on capacity or another. These were the Maiar, whose numbers includes such famous characters as Gandalf, Sauron, and Saruman. The most mighty of all the Ainur was Melkor, whom the elves later named Morgoth, a great Satan-figure for these mythic narratives. Melkor seduced many of the lesser Ainur into his own service, Sauron most significantly; some of these evil demigods took the form of demons, and the Balrogs (also known as "demons of might") and possibly even Dragons are among the most striking examples. It is well worth noting that, here in the early characterizations of these creatures, Tolkien might have chosen to list orcs among the lesser Ainur as well, effectively making them demons or devils, but he does not. Far from considering the Balrog a kindred spirit or even ally, for instance, the orcs of Moria in *The Fellowship of the Ring* seem to fear it and flee from it (Tolkien 1965a, pp. 369–70). However, Tolkien's characterization of orcs and his speculations as to their origins show that he was not comfortable assigning them the role of the actual demon, even if his narratives required that these creatures be thoroughly demonized later.

Regarding the origins of orcs, perhaps it is telling that even Tolkien changed his mind over time, as he seemed uneasy about the ways in which they fit into the mythic histories of Middle-earth. The standard view is that orcs were once elves, who through various means had somehow become ugly, violent, uncouth, and altogether monstrous. As *The Silmarillion* relates the matter, the elves "by slow arts of cruelty were corrupted and enslaved; thus did Melkor breed the hideous race of the Orcs in envy and mockery of the Elves" (Tolkien 2002, p. 47). In *The Two Towers*, the authority of Treebeard is asserted, as he explains to his hobbit guests, Merry and Pippin, that "Trolls are only counterfeits, made by the Enemy in the Great Darkness, in mockery of Ents, as Orcs were of Elves" (Tolkien 1965c, p. 91). Elsewhere in *The Silmarillion*, there is also the surmise that orcs actually *were* elves, specifically the Avari or Dark Elves, which is to say, the ones who did not migrate to the holy realm of Valinor, which is what distinguished the Light Elves from the Dark. As the narrator puts it, "Whence they [the orcs] came, or what they were, the Elves knew not then, thinking them perhaps to be Avari who had become evil and savage in the wild; in which they guessed all too near, it is said" (Tolkien 2002, pp. 103–4). If orcs were merely another race of elves, however, it would be much more difficult for their demonization to be tolerated. At least, one would hope so.

The hypothesis that orcs are simply different races or types of elves probably does make the most sense in accordance with Tolkien's overall *legendarium*, if only because orcs appear in these tales after elves but before men, and the special hatred that the elves bear toward orcs, and vice-versa, could almost be taken as a personal grudge. However, as Dimitra Fimi has elaborated, "the thought that the hideous and malicious Orcs were once Elves—the 'highest' beings of Middle-earth—became increasingly unbearable to Tolkien" (Fimi 2009, p. 155). In fact, in several posthumously published manuscripts written in the 1950s and 1960s (see, e.g., Tolkien and Tolkien 1993, pp. 408–25), during which period Tolkien was endeavoring to revise his earlier *Silmarillion* legends in order to make them more internally consistent and compatible with *The Lord of the Rings*, Tolkien entertained a number different ideas regarding the origins and characters of his orcs. Of the more bizarre explanations, Tolkien briefly considered the possibility that orcs were automatons, robots or puppets controlled by Morgoth or Sauron, without free will, languages, or thoughts of their own. This was an admittedly unlikely scenario, especially after readers had already been exposed to various goblins and orcs in *The Hobbit* and *The Lord of the Rings* who clearly had their own views. Whatever else orcs may be, they are most assuredly sentient; moreover, the orcs we meet in Tolkien's writings are imbued with fears, desires, values, families, and even cultures. Tolkien did toy with the idea that orcs might be lesser Maia, which was certainly possible given that Balrogs were already so understood, but he abandoned that notion as well. It seems that the orcs were far too *human* to be categorized as angels or demons.

Indeed, if we had to make a case for which of the various origins stories were most likely to be believed by Tolkien himself, the best bet seems to be that orcs are some form of human being. Rather than being tortured, twisted, or corrupted versions of elves, they were more likely corruptions of men. Among the unfinished writings published after Tolkien's death, there is even the vague suggestion that orcs *were* a kind of man, distant cousins of the Drúedain or related to the Púkel Men who appear in *The Return of the King*: "some thought, nonetheless, that there had been a remote kinship, which accounted for their special enmity. Orcs and Drûgs each regarded the other as renegades" (Tolkien 1988, pp. 401–2). And, as Christopher Tolkien concludes the discussion in *Morgoth's Ring*, "This would appear to be my father's final view on the matter: Orcs were bred from Men" (Tolkien and Tolkien 1993, p. 421).

There is one crucial philosophical or religious point in the various arguments concerning the origin of orcs that clearly troubled even Tolkien himself. To wit, their very existence shows they have value and are worthy of being. To put it another, less formal way, one could say that by their very nature, it seems, orcs must have souls; furthermore, being so endowed means that they must be, in theory at least, redeemable. As I have discussed in my article, "Let Us Now Praise Famous Orcs," the origin story of the dwarves as told in *The Silmarillion* offers a powerful test case, one that calls into question any view of the orcs as merely soulless monsters. There I pointed out that,

> An article of faith in Tolkien's world is that only God (in the Elvish, Eru or Ilúvatar) can *create*, and the evil ones—whether Melkor (a.k.a. Morgoth, Tolkien's original Satan figure), or Sauron (Melkor's acolyte and successor), or Saruman (who apparently breeds his own Orcs or "half-Orcs")—can only *pervert* that creation. To put it another way, no new "souls" or "spirits" can be created. Frodo explains as much to Sam when he states: "The Shadow that bred them [the Orcs] can only mock, it cannot make: not real new things of its own. I do not think it gave life to the Orcs, it only ruined them and twisted them" [1965b, p. 201].
>
> Indeed, this principle is dramatized and made perfectly clear in *The Silmarillion* in explaining the existence of the Dwarves. Aulë, a Vala (or "good" god) who longs to share his great knowledge with pupils and becomes impatient waiting for the Elves to awaken, actually creates Dwarves, but they are merely as clay figurines or puppets with no independent being. Ilúvatar chastises Aulë for attempting a thing "beyond thy power and thy authority," but even so grants his wish by giving his Dwarves life [pp. 37–38]. What this episode underscores is that not even the most powerful beings in the world—the Valar—can create new beings or imbue creatures with life. What this also means, of course, is that anything that in fact *has life*, has it with the tacit if not explicit approval of Ilúvatar. As Tolkien concedes in a letter, drafted but unsent, "by accepting or tolerating their making—necessary to their actual existence—even Orcs would become part of the World, which is God's and ultimately good" [1981, p. 195]. Hence, like Men and Elves, Orcs are in a way also the "Children of Ilúvatar. (Tally 2010, pp. 18–19)

By their very existence, then, orcs cannot be viewed as literal demons, yet in the stories, they are demonized throughout and dispatched thoroughly without pause or pity.

The extent to which the orcs are demonized, by the other characters if not by the author himself, can be measured by the vastly different treatment of orcs when compared to other characters. Notably, in the midst of terrible bloodshed, Legolas and Gimli maintain a friendly competition to see who can kill the most orcs. This grisly entertainment would seem almost inhuman were it not for the demonization of the enemy in the case. Contrast the positive glee these heroes express when killing orcs to the famous scene in which Sam for the first time witnesses a battle between armies of men. Looking upon the corpse of a "swarthy" Southron soldier, who had been cut down while fleeing, his "brown hand" still clutching a broken sword, Sam "wondered what the man's name was and where he came from; and if he was really evil at heart, or what lies or threats had led him on his long march from his home; and if he would not really have rather stayed home in peace" (Tolkien 1965c, p. 301). In *The Lord of the Rings*, Sam witnesses orcs both living and dead, but never does he wonder about their motivations and preferences, and needless to say, despite frequently longing for home and peace himself, Sam never considers what potential "lies and threats" have brought his own friends to wage war on diverse peoples and races of the South and East. Later, after the war had ended, Aragorn (now King Elessar) releases the Easterlings who had surrendered on the battlefield, makes peace with the swarthy men of the South, and frees the thralls of Mordor, granting them lands in that region (Tolkien 1965b, pp. 266–667), but no reference is made to any such accommodations or humane treatment of orcs. It is assumed that the orcs of Mordor simply die off after the ring was destroyed, but, as noted above, that seems rather unlikely given what the reader would have gleaned about orcs and their character from earlier scenes. Moreover, living orcs are not even taken hostage or held as prisoners of war by the heroes, who instead happily slaughter the enemy even as they recognize the baleful effects of war on men and elves. Within these pages, Tolkien's characters may view even humans in the service of "evil" as being potentially good—note Frodo's sympathy and kind treatment of the treacherous renegade Wormtongue, for example—but the reigning assumption is that orcs must be inherently evil, demons to the end.

3. Sympathy for the Devils

If Tolkien's orcs appear to be merely one-dimensionally evil beings, or even worse, simplistic and racist caricatures, it is worth noting that Tolkien himself had his concerns about the matter. For example, Shippey has pointed out that, "though he became increasingly concerned over the implications of the orcs in his story, and tried out several explanations for them, their analogousness to humanity always remained clear" (Shippey 2000b, p. 186). Elsewhere Shippey had conceded that "Orcs entered Middle-earth originally just because the story needed a continual supply of enemies over whom one need feel no compunction" (Shippey 2003, p. 233), but Tolkien could apparently not resist "fleshing out" these default enemies with almost the same sort of cultural and historical detail with which he had made his elves and men so compelling.

For one thing, as noted above, he gives different groups of orcs distinctive cultures, languages, and even families. In *The Hobbit*, for instance, Gandalf declares, "The Goblins are upon you! Bolg of the North is coming, O Dain! whose father you slew in Moria" (Tolkien 1982, p. 281); the actual battle in which Bolg's father, Azog, is killed by Dáin Ironfoot is described in Appendix A to *The Lord of the Rings* (see Tolkien 1965b, p. 392). Orcs can bear grudges and be motivated by vengeance just as humans can. In *The Two Towers*, Tolkien includes a scene in which three different groups of orcs—one from Mordor and in service to Sauron, one from Isengard representing Saruman's forces, and a third group of "Northerners" who want no part of such politics, but who (as one says) "have come all the way from the Mines and wish to kill, and avenge our folk. I wish to kill and go back north" (Tolkien 1965c, p. 43)—whose very languages, not to mention allegiances and motives, are completely different. The narrator observes that the different orcs speak in the "Common Tongue," for they did not know each other's native language, and the debate they hold in this lingua franca reveals their vastly different aims and allegiances. Shippey even points out that the basic sense of morality—thei views of good and evil, for instance—aligns with that of the heroes, even if, in practice, the orcs engage in immoral activities. As Shippey puts it, the orcs "have a clear idea of what is admirable and what is contemptible behavior, which is exactly the same as ours" (Shippey 2000a, p. 133). Far from being mindless drones, orcs are "rational, incarnate beings" (Tolkien 1981, p. 195), with what we might recognize as deeply *human* feelings, perhaps even more so than the elves, whose near-perfection marks them with a profound alterity.

Later in *The Two Towers*, Tolkien depicts a scene in which two orc captains are discussing the war that they find themselves waging, and each expresses not only his concerns over its potential failure, doubting the word of their own leaders as to its inevitable success and complaining about the circumstances of their own service. Moreover, these two express the sincere desire to live free, without "Big Bosses" to rule them, which is a far cry from the notion that all orcs are mindless slaves or minions. True, the freedom they seek is to become itinerant raiders and pillagers, but their desire for autonomy and independence clearly indicates that they are not slaves to greater powers, whether evil or not. In fact, by complaining about their jobs and their supervisors, these orc soldiers seem more realistically human than many of the heroic men fighting against the armies of Mordor.

Of course, the question of race is part of the problem when examining the role of orcs in Tolkien's world. In this fantasy universe, the "races" usually involve types of beings, such that elves, men, and dwarves each constitute a separate race, yet within these racial categories, there exist other racialized hierarchies (Light Elves versus Dark Elves, for instance, or even the various elven kinship groups, such as the Vanyar, the Noldor, the Teleri, and so on). Among men, and orcs may well be merely corrupted men or perhaps another race of men, Tolkien clearly distinguishes a number of different racially identifiable cultures. But regardless of the specific culture or kinship group they belong to, orcs are almost invariably described as "swart" and "slant-eyed," to the extent that one cannot help finding the characterization offensive at times, all the more so if one is familiar with Tolkien's description of orcs as being Mongol-like in appearance. In a 1958 letter, Tolkien averred that "The Orcs are definitely stated to be corruptions of the 'human' form seen in Elves and Men. They are (or were) squat, broad, flat-nosed, sallow-skinned, with wide mouths and slant eyes: in fact degraded and repulsive versions of the (to Europeans) least lovely Mongol-type" (Tolkien 1981, p. 274). By granting that orcs bore the appearance of Mongols, Tolkien emphasizes their basic humanity even as he underscored their profound Otherness when compared to the Northern European physical types comprising his various heroes. Although the racial stereotyping is problematic, this nevertheless allows readers to see orcs as discernibly human, if also demonized by their enemies.

Admittedly, Tolkien's own texts are somewhat inconsistent on this matter. For example, even though *The Hobbit* and *The Lord of the Rings* contain scenes in which orcs are shown to operate in well-organized societies, ones that can be completely independent of such "Big Bosses" as Saruman and Sauron, for example, Tolkien bizarrely depicted the orc armies as scattering like mindless insects after the destruction of the Ring: "As when death smites the swollen brooding thing that inhabits their crawling hill and holds them all in sway, ants will wander witless and purposeless and then feebly die, so the creatures of Sauron, orc or troll or beast spell-enslaved, ran hither and thither mindless, and some slew themselves, or cast themselves in pits, or fled wailing back to hide in holes and in dark lightless places far from hope" (Tolkien 1965b, pp. 243–44). Needless to say, such a fate makes little sense given the conversations already depicted among the orcs, but this does serve the narrative function of allowing the war to end at the very moment that Sauron's power is overthrown. Such a fantasy makes for a neat, simple narrative of victory or defeat, and allows the characters to avoid the long, messy aftermath of battle, and the far more complicated process of rebuilding and reorganizing the geopolitical frameworks of a postwar world.

Tolkien was reluctant to pronounce orcs "irredeemably bad" (Tolkien 1981, p. 195), although he could not really envision any real salvation for them, but even the most evil creatures, in theory, ought to have redeeming qualities. As a survivor of the Great War and the father of a Second World War veteran, Tolkien also exhibits a knowing ambivalence towards the horrors of battle, even amid the tremendous bloodshed of his tales, and there should be at least grudging respect for the orc warriors, although one must perhaps read between the lines to find it. Although Tolkien's readers do not necessarily sympathize with the orcs directly, they can hardly have missed scenes such as those I have discussed, in which the basic humanity of orcs, in both the good and bad senses of the word "human," is on display. However, the narrative structure and plot requires an endless supply of enemies to be defeated, in which case the literal demonization of the enemy—orcs *as* demons—serves a valuable purpose. As Shippey has pointed out, recasting the origins of the orcs and of their behaviors in the books "would have involved, to be consistent, a complete revision of all his earlier work" (Shippey 2003, p. 234). The unlikely end of the orcs at the conclusion of the War of the Ring allows for the sort of narrative closure that most real-world wars cannot. Here demonization becomes as "strategy of containment," as Fredric Jameson famously called it (Jameson 1981), which ideologically delimits the narrative field in order to make the story more easily comprehended.

4. After the Wars

Tolkien's two great completed works of fantasy feature warfare, but in each case, the depiction of the fighting is mostly ambiguous. In *The Hobbit*, for example, the Battle of the Five Armies would appear to be the climactic event of the novel, except that most of it takes place, as it were, *off camera*, since the protagonist and eponymous hero, Bilbo Baggins, is knocked unconscious early on in the great skirmish. When he awakens, the war is over, and the leader of the "good" forces, the dwarf King Thorin Oakenshield, lies wounded and dying, hanging on only long enough to express his admiration for the hobbit's pacifism and humility. Not that Tolkien himself is a pacifist exactly; he seems to recognize that some wars may be necessary, and in any case, like Kurt Vonnegut, he knows that wars are inevitable so long as humans are imbued with human nature. But Tolkien certainly does not celebrate warfare. Good warriors and leaders, such as Aragorn, do their work out of a sense of duty, but do not seek renown on the battlefield. In *The Lord of the Rings*, both Éowyn and Théoden come to realize that their desire for glory in battle was wrongheaded, and, while many characters are regarded as great warriors, they generally fight only when necessary, taking little pleasure in the fighting. (Here, Legolas's and Gimli's orc-killing game stands out in sharp relief to the more sober, even grim sense of duty seen in Aragorn, Faramir, or Gandalf.) As noted above, King Elessar actually forgives the people (i.e., the men, but not orcs) of Mordor, allowing them to live and to thrive in their homelands. Only the demons, the demonized enemies, are dispensed with at the conclusion of Tolkien's two novels. Their defeat, presumably, must be total.

It is not so simple in the real world, after all. The rank artificiality of these forms of demonization becomes all the more apparent when a given conflict ends and the ideological commitments of a postwar political order are established. Almost immediately after World War II, within days or weeks at most of the end of the hostilities in Europe and the Pacific, Americans were expected not only to stop demonizing the Germans and the Japanese, but to offer sympathy and aid to them. At the same moment, many people in the United States, France, and Great Britain found that they were now supposed to shift their allegiances away from former Allies. Studs Terkel's monumental oral history of World War II, *The Good War*, details some of these paradoxes. As Dellie Hahne, a retired music teacher and one of Terkel's interlocutors recalled,

> The OWI, Office of War Information, did a thorough job of convincing us our cause was unquestionably right. We were stopping Hitler, and you look back at it and you had to stop him. We were saving the world. We were allied with Russia, which was great at that time. Germany had started World War One and now it had started World War Two, and German would be wiped off the face of the map. A few years later, when we started to arm Germany, I was so shocked. I'd been sold a bill of goods—I couldn't believe it. [...] As soon as the war was over we dropped Russia. During the war, I never heard any anti-Russia talk. (Terkel 1984, pp. 117–18)

It is remarkable how quickly, in the minds of the public, an ally can become an enemy and vice versa, but Hahne goes on say that her "disillusionment was so great, that was the beginning of distrusting my own government" (Terkel 1984, p. 118).

To offer another example from the same moment, consider a statement from a well-known journalist, the *Chicago Tribune*'s Mike Royko. Royko was too young to fight in World War II, but he fought in the Korean War, where he saw clearly just how absurdly insubstantial the earlier demonization of the enemy had been. "I didn't know anyone who was in Korea who understood what the hell we were doing there," he told Terkel. As he explained, "We were over there fighting the Chinese, you know? Christ, I'd been raised to think the Chinese were among the world's most heroic people and our great friends. [...] I was still mad at the Japs. The Japanese are now our friends, our pals. I'm going from Japan to Korea, where I'm supposed to fight the Chinese, who are now our enemies. A few years earlier, I was mad at the Japanese and I was supposed to love the Chinese. Now I gotta love the Japanese and hate the Chinese. (Laughs.) That's when I decided something's wrong"

(Terkel 1984, pp. 137–38). One of the most telling things about these observations is that both Hahne and Royko, in their moment of revelation, discovered that "something's wrong," which in turn caused them to distrust their own government, as well as other sources of information, when they saw the eerie reversibility of the demonization of the enemy.

The propaganda of the war machine finds outlets throughout mass culture, not merely through the news media or official government reports. In Terkel's *The Good War*, legendary film critic Pauline Kael complained about the egregious representation of the enemy in films from that period. Films, like novels and other forms of narrative, helped to shape the way both allies and enemies would be viewed, which in turn shaped how the entire narrative of the war would be understood. As Kael put it,

> Oh, I hated the war movies, because they robbed the enemy of any humanity or individuality. In all these films you were supposed to learn a lesson: even the German or the Japanese who happened to be your friend, even the one who was sympathetic, had to be killed because he was just as dirty as the others. Even those who were trapped trying to save American lives were weaklings and untrustworthy. We had stereotypes of a shocking nature. They could never be people, who were just caught in the army the same way Americans were and told what to do. They always had to be decadent, immoral people, sneaks. (Terkel 1984, p. 137)

The demonization of the enemy, while quite effective for ideological—which is also to say, for narrative—purposes, rings hollow to those who can read beyond the surfaces. But in oversimplifying matters, this trope also made the war all the more cognizable or *sensible* to the soldiers and, moreover, to the average citizen.

Tolkien's depiction of the orcs at the end of *The Lord of the Rings* is, in my view, clearly an error, given what the reader would have gleaned about orcs and their cultures in those revealing chapters of *The Two Towers* mentioned above. Moreover, Tolkien's presentation of the orcs' origins in *The Silmarillion* and other posthumously published writings indicates that he was well aware of their "humanity," if we may call it such. Yet in creating the orcs as a race to be demonized in wartime, Tolkien demonstrates the perverse effectiveness of this form. He also proved himself able to see beyond the mere demonization of the enemy, by showing that whatever demonic or orcish behavior there was to be found in the world, it was not limited to the ranks of the enemies. As he famously put it in a wartime letter to his son Christopher, "I think the orcs as real a creation as anything in 'realistic' fiction," before adding, "only in real life they are on both sides, of course" (Tolkien 1981, p. 82).

This acknowledgement cannot stand long without calling into question the entire ideological program associated with demonizing the enemy, which at least suggests a crack in the armor, a scarcely visible yet undoubtedly real utopian element in the martial narratives of both Tolkien's fantasy novels and the stories of the World Wars. From this fissure, one can imagine, might emerge a more powerful sense of sympathy with one's fellow man, during times of war and times of peace, in which the demonic characteristics for the moment evanesce, and the face of our shared humanity shines forth. In this moment, our fellow "orcishness" may also be acknowledged, along with the profound desire for freedom from "Big Bosses" and other repressive authorities. That Tolkien allows this image of freedom to be voiced by disgruntled orc soldiers, Shagrat and Gorbag, indicates his own, perhaps unconscious sense that "both sides" deserve respect and sympathy.

Funding: This research received no external funding.

Conflicts of Interest: The author declares no conflict of interest.

References

Croft, Janet Brennan. 2004. *War and the Works of J.R.R. Tolkien*. Westport: Praeger.
Fimi, Dimitra. 2009. *Tolkien, Race, and Cultural History: From Fairies to Hobbits*. New York: Palgrave Macmillan.
Fussell, Paul. 1975. *The Great War and Modern Memory*. Oxford: Oxford University Press.
Garth, John. 2003. *Tolkien and the Great War: The Threshold of Middle-Earth*. London: HarperCollins.

James, Robert Rhodes. 1965. *Gallipoli*. New York: Macmillan.
Jameson, Fredric. 1981. *The Political Unconscious*. Ithaca: Cornell University Press.
Shippey, Tom. 2000a. *J.R.R. Tolkien: Author of the Century*. Boston: Houghton Mifflin.
Shippey, Tom. 2000b. Orcs, Wraiths, Wights: Tolkien's Images of Evil. In *J.R.R. Tolkien and His Literary Resonances*. Edited by George Clark and Daniel Timmons. Westport: Greenwood, pp. 183–98.
Shippey, Tom. 2003. *The Road to Middle-Earth*, Rev. and Expanded ed. Boston: Houghton Mifflin.
Tally, Robert T., Jr. 2010. Let Us Now Praise Famous Orcs: Simple Humanity in Tolkien's Inhuman Creatures. *Mythlore: A Journal of J.R.R. Tolkien, C.S. Lewis, Charles Williams, and Mythopoeic Literature* 29: 3.
Terkel, Studs. 1984. *The Good War: An Oral History of World War II*. New York: New Press.
Tolkien, John Ronald Reuel. 1965a. *The Fellowship of the Ring*. New York: Del Rey.
Tolkien, John Ronald Reuel. 1965b. *The Return of the King*. New York: Del Rey.
Tolkien, John Ronald Reuel. 1965c. *The Two Towers*. New York: Del Rey.
Tolkien, John Ronald Reuel. 1981. *The Letters of J.R.R. Tolkien*. Edited by Humphrey Carpenter. Boston: Houghton Mifflin.
Tolkien, John Ronald Reuel. 1982. *The Hobbit*. New York: Del Rey.
Tolkien, John Ronald Reuel. 1988. *Unfinished Tales: The Lost Lore of Middle-Earth*. New York: Del Rey.
Tolkien, John Ronald Reuel, and Christopher Tolkien. 1993. *Morgoth's Ring*. Edited by Christopher Tolkien. Boston: Houghton Mifflin.
Tolkien, John Ronald Reuel. 2002. *The Silmarillion*. Edited by Christopher Tolkien. New York: Del Rey.
Tolkien, John Ronald Reuel. 2014. *Beowulf: A Translation and Commentary*. Edited by Christopher Tolkien. Boston: Houghton Mifflin.

© 2019 by the author. Licensee MDPI, Basel, Switzerland. This article is an open access article distributed under the terms and conditions of the Creative Commons Attribution (CC BY) license (http://creativecommons.org/licenses/by/4.0/).

Article

How Can You Not Shout, Now That the Whispering Is Done? Accounts of the Enemy in US, Hmong, and Vietnamese Soldiers' Literary Reflections on the War

David Beard

Department of English, Linguistics, and Writing Studies, University of Minnesota Duluth, Duluth, MN 55812, USA; dbeard@d.umn.edu

Received: 21 June 2019; Accepted: 22 October 2019; Published: 1 November 2019

Abstract: As typified in the Christmas Truce, soldiers commiserate as they see themselves in the enemy and experience empathy. Commiseration is the first step in breaking down the rhetorical construction of enemyship that acts upon soldiers and which prevents reconciliation and healing. This essay proceeds in three steps. We will identify first the diverse forms of enemyship held by the American, by the North Vietnamese, and by the Hmong soldiers, reading political discourse, poetry, and fiction to uncover the rhetorical constructions of the enemy. We will talk about both an American account and a North Vietnamese account of commiseration, when a soldier looks at the enemy with compassion rooted in identification. Commiseration is fleeting; reconciliation and healing must follow, and so finally, we will look at some of the moments of reconciliation, after the war, in which Vietnamese, Hmong and American soldiers (and their children and grandchildren) find healing.

Keywords: enemyship; rhetoric; reconciliation; commiseration; Vietnam/Vietnamese; Hmong; war

---

The critical reflections at the core of this essay begin with a conversation between a student and I, after my course (in multigenre writing through the Vietnam War) was over and the student had graduated, stopping just to say "hi".

The student enjoyed the class, they said, but they wanted to encourage me to talk about "the other side" of the war. I asked whether they had any suggestions. They talked about protest movements, Kent State, American popular music against the war.

It occurred to me, in that moment, that the student imagined that "both sides" of the Vietnam war included the hawks who sent our military into war and the hippies who protested it. Both sides of the war were inside the United States. As I had taught the class, and as our popular culture had reinforced within the student's mind, the Vietnamese were not, for this student, one of the "sides" of the war.

I'm not entirely sure that the Vietnam war is reducible to an experience of "sides". My student's intuition that there were two "sides" to the American experience of the war could be pulled further—maybe, within the U.S., there were more than two sides. Those who were "for" the war within the U.S supported it for diverse reasons; those who were against the war resisted it for diverse reasons, too. Maybe there were five or six "sides" to the war, even, within the United States.

In Vietnam, too, the war was built from more than two "sides"—the American soldiers who had been the center of my class entered the war with allies, and those allies were more than "on our side". The North Vietnamese had allies, too, invested in the war for more than one reason.

I went home to revise the class: the next iteration of the class complicated our sense of the "sides" of the war by more deeply addressing the North Vietnamese and Hmong soldiers who fought in the war. This essay, for this special issue of *Humanities* on war in literature, brings American, Hmong, and Vietnamese representations of the enemy into dialogue as we explore the themes of commiseration and reconciliation.

1. About Enemyship: The Rhetorical Construction of the Enemy Complicates Commiseration

Accounts of "enemyship" focus on the ways that political leaders use the construction of an enemy to bring unity to a (typically national) community. In *Enemyship: Democracy and Counter-Revolution in the Early Republic*", Jeremy Engels demonstrates the rhetorical process by which politicians construct "mutual antagonism for an enemy, resulting in a solidarity of fear, a community of spite, a kinship in arms, and a brotherhood of hatred" (Engels 2010, p. 13). To justify a war, the United States needed to project "fears outward onto an enemy who had to be eliminated" (Engels 2010, p. 20). If friendship brings a people together, enemyship unites them, too, in opposition to someone else, real or imagined.

Frank and Park connect enemyship to foundational myths; in examining the political discourses of Korea, they examine the ways that "foundational myths are formed, the trajectories they take, the enemyships they create" (Frank and Park 2018, p. 221). Given that enemyship is born and given structure by foundational myths, and that the foundational myths will be different across either side of the battlefield, we can conclude that enemyship in war is asymmetrical. In the Korean War, the Koreans were shooting at American soldiers for reasons different from the reasons that the Americans were shooting at the Koreans. Soldiers on one side believed that they were repelling an invader in what they now call the "Great Fatherland Liberation War". On the American side, soldiers were holding a Communist ideology at bay on foreign shores.

Such asymmetry is also evident in the Vietnam War. We call the conflict "the Vietnam War", while Vietnamese people refer to the same conflict as "the American War", implying a symmetry. However, there is no more symmetry in the Vietnam conflict than there was in the Korean conflict. The North Vietnamese construction of their enemy (the Americans) is not symmetrical to the American construction of their enemy, the Communist Vietnamese. And the asymmetry is complicated again by a third population, our allies in the Secret War, the Hmong. The Hmong construction of their enemy differs from both the American and Vietnamese sense of enemyship.

This essay draws our attention to literature which shows soldiers in commiseration in a time of war, despite the rhetorical and ideological forces driving them against each other. Commiseration, as a form of empathy, begins with seeing the enemy as similar to ourselves: *we are all soldiers here*. This is the first step in breaking down the rhetorical construction of enemyship that acts upon soldiers. After commiseration, soldiers can move toward reconciliation.

This essay proceeds in three steps. We will identify first, the diverse forms of enemyship held by the American, by the North Vietnamese, and by the Hmong soldiers, reading political discourse, poetry and fiction to uncover the rhetorical and ideological constructions of the enemy.[1] We will talk about both an American account and a North Vietnamese account of commiseration, when a soldier looks at the enemy with compassion rooted in identification. Commiseration is the first step toward healing. Finally, we will look at some of the moments of reconciliation, after the war, in which Vietnamese, Hmong and American soldiers (and their children and grandchildren) find healing.

---

[1] For these claims, we will look at poetry and literature both by poets and authors as well as by writings of soldiers. Of special note are texts from *Note on Captured Documents*, which are a unique set of poems. "American military units captured documents—among them a variety of military communications, as well as personal diaries, letters, and, surprisingly, a great deal of poetry written by members of the various revolutionary forces. These were sent to Saigon for analysis and translation, grouped into batches, and microfilmed on 35-mm film stock. (The originals were lost in 1975.) The microfilm copies were housed in the National Archives in Washington, D.C., and after the war they eventually were declassified" (vii–viii). The collection is nineteen miles of microfilm. The volume of poetry published from this microfilm is especially useful for clarifying a soldier's perspective. "The effect of this poetry is to humanize the soldiers who fought on the side of the revolution in such a way as to help dispel the stereotypes created by the United States military and the American media during and after the American war in Vietnam" (p. xiii).

1.1. The American Sense of Enemyship, 1955–1975

While some American soldiers entered Vietnam with a sense of nationalism and heroism, many were reluctant draftees. American construction of the enemy in the North Vietnamese was energized by two forces: by political ideology and by racist experience. We will discuss each in turn.

American political ideology constructed the North Vietnamese as a proxy for Communism. The North Vietnamese had not invaded the United States, nor did they intend to do so, but Communism was a global threat, manifest in the "domino" theory. The threat posed by North Vietnam was indirect and a construct of Cold War propaganda.

The Gulf of Tonkin Resolution becomes a moment in which the U.S. government could argue that the North Vietnamese were no longer only an ideological threat. As Richard Cherwitz demonstrated (in a series of articles on the Gulf of Tonkin resolution[2]), Johnson's administration took the opportunity of the crisis in the Gulf of Tonkin to remake an ideological opponent into a physical threat.

In terms of enemyship, then, the American soldiers were, in a way, shooting at Communism by shooting at the North Vietnamese. But time in country would wear on the soldiers, and they would eventually not only shoot at North Vietnamese; they would shoot at all Vietnamese. Racism became part of the experience of enemyship of American soldiers.

The lived experience of a guerilla war disoriented American soldiers; they ceased firing only upon the Viet Cong and simply began shooting the Vietnamese. As Jean Paul Sartre noted in his work against the Vietnam war, "The armed forces of the United States torture and kill men, women and children in Vietnam because they are Vietnamese" (Sartre 1968, p. 82). The guerilla nature of the war, in the end, eroded the ability of the American soldiers to determine which Vietnamese people were friend or foe.

Sartre gives a rich and violent description of the change in the behaviors of U.S. soldiers:

> (T)he racialism of the Yankee soldiers from Saigon to the 17th parallel has increased. The young Americans torture without repugnance, shooting at unarmed women for the pleasure of completing a hat-trick: they kick the wounded Vietnamese in the testicles; they cut off the ears of the dead for trophies. The officers are worst: a general was boasting in front of a Frenchman who testified at the Tribunal of hunting the Viet Cong from his helicopter and shooting them down in the rice fields. They were, of course, not NLF fighters, who know how to protect themselves, but peasants working in their rice fields. In these confused American minds, the Viet Cong and the Vietnamese tend to become more and more indistinguishable. (Sartre 1968, p. 81)

Sartre hammers the description home: "A common saying is 'The only good Vietnamese is a dead one,' or, what comes to the same thing, 'Every dead Vietnamese is a Viet Cong'" (Sartre 1968, p. 81). At some point, for some soldiers, they ceased shooting at specific Vietnamese as proxies for Communism and started shooting at anyone who was not visibly American.

Sartre's account has been borne out by historical research. As Turse (2013) explores in *Kill Anything That Moves: The Real American War in Vietnam*, the widespread deaths of civilians at the hands of US soldiers in Vietnam were no accident. Turse counts 65,000 North Vietnamese and 3.8 million South Vietnamese civilians dead by the end of the war—some were killed by "friendly fire", but many were simply murdered. Col. David Hackworth was quoted (by Patricia Sullivan (2009) in the *Washington Post*) as claiming that "My division in the Delta, the 9th, reported killing more than 20,000 Viet Cong in 1968 and 1969, yet less than 2000 weapons were found on the 'enemy' dead. How much of the 'body count' consisted of civilians?" In different ways, the demands for high body counts (for purposes of creating a narrative of American success to deliver to the media back home) gave soldiers permission

---

[2] Cherwitz (1978, 1980) makes these arguments in "Masking Inconsistency: The Tonkin Gulf Crisis" and in "Lyndon Johnson and the 'Crisis' of Tonkin Gulf: A President's Justification of War".

to shoot any Vietnamese. This policy converged with the psychology of the individual soldier (feeling under threat from every direction) to encourage the murder of civilians. The military and the media incentivized what fear accelerated: a desire to kill anyone who wasn't obviously an American.

All of that said, the experiences of soldiers are diverse, and this short essay cannot be exhaustive. (For example, enemyship was not always central to the solder's experience; for some soldiers, enemyship mattered less than staying alive long enough to come home.) In terms of the rhetorical processes of enemyship, though: for two decades, the enemies of many American soldiers of the Vietnam war were "Communism", or "the Vietnamese", as a racial category.

1.2. The North Vietnamese Sense of Enemyship, 1887–1975

The sense of enemyship among the North Vietnamese soldiers was radically different from the sense of enemyship among the American soldiers. We will point to two salient features of the rhetorical and ideological construction of the enemy among the North Vietnamese soldiers. First, the North Vietnamese understood the war as the next phase in a century-long war against colonial powers (of which the United States was just one). Second, the Vietnamese understood the war as a war to repel invaders, and their work as soldiers was to protect their nation, envisioned as their lover, from these invading forces. We will discuss each in turn.

First: for North Vietnamese soldiers, the conflict did not begin with the arrival of U.S. advisors in 1955 or with formal U.S. military participation in the war in 1964. Rather, in the lived experience of some of its soldiers, the beginning of the war dated to 1946 (the first "Indochina war" against France). For others, the war began with the 1887 formal recognition of Vietnam as "French Indochina" (the moment when the Vietnamese lost control over their home). Soldier and poet Duc Thanh tells us, in "In the Forest at Night", that he is "the son of the Vietnamese, under siege for a hundred years By the French and Americans" (Nguyen and Weigl 1994, p. 45). For Duc Thanh, the war is not a war against the United States. It is not a war to advance Communism (as American propaganda claimed). Duc Thanh fought a war against colonial powers.

Huang Loc names his colonial enemies with rancor in "Condolence to a Friend". Writing from the Quang Tri campaign in 1972, he asks "Who took that fatal shot? What gun hit the mark? Please, sacred spirit, show me The murderer, call out his name". The answer is cold and hard, and it makes clear the Vietnamese experience of the war: "He's an imperialist. He's a colonialist. He's a bandit" (Bowen 1998, p. 47). The enemy is not an American, a Yankee who must go home. The American War, in the minds of its soldiers, was just one more manifestation of the century-long fight for freedom from the colonizers.

Second: the enemy, in the mythic narrative of the Vietnamese soldiers, comes to attack the homeland whom the soldiers must defend as they would defend a lover. Nguyen Dinh Thi writes a poem addressed to a lover back home, using that form of address to explain his experience of war. In "Remembering", he notes, "I love you as I love our country, In pain, hardship and with great passion. Every step I take you are in my thoughts, Every meal I eat, every night I sleep" (Bowen 1998, p. 15). That passion is with him every day; it fuels his efforts in war. This love of country, imagined as a romantic love, is powerful: "We'll fight all our lives for our love. We love each other, and we are proud to be human" (Bowen 1998, p. 15). The impulse to defend a lover against an invader is deeply human.

As among the Americans, motivations for fighting in war are diverse; I offer here only a sample. At a rhetorical level, some of the North Vietnamese soldiers fought the war to protect their nation (envisioned as their lover) from colonialism.

1.3. The Hmong Sense of Enemyship, 1910–1975

The Secret War, in Laos, complicates the diverse experience of enemyship in the Vietnam War. The Hmong brought their own stories to their experience of enemyship. During the Hmong struggle for self-determination against a backdrop of shifting colonial powers, the nature of the enemy shifted.[3]

The Hmong had rebelled against the French colonial powers from 1910 to 1912 (in the conflict called "Mi Chang's rebellion"), and from 1918 to 1921 (called the "War of the Insane" by the French). Both rebellions were suppressed by the French. In World War II, the French shifted from enemy colonizer to ally, as the Hmong sided with the French to push Japanese occupiers out.

After WWII, between 1946 and 1954, Hmong led by Touby Lyfoung resisted the North Vietnamese, while Hmong led by Faydang Lobliayao resisted French colonial rule. In both cases, the Hmong were fundamentally seeking autonomy. Touby Lyfoung believed that autonomy was better preserved by alliance with the French against the Communist North Vietnamese; Faydang Lobliayao believed that autonomy was better preserved by alliance with the North Vietnamese against the French.

When Vang Pao formed alliances with the United States, he was, like Lyfoung, allying with the western colonial power against the Communist colonial power. In return, the U.S. airlifted roughly 40 tons of food per month to Hmong communities and funded new schools throughout the remote regions of Laos, training Hmong girls as nurses and medics to care for wounded soldiers and increasing Hmong literacy.

While Americans and North Vietnamese were "taking sides" against each other, the Hmong found that the war came to them. Lao poet Bryan Thao Worr's claim that "There were refugees Who to this day cannot explain why they were the enemy When the war came" (Moua 2002, p. 98) makes sense when we see the Hmong as participants in someone else's war narrative, rather than protagonists of their own war story. Hmong served as allies of the United States in fighting the Secret War, but they were, in many ways, fighting a different war, than their American allies fought.

On the one hand, some Hmong saw the Americans as allies against Communism: Mai Der Vang asks "Do you think of your missing wife, how the Pathet Lao dragged her naked, screaming, and bleeding by her long black hair deep into forest shadows" (Der Vang 2017, p. 7). Pathet Lao were a communist political movement in Laos; the Hmong were allies of the U.S. against Pathet Lao, and so against Communism, in the Secret War.

> And yet, there was little affection for the Americans: Mai Der Vang asks
>
> Do you think of the American
>
> returning to the coffee cup
>
> new linens
>
> in a warm bed
>
> pulling into the driveway? (Der Vang 2017, p. 7).

The Hmong sacrifices in the Vietnam war dwarfed American sacrifices. By war's end in 1975, nearly 40,000 Hmong soldiers had been killed or were missing in action—totaling approximately one-fourth of all Hmong men and boys. For point of comparison, the US death total in Vietnam was about 58,000 when the total US population was 200,000,000. Hmong soldiers, many of whom were children when they were asked to bear arms, resented the Americans who could go home to comfortable lives.

Bryan Thao Worr tell us that, in retrospect, other soldiers (not the Viet Cong, nor even the Americans who left them behind) were not the real enemy of the Hmong. Instead, the Hmong people "are victims of fat tigers and foreign policy" (Moua 2002, p. 98). In this way, Hmong experience of the war and of enemyship was their own.

---

[3] This history is traced in broad strokes from (Hillmer 2010; Her and Buley-Meissner 2012).

At this point, I'd like to pause and note the ways that the rhetorical study of enemyship changes our understanding of war. War is often metaphorically understood in terms of games. Board games have for centuries appeared to model warfare. But when two players meet to play chess, they have symmetrical objectives in the same system. Player push their pawns across the board hoping to achieve checkmate, victory on the battlefield. When paintball players meet to wargame, each team seeks to capture the flag of their opponent's team. But the perspective of enemyship reminds us that real war doesn't work that way. War is asymmetrical, even chaotic, in this light.

A slow walk through the distinctions between American, North Vietnamese, and Hmong rhetorical constructions of enemyship demonstrates how impoverished this "two sides" conception of war is. In the next section, I will map the implications of the study of "enemyship" for the possibility of commiseration on the battlefield.

2. Commiseration on the Battlefield

I have sketched here the ways that soldiers from three communities envisioned their enemies in war. It might feel like these soldiers were fighting three different wars, where the only common ground was the battlefield. On the battlefield, though, commiseration was possible.

In the broader history of warfare, the prototypical moment of commiseration is the Christmas Truce of World War I, in which "soldiers began to brave No Man's Land, shaking hands, exchanging gifts and pictures, mutually complaining about the war, and kicking a ball around" (McDaniel 2015, p. 92). In these moments, the soldiers on both the German and British sides of the front paused and saw themselves in the enemy. They both celebrated, even played, with each other—but they also used this time to "repair their trenches as well as collect and bury the dead"—very, very human acts made possible because the Germans and British soldiers saw past the rhetorical construction of the enemy. Instead, they saw in each other their common Christianity and their common exhaustion as soldiers. They looked across No Man's Land and saw people like themselves (instead of enemies).

Given all that we have said about enemyship in the Vietnam war, it's not surprising that there could be no collective moment like the Christmas truce. There is no common identity, like religion, that binds North Vietnamese, Hmong, and American soldiers. But there are individual moments of commiseration across individual soldiers. To see those moments, we will look briefly at poetry by Nguyen Duy, who served in the North Vietnamese National Guard, and at a seminal short story by Tim O'Brien from the classic novel, *The Things They Carried*.

In "Stop", Nguyen Duy talks about the "ranger with the face of a child" whose "shot just missed" him. He's very aware that as the soldier flees, Duy has the upper hand: "If my finger moved half a millimeter, he'd be dead" (Bowen 1998, p. 133). But doesn't want to press that advantage. After all, "if the situation had been reversed, and I ran in front empty-handed, and he ran behind, M16 in hand, very likely I'd have died". Duy reaches a moment of commiseration as he becomes able to see himself in the American soldier.

Tim O'Brien also experiences commiseration through identifying with the enemy. In "The Man I Killed", O'Brien identifies with the North Vietnamese soldier whom he encountered on a trail and whom he killed with a grenade. He finds that man was "a scholar, maybe", resonating with O'Brien's narrator's identity as a student. He asserts that the man he killed was "born, maybe, in 1946", the same year the author was born, and that "he liked books" (O'Brien 2009, p. 118), like O'Brien.

O'Brien's narrator projects his psyche onto the man he killed: "the young man would not have wanted to be a soldier and in his heart would have feared performing badly in battle ... He had no stomach for violence" (O'Brien 2009, p. 119) We know these to be traits of O'Brien's narrator, who also "was afraid of disgracing himself, and therefore his family and village" (O'Brien 2009, p. 119). In earlier chapters of the novel, it is clearly established that Tim does not want to go to war; rather, he is afraid of being thought a coward.

When Tim O'Brien's narrator writes that the man he killed "hoped the Americans would go away" (O'Brien 2009, p. 119), he likely speaks truth about the North Vietnamese soldier. He also projects his own hopes onto the enemy. Neither one of them wanted the Americans to be there.

In looking at the enemy and seeing himself, O'Brien does the same work that Nguyen Duy does, placing himself in the place of the other. The soldiers reject the rhetorical and ideological construction of the enemy and understand that their enemy struggles as they do. And so they experience commiseration.

Seeing yourself in someone else is the first step toward commiseration. Commiseration may not be enough, though. In the Christmas Truce, "parts of the trench line did continue to shell each other on Christmas, and [...] soldiers died on that day" (McDaniel 2015, p. 92), while after the Truce, "propaganda touting the barbarity of the enemy increased in quantity and viciousness" (McDaniel 2015, p. 92). Commiseration is ephemeral, and violence remains. Both Duy and O'Brien tell stories of killing their enemy despite the experience of commiseration. We need more; beyond commiseration, we need reconciliation and healing.

3. After the War, Healing at the Memorials to the War

Commiseration can occur, however fleetingly, on the battlefield, but reconciliation cannot occur in the moment of war. Reconciliation comes after, but it does not come easily. The scars of war run deep after the battle stops, as Hmong, American and Vietnamese poets alike have felt their lives and land damaged long after the war.

Among Hmong poets, in "Declassified", Mai Der Vang tells us about the "vividness of saffron and canary arriving as small showers". Vang references claims that the USSR sprayed Vietnam and Laos with chemical weapons in 1981—long after the official end of hostilities, visible as a kind of yellow rain that dried as a yellow powder (Der Vang 2018).[4] Abandoned munitions remind Bryan Thao Worr of war: "Grenade fishing in the aftermath of Phou Pha Thi Has lost its novelty To the man with a bullet fragment rattling In his body, slowly tearing him apart". (Moua 2002, p. 99).

Among Vietnamese poets, bones speak of the wounds not healed: Van Le's meditation on "Quang Tri", a provincial capital that suffered attack in the 1968 Tet Offensive, opens with the observation that "everywhere we dug there were white bones ... What kind of foundation would they make for our house? "Were they our bones or their bones?" Van Le answers: "There are no American bones here. The Americans left years ago and took their bones with them. These skeletons, scattered all over our land, Belong only to Vietnamese" (Bowen 1998, p. 121).

Healing comes hard when the ground beneath your feet reopens the wounds, burns and blisters, and more than a half century later, the pain is still coming to light. Mai Der Vang exhorts: "May this secret war ... burn and blister under its own nakedness", as it comes into view for American, Hmong, and Vietnamese alike (Der Vang 2018). Reconciliation seems unlikely when so many hurts have yet to heal.

And yet: pilgrimage has made healing possible. The Vietnam Memorial in Washington, D.C. is, first and foremost, the site of postwar reconciliation between American soldiers in the Vietnam War and the American public. The site houses multiple works of sculpture: [a] the abstract Maya Lin memorial wall that captivated the American imagination in 1982, [b] the "Three Servicemen" statues sculpted by Frederick Hart in 1984, honoring the veterans from the branches of the military active in Vietnam, and [c] the Glenna Goodacre "Women's Memorial", honoring the women who served in the war, dedicated in 1993. As the site incorporates additional statuary, more Americans experience healing and resolution in the Memorial grounds.

---

[4] Some scientists insisted that the yellow rains were bee feces, dropped by swarms moving through the jungle. Six years after the fall of Saigon, the lens of the war still frames discussions of yellow pollen appearing on tree leaves; it is hard to move forward when the landscape reminds you of war.

Bobbie Ann Mason's novel *In Country* offers an account of the struggles of those born after the war to understand the experiences of their veteran fathers and uncles. Visiting the memorial is the crescendo of understanding the war. In the novel, the protagonist, young Sam, touches her father's name, which she shares. She "touches her own name. How odd it feels" (Mason 1986, p. 245). Similarly, in "Facing It" by Yusef Komunyakaa, the poet goes "down the 58,022 names/half-expecting to find my own in letters like smoke" (Komunyakaa 2001, p. 234). Citizens who have never been to Vietnam feel connected to the veterans who lost their lives.

The wall, and the healing that the wall makes possible, is experienced by soldiers, by citizens who stayed home, and by the generations born after the war's end. As Mason writes it, "How odd it feels, as though all the names in America have been used to decorate this wall" (Mason 1986, p. 245)—all Americans can feel reconciliation at the wall.

Perhaps more strikingly, North Vietnamese soldiers also feel healing in visiting the Wall. Nguyen Duy, who served for a decade as a member of the North Vietnamese National Guard, visits the Memorial in a poem filled with religious imagery, noting that "heaven's eyes stare" as "a Wailing Wall sings cries of the dead". At the wall, he feels "a time of chaos, sun and moon trading places" (Duy 1999, p. 227). We expect American veterans to experience healing and reconciliation at the wall, but that a Vietnamese soldier experiences the same may surprise us.

Duy finds that the rhetorically constructed narratives of enemyship slip away when he visits the wall. Instead, "this grief deepens, this agony endures". Reconciliation comes at the wall because Duy recognizes that the war was "a game for some, heartache for all" (Duy 1999, p. 227), American and Vietnamese alike. Enemyship dissolves, and a healing deeper than the typically fleeting experience of commiseration.

4. Healing Still Ahead

I wrote this essay as part of the project of deepening my class in multigenre writings about Vietnam.[5] In revising my class, I wanted to incorporate the Hmong experience to complicate the accounts of American and Vietnamese soldiers. In writing this essay, I have a final goal: to exhort us to remember that there is work ahead in achieving reconciliation. I live and teach in Minnesota, near one of the largest Hmong communities in the world—perhaps that experience more than anything reminds me of the healing ahead.

The Hmong experience of the Vietnam war is marginalized. The war was called "the Secret War", and for many, it is still a secret. The complex on the National Mall (that includes the Maya Lin, Frederick Hart, and Glenna Goodacre sculptures) honors U.S. Veterans, but it does not honor or even acknowledge our Hmong allies.[6]

Several local memorials to Hmong participation in the war do exist in the cities where Hmong refugees have settled. For example, the *Lao, Hmong and American Veterans Memorial* has been built in Sheboygan, WI. A community of six thousand Hmong (in a city with a population of fifty thousand) worked with the City of Sheboygan to produce the memorial. Similar memorials exist in Wausau, WI (population 40,000, with about 10% of that population Hmong) and in St. Paul, MN, whose Hmong population of 30,000 people is roughly ten percent of the city's population. These memorials are striking and powerful but still marginal in the American process for healing from the war.

---

[5] The project of more deeply internationalizing my courses has been supported by the Global Programs and Strategy Alliance of the University of Minnesota, whose "Internationalizing the Curriculum" has supported my work. Visit https://global.umn.edu/icc/about/index.html for more information.

[6] Hmong veterans have been recognized, in the *Laos and Hmong Memorial*, or *Lao Veterans of America Monument*, which rests in Arlington National Cemetery—geographically distant from the Mall. This monument is primarily visited by veterans and their families and so is not part of most visitors' experience of the war in Washington, D.C.

Millions of Americans and North Vietnamese alike will not experience reconciliation or healing with Hmong participants in the Secret War until the Secret War becomes part of the public, national, memorial discourse on the war.[7]

After all, we call Hmong participation in the Vietnam War "the Secret War", but it wasn't long ago that the Vietnam War was our national secret, the war we didn't want to talk about, at all. But we have come to speak of the war, we have found our tongue, and we must keep speaking until reconciliation is possible for all. Hmong poet Bryan Thao Worr tells us in "The Last War Poem" that we must speak:

> How can you not have words for the war of whispers?
>
> How can you not shout, now that the whispering is done?
>
> And I swear, each time I break this promise, that the next time
>
> Will be the last word I write about this damn war. (Moua 2002, p. 98)

The closure we need to enable Bryan Thao Worr to keep his promise will come from breaking down the rhetorical construction of enemyship. We will stop seeing the North Vietnamese as enemies, the Hmong as the allies we refuse to acknowledge. Beginning with what this special issue of *Humanities* calls "commiseration", we can move into reconciliation where, perhaps, we all can heal.

Funding: This research received no external funding.

Conflicts of Interest: The author declares no conflict of interest.

References

Bowen, Kevin, ed. 1998. *Mountain River: Vietnamese Poetry from the Wars: 1948–1993, A Bilingual Collection*. Amherst: University of Massachusetts Press.

Cherwitz, Richard A. 1978. Lyndon Johnson and the "Crisis" of Tonkin Gulf: A President's Justification of War. *Western Journal of Communication* 42: 93–104. [CrossRef]

Cherwitz, Richard A. 1980. Masking Inconsistency: The Tonkin Gulf Crisis. *Communication Quarterly* 28: 27–37. [CrossRef]

Der Vang, Mai. 2017. *Afterland: Poems*. New York: Farrar Straus & Giroux.

Der Vang, Mai. 2018. Declassified. *West Branch Wire*. Available online: https://www.bucknell.edu/west-branch-wired/winter-2018/monica-sok/mai-der-vang (accessed on 12 October 2019).

Duy, Nguyen. 1999. *Distant Road: Selected Poems of Nguyen Duy*. Translated by Chung Bá Nguyễn, and Kevin Bowen. Willimantic: Curbstone Press.

Engels, Jeremy. 2010. *Enemyship: Democracy and Counter-Revolution in the Early Republic*. East Lansing: Michigan State University Press.

Frank, David A., and WooSoo Park. 2018. Syngman Rhee, Robert T. Oliver, and the Symbolic Construction of the Republic of Korea during the Global Cold War. *Rhetoric Society Quarterly* 48: 207–26. [CrossRef]

Her, Vincent K., and Mary Louise Buley-Meissner. 2012. *Hmong and American: From Refugees to Citizens*. St. Paul: Minnesota Historical Society Press.

Hillmer, Paul. 2010. *A People's History of the Hmong*. St. Paul: Minnesota Historical Society Press.

Komunyakaa, Yusef. 2001. *Pleasure Dome: New and Collected Poems*. Middletown: Wesleyan University Press.

Mason, Bobbie Ann. 1986. *In Country*. New York: Harper Collins.

McDaniel, Kathryn N. 2015. Commemorating the Christmas Truce: A Critical Thinking Approach for Popular History. *The History Teacher* 49: 89–100.

Moua, Mai Neng, ed. 2002. *Bamboo among the Oaks: Contemporary Writing by Hmong Americans*. St. Paul: Minnesota Historical Society Press.

Nguyen, Thanh T., and Bruce Weigl, eds. 1994. *Poems from Captured Documents*. Amherst: University of Massachusetts Press.

---

[7] It may be unusual to advocate in a scholarly article, but I believe this is important.

O'Brien, Tim. 2009. *The Things They Carried*. Boston: Houghton Mifflin Harcourt.
Sartre, Jean-Paul. 1968. *On Genocide*. Boston: Beacon Press.
Sullivan, Patricia. 2009. Julian J. Ewell. 93, Dies; Decorated General Led Forces in Vietnam. *Washington Post*. August 5. Available online: http://www.washingtonpost.com/wp-dyn/content/article/2009/08/04/AR2009080403187.html (accessed on 24 October 2019).
Turse, Nick. 2013. *Kill Anything That Moves: The Real American War in Vietnam*. New York: Metropolitan Books.

 © 2019 by the author. Licensee MDPI, Basel, Switzerland. This article is an open access article distributed under the terms and conditions of the Creative Commons Attribution (CC BY) license (http://creativecommons.org/licenses/by/4.0/).

Article

The Making of a Terrorist: Imagining Combatants' Points of View in Troubles Literature

Stephanie Callan

Department of English, Spring Hill College, Mobile, AL 36608, USA; scallan@shc.edu

Received: 11 January 2019; Accepted: 6 February 2019; Published: 8 February 2019

Abstract: This article analyzes portrayals of paramilitary fighters in Irish literature from the Troubles (1968–1998). While the conflict between Protestant loyalists and Catholic nationalists has provoked many literary responses, most focus on noncombatants. This article reads Edna O'Brien's novel *House of Splendid Isolation* (1994) and Anne Devlin's story "Naming the Names" (1986), two texts that succeed in portraying paramilitary characters as complex individuals who are not wholly defined by their violent acts, but each reaches a limit of imagination as well. In *House of Splendid Isolation* the paramilitary character Mac chooses silence over justifying himself to a hostile audience, and in "Naming the Names" the stream of consciousness style becomes increasingly fragmented, suggesting the paramilitary narrator is on the verge of a breakdown. As a result, both characters remain enigmatic, with aspects of their motives and thinking not fully intelligible. Both texts show that it is a struggle for a noncombatant to understand a paramilitary's point of view, but these texts make readers want to engage in that struggle.

Keywords: Irish literature; Northern Ireland; political conflict; terrorism; Edna O'Brien; Anne Devlin; fiction

---

1. Introduction: Historical and Literary Contexts for the Troubles

Although Irish writers have responded to the Troubles with astonishing creativity, sympathetic renderings of a fighter's point of view are relatively rare in their work. Elmer Kennedy-Andrews's study of Troubles fiction (2003) shows that it is much more common to focus on noncombatants trying to cope with the violence. While he does discuss some novels that depict a terrorist's mindset, most of those are thrillers, which tend to paint the fighters as uncomplicated villains and monsters. Michael L. Storey's survey of short stories depicting the Troubles also finds them focusing mostly on themes that emphasize noncombatant experiences, including "the devastating physical, social, and psychological effects on innocent people; and the moral decisions and actions that acts of sectarian violence force upon civilians" (Storey 2004, p. 155). In fiction, there are multiple examples of young men who are sympathetic because they struggle to get out of their associations with the IRA, such as Cal in Bernard MacLaverty's novel of the same name or Brendan in Jennifer Johnston's *Shadows on Our Skin*. However, there are few attempts to imagine the mind of a person who does not want to get out of such a paramilitary organization, who is convinced that fighting is the right course of action. This article examines texts by Edna O'Brien and Anne Devlin that tackle this project, analyzing both how they humanize combatants and how they strain to fully account for a paramilitary's motives. As a result, these texts speak to the importance of trying to understand an enemy's perspective and the difficulties in doing so.

The Troubles are not a typical war in key respects; even deciding whether to call them a war is complicated. Scholars use a variety of terms to characterize this event, including "political violence" (Kennedy-Andrews 2003, p. 7), "terrorist campaign" (Dingley 2009, p. 10), and "civil war" (Fitzduff and O'Hagan 2009). Lasting from 1968 to 1998, the Troubles were a period of armed conflict between

Catholic nationalists, who want the entire island of Ireland to be one country independent of Britain, and Protestant loyalists, who want Northern Ireland to remain part of the United Kingdom. In the late 1960s, tensions between Catholic and Protestant communities boiled over into frequent rioting, and the Northern Irish police were unable to control the violence. As a result, British troops were mobilized to help keep the peace in Northern Ireland. The conflict was further complicated by the involvement of paramilitaries, or illegal armed militias, on both sides: the most important nationalist paramilitary group is the Irish Republican Army (IRA), and the two most important loyalist paramilitaries are the Ulster Volunteer Force and the Ulster Defence Association. The IRA saw themselves in a war for independence while the police and army saw themselves as restoring law and order. While acts of violence by loyalist paramilitaries were deplored by the government, in practice the state's tactics often focused on the nationalist paramilitaries as they were the greater threat to the existing government. For example, under the policy of internment, or imprisoning suspected paramilitaries without trial, 1874 Catholics were jailed as compared to 107 Protestants (Melaugh). Calling the Troubles a "civil war"—which they do resemble in that two factions of Northern Irish citizens were fighting each other—makes the nationalist side seem as legitimate as the government's, which loyalists would object to. But describing the conflict as a police action in response to terrorism denies legitimacy to the nationalist side, which they find unacceptable.

Critics have noted that much Troubles literature reinforces common perceptions of the violence as fundamentally irrational, driven by blind sectarianism and tribalism. As Laura Pelaschiar describes, the typical paramilitary character is "a macho-man in love with guns, naturally violent, sexually disturbed and often connoted by visual defects" (Pelaschiar 2009, p. 58). In this essay, I call attention to some notable attempts to move beyond such familiar stereotypes in order to acknowledge that the motives for violence are more complicated than the "terrorist" stereotype allows. Pelaschiar's description suggests that there is a strong association between masculinity and violence in Troubles literature as well. When women characters appear, they frequently stand for "the sacred realm of private feeling and personal relationships," which is positioned as the opposite of the "macho-man" paramilitary arena (Kennedy-Andrews 2003, p. 17). The texts by Edna O'Brien and Anne Devlin discussed in this essay challenge this gender binary: they feature women characters who have complicated relationships to violence and they are written by women authors who are interested in understanding a paramilitary's point of view, not just rejecting it. Their departure from the general pattern may partially explain why these texts have received limited critical attention, but it is also what makes them relevant for the current moment. Recently, a critical conversation has developed about ways that literary representations of Troubles violence are changing in the "post-conflict" years since the Good Friday Agreement was signed in 1998. Critics, including Pelaschiar, are bringing attention to the ways that recent literature is diversifying and complicating its representations of violence. This essay takes another look at literature written during the Troubles in the light of these arguments and finds that some efforts to challenge the prevailing view of the violence as merely irrational and disturbed were already underway in the 1980s and 1990s, adding historical depth to this critical conversation.

The view of Troubles violence as irrational was fostered not just by people outside Northern Ireland, but by the many Protestant and Catholic noncombatants living through the Troubles in their own communities. When thinking about attempts to imagine "the enemy" in Troubles literature, then, we should consider not just divisions between Protestants and Catholics, but also divisions between noncombatants and combatants within the same community. This division between combatants and noncombatants is inflected by class: paramilitary members came primarily from the working classes, for several reasons. Working-class neighborhoods took the brunt of the violence during the Troubles, both in terms of rioting and the police crackdowns in response. Some residents turned to paramilitaries because they saw these organizations as necessary for communities that the police had failed to protect. Segregation was also most pronounced in the working class. Protestants and Catholics lived in separate neighborhoods, sent their children to separate schools, and worked for separate employers, as well as attending separate churches. With so little social contact, the historical distrust between these communities only became more entrenched, and it was easy to believe that people on the other side of the divide were uniformly hostile to oneself and one's community. Even years after the Good Friday Agreement, "most social integration begins only in adulthood and usually correlates with education level via universities, civil service, and the private sector, which are bound by anti-discrimination regulations" (Knobel 2011, p. 90). Members of the Protestant and Catholic middle classes were more insulated from the violence and more likely to encounter each other professionally. They were much less likely to support the fighting, though they still identified as Catholic and Protestant. For a middle-class Catholic just trying to work and raise a family in the midst of bombings and assassinations, an IRA member could seem as threatening and as responsible for perpetuating the violence as Protestants on the other side.

It is the divide between noncombatant nationalist and IRA paramilitary that is most relevant for O'Brien's and Devlin's work. Both authors come from middle-class nationalist backgrounds and write texts that reach across the combatant-noncombatant divide to imagine complex paramilitary characters. Crossing this divide is more challenging than it might seem at first; as Elmer Kennedy-Andrews asks, "How can the typically middle-class, educated, liberal writer, physically removed from the conflagration, understand the underlying causes of discontent or the need for urgent action?" (Kennedy-Andrews 2003, p. 15). Seamus Heaney examines the ways some middle-class nationalists distance themselves from paramilitaries in his poem "Whatever You Say Say Nothing" (1975). With each news report of another violent incident, noncombatants engage in an elaborate performance designed to show that "we" are not like "them": the paramilitary "terrorists" who keep stoking the conflict. Heaney describes the noncombatants as "Expertly civil tongued with civil neighbors/On the high wires of first wireless reports," trading "sanctioned, old, elaborate retorts" such as "Oh, it's disgraceful, surely, I agree" and "Where's it going to end?" (Heaney 1988, pp. 212–13). This performance is both precarious like a high-wire act and predictable as a long-established custom, and it reassures the middle-class speakers that they and their neighbors are "civilized" enough to know better than to resort to violence. The rest of the poem, however, challenges this self-image, pointing out ways that middle-class nationalists are implicated in the conflict and criticizing the habit of saying elaborate nothings in a vain attempt to keep the peace. "Punishment" (1975) further elaborates on this theme, suggesting that saying nothing may actually make one complicit with the violence one claims to deplore. The poem draws an analogy between modern Irish women who were tarred and feathered by nationalist paramilitaries for fraternizing with enemy soldiers and an Iron Age woman caught in adultery and sacrificed to a goddess. While the speaker feels compassion for the Iron Age woman, he also admits, with painful honesty, that he "would have cast [...] the stones of silence," just as he "stood dumb" at the sight of the women shamed in public during the Troubles (Heaney 1988, p. 193). Saying nothing to stop such ritual punishment is almost as bad as actively throwing stones, the speaker guiltily acknowledges. This poem also alludes to the performance of civility, this time with the oxymoron of "civilized outrage," suggesting that Northern Irish expectations of civilized behavior prevent the speaker from expressing his emotions more directly. Heaney's poems give insight into the ways that the weight of custom urges middle-class noncombatants not to engage with combatants' perspectives seriously or publicly. In creating nuanced portraits of paramilitary fighters, then, both Edna O'Brien and Anne Devlin are working against this cultural pressure.

2. *House of Splendid Isolation*

Edna O'Brien dramatizes the struggle of a middle-class noncombatant to relate to a paramilitary soldier in her novel, *House of Splendid Isolation* (1994). The novel focuses on two main characters: Josie, an elderly woman living alone in a big country house, and Mac, short for McGreevy, a paramilitary who escapes police custody and invades Josie's home while pursuing his next mission. At first, Josie is terrified and thinks Mac will surely kill her before he leaves. As a lady of a big house, Josie belongs to a different class, though we later find out that she worked as a maid as a young woman and only married into the property. More importantly, Josie has the distaste for violence and liberal humanist values that are characteristic of the middle class, and initially she positions herself as morally superior to Mac. His viewpoint is so unlike hers, she reflects in one memorable passage, that they might as well be speaking different languages: "The saddest bit is that we're the same stock, the same faith, we speak the same tongue and yet we don't. . . . Words like justice or love or bread turned inside out or outside in" (O'Brien 1994, p. 87). And yet, as this passage also points out, Josie and Mac have much in common: they are both Catholic, both Irish, and, in fact, they both revere nationalist ideals. Over the course of the novel, Josie abandons her idea that Mac is completely different from her and becomes more and more interested in him as a complex, flawed human being.

One important way the novel shortens the distance between Josie and Mac is by holding Josie's political views up for scrutiny. At one point, Josie shows Mac the diary of her uncle, who fought in the 1921 war for Irish independence and was killed by the British. When Mac asks why she showed him the book, she explains that she wants him to know that "we are on the same side," but quickly follows that by saying, "What they did then was different" (O'Brien 1994, p. 85). Like other citizens of the Republic of Ireland in this novel, Josie wants to admire the revolutionaries of 1916 and 1921 while deploring Mac and other paramilitaries for causing the deaths of innocents. Mac immediately challenges her, saying "It's exactly the same," and while Josie sticks to her position that harming innocent people is wrong, the novel shows that insisting the revolutionaries were different than the present-day IRA is a flawed argument. Indeed, the main difference is that those previous conflicts are safely in the past, which makes the soldiers that much easier to romanticize: "Politics were one thing when brave men were shot long ago for their beliefs, or brave women hid volunteers in settle beds or churns, but politics had become a racket, hijacking, robberies, mindless assassinations" (O'Brien 1994, pp. 53–54). When Josie thinks of the past, she thinks of sacrifice and bravery, but when she thinks of the present, she sees the collateral damage and mixed political motives that also come with war and that, realistically, were probably going on in 1921 as well. In this way, the novel raises the uncomfortable thought that the difference between a war for independence and pointless acts of violence is primarily in the eye of the beholder. Josie doesn't believe that the IRA's ongoing attacks are worthwhile, but Mac believes he is fighting to save his country, just as the revolutionaries of the past did (O'Brien 1994, p. 85).

Josie comes to know Mac better over the course of the novel, but she still struggles to reconcile her experience of him with her knowledge of the violent acts he has committed and plans to commit again. She thinks, "I like everything about him except what he does" (O'Brien 1994, p. 98): he is considerate within the constraints of his mission, bringing her tea and seeing her comfortably settled, though he won't let her leave the house. More importantly, he comes across as authentic, honest, and unapologetic for his beliefs. Josie has difficulty making this side of him fit with what she knows of his paramilitary career, and indeed indulges in the fantasy that through their conversations, "something would happen . . . A sea change . . . I'd save you" (O'Brien 1994, p. 111). This illusion is shattered when a neighbor snoops around the house and Mac's frightening reaction—holding Josie against a wall and interrogating her—makes it clear that he puts the success of his mission above consideration for her (O'Brien 1994, p. 110). As Josie tries to make Mac's different aspects fit together in her mind, she wonders if he is mad (O'Brien 1994, p. 99), if insanity could explain why he has sides to his personality that seem as different to her as Dr. Jekyll and Mr. Hyde. But the novel shows that Mac is rational; he just makes choices to steal, intimidate, and attack that Josie could never imagine herself making.

Josie, and to some extent the novel, never succeeds in synthesizing Mac's different aspects into one coherent portrait. At the end of the book, there are still more questions than answers about why Mac commits the violent acts that he does, how he reconciles those decisions with his love of "justice" and hope for "peace" (O'Brien 1994, pp. 98–99). But Josie does not need answers to these questions in order to want Mac to live. Simply recognizing that there are different aspects to his character is enough. In the final sequence of the novel, the police track Mac to Josie's house and raid it in the early morning. As Mac and the police trade gunfire, Josie goes out to "mediate" in hopes of convincing the police not to kill Mac (O'Brien 1994, p. 204). She thinks, "His life has many chapters to it and many evolutions.

They do not know that. But she knows it, because she knows him" (O'Brien 1994, p. 205). Because she has seen another side to Mac, she knows he is capable of more than just fighting and destruction, and she wants him to have that chance for another "chapter" in his life. The other noncombatant characters in the novel refer to Mac and other paramilitaries as "thugs," "sickos," and "psychopaths." Their view of Mac is one-dimensional, as someone who is wholly defined and consumed by the violence that he does. But the novel encourages us to see Mac as a complex human being. It does not deny the fear and damage his violent acts cause, but it insists that there is more to him than just that violence.

3. "Naming the Names"

In "Naming the Names" (1986), Anne Devlin's short story about a female paramilitary, there is no middle-class character like Josie struggling to understand a combatant. Instead, because the story is narrated in first person and incorporates stream-of-consciousness techniques, readers are put in Josie's position, trying to comprehend how the main character, a young woman named Finn, could commit a devastating act. Finn's decision to deceive her lover and lead him into an IRA trap is all the more shocking because, at the beginning of the story, she seems like a noncombatant, holding down a job in a bookstore and going about her life. The story seems like it will be about the familiar theme of noncombatants trying to live as normally as possible in the midst of bombings, police actions, and paramilitary retaliation. The first half of the story also relates Finn's growing relationship with a young Protestant man, a judge's son, and because Finn is Catholic, we suspect this relationship will be disrupted by politics and political violence. Such "romance across the divide" stories are also common in Troubles literature (Cleary 2001, p. 112). Our awareness that Finn is a nationalist paramilitary like Mac dawns slowly. After a reunion with her young man in the park that turns into a quarrel, the judge's son turns up dead, and the police take Finn in for questioning. Her responses to their interrogation lead readers to the chilling realization that Finn deliberately took the judge's son to the park knowing the IRA would be waiting: as a judge's son, he makes an appealing political target. In this way, the story transforms Finn from an ordinary young woman into a paramilitary before our eyes.

The story also gives insight into the history behind Finn's eventual decision to join the IRA. The major factor is her grief over what has happened to her neighborhood, the Falls Road, during the Troubles. In her memories of childhood, the street is so safe that when she wanted to go to the park, she could simply stand on the street corner and wait for a passer-by to take her hand and help her cross the street (Devlin 1986, p. 105). But everything changes in the August 1969 riots. Finn sees gangs from the nearby Protestant neighborhood, Shankill, setting fire to buildings and looting. Her main concern is helping any residents to escape, especially her grandmother. Betrayal is added to violence when she sees police in armored vehicles "moving slowly down Conway Street towards the Falls Road with the crowd behind them, burning houses as they went" (Devlin 1986, p. 112). The implication is that the police are indifferent to the harm being done to this neighborhood since they allow the riot to continue behind them. Later, Finn learns that a neighbor with IRA ties carried her grandmother to safety that night and helped many others besides (Devlin 1986, p. 114). It seems that the IRA is better able to protect Finn's community than the police, which helps us understand her decision to volunteer. When the police press her for names of other IRA members after the murder, she responds by naming the streets in the Falls: "'Abyssinia, Alma, Balkan, Belgrade, Bosnia,' naming the names: empty and broken and beaten places. I know no others" (Devlin 1986, p. 118). From Finn's perspective, the real crime is what has been done to the people on these streets: the arrests, gassings, and rubber bullets in the name of law and order, and the home-destroying riots that were tacitly allowed by the police. Just as Josie liked "everything" about Mac "except what he does," there is much to like about Finn as well, including her concern for the vulnerable and her fierce sense of justice.

While anger and grief over such destruction is not hard to understand, Finn's choice to turn another human being into a target is still alarming. In the timeline of the story, the riots in her neighborhood happen years before she meets the judge's son, and there are hints in the story that Finn viewed the young man as a target from the beginning of their relationship: the first time she sees his name, she recognizes it and goes out of her way to meet him (Devlin 1986, p. 97). The narration of their relationship is carefully crafted so that descriptions imply a budding romance as much as they imply the darker intention of getting close enough to someone to be able to use him for the IRA's ends. For example, when Finn goes to meet him on the night he will be killed, her stomach is in knots, which seems just as likely to be from nervousness at seeing him again after a three-week hiatus in their relationship as it is from the difficulty of maintaining a deception that will end in his death. Both Fiona McCann and Shamara Ransirini see this merging of personal romantic motives with political ones as central to the text's feminist message: there is no separating the personal from the political for Finn (McCann 2012; Ransirini 2015). In this story, though, the refusal to prioritize either the personal or the political over the other results in a terrible realization: Finn both has real feelings for the judge's son and decides to make him into an IRA target.

After the abduction, Finn pays a heavy price in guilt and the increasingly fragmented narrative shows that she is under severe mental strain, possibly even having a breakdown. She sleeps poorly and begins to see and hear things that aren't there, which the story renders through stream of consciousness. These moments are comparable to the way Virginia Woolf represents the consciousness of the shell-shocked World War I soldier, Septimus Smith, in *Mrs. Dalloway*. At points, Septimus hallucinates that the birds are singing in Greek, or that his dead friend Evans is walking towards him. As Vicki Mahaffey points out, the best stream-of-consciousness writing not only depicts subjective experience in the moment but also makes us aware of the viewpoint character's limitations by showing us how their experience relates to larger social realities (Mahaffey 2013, p. 46). In the example of Septimus's hallucinations, the larger social reality is our own understanding of what can plausibly happen in a city park, which allows us to realize that we should read the Greek-singing birds or the reappearance of a dead man as breaks from reality, even though they seem real to Septimus. "Naming the Names" incorporates similar moments. When the police take Finn to the station for questioning, to her it is as if everything in the store and on the street stops dead, like a freeze-frame in a movie, and only she and the police keep moving. This unrealistic effect is immediately preceded by a time jump: suddenly Finn is remembering the previous day when another IRA member came into the store and she told him she would get the judge's son to the park (Devlin 1986, p. 108). Because of the jumps in time, there are two possible larger realities we might recognize behind Finn's perception: the bystanders could have abruptly frozen in astonishment at seeing the police apparently arrest her, or to Finn's guilty conscience, it could be like they stopped at the moment she planned to hand the judge's son over to the IRA, as if they knew the decision she had made and were shocked into immobility.

These abrupt jumps through time continue in the interrogation sequence when Finn answers questions about the present with memories of the past. For instance, when the police press her for the names of her conspirators, she responds with a memory of her father and grandmother (Devlin 1986, p. 116). When her ex-boyfriend Jack comes to see her near the end of the story, he wants to know how Finn could lead someone she knew into a trap and questions his relationship with her: these concerns are exactly what we would expect from someone who cares about Finn. But Finn's responses are fragmentary and disconnected from the present: when Jack says, "I loved you once," her response is "Once, once upon a time" (Devlin 1986, p. 118). The sing-song repetition of "once" and the classic opening to a fairy tale all seem out of step with the serious situation and suggest a mind clutching at single words because the whole truth is too overwhelming. Jack is "puzzled" when Finn says "You should never have let me go!" because, as he points out, she was never very happy in their relationship (Devlin 1986, p. 118). Finn's words make more sense in the context of an earlier passage about a nightmare so disturbing that Jack described it as a "fit" (Devlin 1986, p. 115). On waking from it Finn behaves strangely, asking Jack to cover up all the mirrors so that she can't see anything in them. She also clings to him, having him take her to the bathroom and hold her hand as she falls asleep again. It is at this point that she asks him not to let go of her hand, no matter what happens, but when the nightmare returns and Finn begins to struggle and say, "Let go of me!" he releases her

(Devlin 1986, p. 116). Immediately after Finn recalls this, she blacks out in the interrogation room and loses time, which suggests that the memory is still deeply disturbing to her, but Jack has no way of making this connection when she talks to him at the end of the story. He can only recognize that Finn's mind is somewhere other than the present, watching her and asking "Where are you, Finn?" (Devlin 1986, p. 118).

Finn is clearly experiencing mental strain, which could easily be attributed to overwhelming guilt. Such guilt is important for making her sympathetic to a noncombatant audience. We expect we would be crippled with fear and shame if we were responsible for the death of another human being. But the story also incorporates signs of mental distress from before she met the judge's son, when she was still living with Jack. The nightmare that so disturbs Finn occurs before they break up, and Finn also recalls some extreme outbursts, such as throwing milk or dishes against the walls, locking herself in the bathroom, or running out of the house. Jack's behavior does not seem to cause these incidents, as Finn describes him as always staying calm and giving her space (Devlin 1986, p. 102). Reconstructing the chronological order of events reveals that she first lived through the Troubles riots of 1969, then had several alarming episodes during her relationship with Jack, which ended, and only after that encountered the judge's son. Another possible explanation for her mental distress, then, is that it traces back to her traumatic experiences during the riots. Research has shown that adults in Northern Ireland who experienced conflict-related trauma have a significantly higher rate of mood and anxiety disorders than other adults. In fact, the rate of PTSD among adults is higher in Northern Ireland than it is in most other countries, including the United States (Bunting et al. 2013). However, the story fosters the impression that guilt causes Finn's distress with its manipulation of time: she doesn't recall her most extreme memories until after the police take her in for questioning, so to readers, she seems more and more distraught after we learn of the judge's son's death, which strengthens the idea of a guilty conscience. A second reading, however, reveals the story's artful construction, which both shows that Finn is affected by Troubles-related trauma and includes the signs of guilt that make her sympathetic.

4. The Limits of Understanding in Devlin and O'Brien

While trauma is a historical effect of the Troubles, there is a problematic implication in reading Finn as more mentally troubled than she seems at first. If she is breaking down, the story could imply that madness is the ultimate explanation for her actions. This, in turn, would short-circuit the attempt to imagine a paramilitary actor not as a one-dimensional "sicko" but as a human being with intelligible motives. Resorting to madness as an explanation, then, could indicate that a noncombatant author or reader has reached the limits of her imagination and cannot get any further with the attempt to understand a combatant's point of view. However, the form of this story is also relevant for this issue because stream-of-consciousness techniques invite us to share Finn's experience as much as they enable us to examine it critically. In stream-of-consciousness writing, "individual experience is exposed as incomplete and distorted, but it is not invalidated" (Mahaffey 2013, p. 42). This makes it a very useful tool for writing a paramilitary character: it can take that character's beliefs and experiences seriously, as worth trying to understand from the inside, while still regarding them critically when needed. One such example in "Naming the Names" occurs when Finn gets into a debate with another clerk at work about increasing Protestant-Catholic segregation in the early years of the Troubles: while the co-worker expresses regret, Finn says it's "inevitable" that Protestants and Catholics should form two separate communities (Devlin 1986, p. 100). It seems she cannot imagine much good coming from contact between Protestants and Catholics, which also informs her decision to betray the judge's son despite her feelings for him: she assumes their relationship will have a bad outcome no matter what she does. As readers, we can recognize the flaws in such an assumption without discounting Finn's other experiences or beliefs. So, while it is important to think carefully about the implications of attributing Finn's actions to mental disorder, the story does avoid simply dismissing her perspective.

In contrast, *House of Splendid Isolation* explicitly denies madness as a possible explanation for Mac's paramilitary activities. At one point, Josie wonders if he might be crazy, but that thought speaks to her difficulties reconciling her different views of him, not to his actual behavior. Later, Mac himself says, "No one in their right minds wants my life and I am in my right mind" (O'Brien 1994, p. 193), indicating a rational understanding of the consequences of his choices. In the place of madness, though, the novel depicts Mac as compartmentalizing his violent acts and avoiding discussion of them: he thinks he has "seen too much and done too much" and admits "some of what he's done he's blocked, he's had to" (O'Brien 1994, p. 13). His conversations with Josie focus on the personal, such as his memories of his wife and daughter. As a result, Josie's sympathetic view of Mac is based on "personal feeling rather than ideological solidarity. She never accepts the moral legitimacy of the IRA man's actions but learns respect for his commitment to an ideal and is attracted to him as a man" (Kennedy-Andrews 2003, p. 251). This focus on the personal allows Josie, and readers, to sympathize with Mac as a human being without condoning his violent acts, but the lack of reflection on Mac's experiences as an IRA member raises the question of how well we finally understand him without much insight into such a significant part of his life. His refusal to speak about his acts as a paramilitary is most extreme at the end of the novel, when Mac is finally captured by the Irish police. They want answers to the same questions that the novel encourages readers to wonder about: "What made him what he is" and what goes on in his mind that allows him to commit bombings and shootings in the name of freedom (O'Brien 1994, p. 209). The detective sergeant who led the manhunt tries to goad Mac into talking: "You could have done a lot for your cause and country, McGreevy ... but all you done was death upon death upon death" (O'Brien 1994, p. 211). However, Mac remains completely silent, choosing not to react at all. The effect is Iago-like: we know all we are going to know about the thoughts behind his life as a paramilitary, and he refuses to explain himself further. Where "Naming the Names" uses stream of consciousness to understand Finn both from the inside and from the outside, at the end of *House of Splendid Isolation* we are forced to recognize that we are viewing Mac almost completely from the outside.

O'Brien makes a similar narrative choice in her later short story "Black Flower" (2011), which features an older ex-paramilitary character with a history similar to Mac's. In this story, Shane the ex-paramilitary also refuses to discuss his violent acts, even with Mona, a sympathetic noncombatant woman who met him in the art class she taught to prisoners. The two talk about art, restaurants, and scenery, but Shane only brings up his deeds as a paramilitary one time: "He said once to her and only once that she herself could be the judge of his actions. He had fought for what he believed in, which was for his country to be one, one land, one people, and not have a shank of it cut off" (O'Brien 2011, p. 82). This decision not to enter into debate over why he did what he did could indicate an awareness that there is not a good justification for the IRA's bombings and assassinations, but the second half of the passage suggests that Shane does have a principle behind his actions: the belief that the entire island of Ireland should be one country, with no part of it "cut off." The overall effect in this short story, as in *House of Splendid Isolation*, is of withholding: Shane and Mac have more thoughts about the justifications for their actions, but because readers never get access to those thoughts, we are uncomfortably aware that our understanding of each character is partial. Both texts register how unsatisfying this situation is by describing each man as wanting to say something he can't articulate: Josie thinks that Mac looks at her "as if there is something he especially wishes to say" (O'Brien 1994, p. 193) and Mona thinks Shane's message is "unfinished, as if he had wanted to say more" (O'Brien 2011, p. 78). Given that the texts never reveal what that something more would be, these lines describe our desires as readers as much as they describe Mac and Shane. We want there to be more explanation because we still don't understand how these characters can justify killing innocent people.

Both Edna O'Brien and Anne Devlin engage in the project of imagining a combatant's point of view, but both their texts reach limits of understanding, marked by the signs of breakdown in "Naming the Names" and the refusal to discuss in *House of Splendid Isolation*. While coming up against such limits is unsatisfying for a reader, the fact that limits are present should not surprise us. Joe Cleary finds signs of "imaginative failure" in many Troubles narratives and argues that they are tied to assuming that any resolution will have to entail "acceptance of the already established state order, something which means that the militant nationalist will eventually either have to repent his opposition to the state or be eliminated and incarcerated by the state security forces" (Cleary 2001, p. 111). O'Brien's and Devlin's characters diverge from this pattern somewhat, because while they are in police custody at the end of each narrative, they do not renounce their politics or their decision to fight. *House of Splendid Isolation* begins with Mac escaping police custody and straightaway planning another bombing; at the end of the novel, there is no reason to believe he won't attempt the same again. At the end of "Naming the Names," Finn takes responsibility for her act, but her tone is neither approving nor regretful: "I only know for certain what my part was, that even on the eve, on such a day, I took him there" (Devlin 1986, p. 119). Even more importantly, Mac and Finn are still the most compelling characters in these final scenes: they do not forfeit our interest or our sympathy simply because they remain in opposition to the state. Rather than achieving closure by having Mac and Finn renounce violence, these narratives leave us with enigmas that at least make us aware that our understanding has reached a limit. This reflects the reality that during the Troubles, the social order was not transformed enough for more common ground between combatants and noncombatants. Thus, while both texts cannot fully account for a combatant's mindset without resorting to the devices of madness or silence, they nevertheless represent those viewpoints as worth struggling to understand and do not force them to conform to the status quo.

Such efforts to understand a combatant's point of view, then, are important beginnings even if they are partial. In the twenty years since the Good Friday Agreement brought an official end to the Troubles, scholars have investigated what we can learn from the peace process that might apply to other conflicts perceived as "terrorism." Many stress how important it was to involve the IRA in negotiations, leading to the principle that "it is always, or nearly always, a good idea to talk to the enemy, even if they are or have historically been seen as terrorists. After all, if those who are engaging in violence are not included in a peace process, is there any hope for peace?" (White 2013, p. 7). The first step in opening such a conversation is to imagine the "enemy" as a human being who can be understood and reasoned with. It is also significant that these literary efforts to imagine IRA characters come from authors with Catholic nationalist backgrounds, mirroring the role that noncombatants, including clergy and non-governmental organizations, played in building trust and keeping channels of communication open to the paramilitaries during the peace process (Knobel 2011, p. 94). The ultimate goal is for nationalists and loyalists to understand each other's perspectives well enough to negotiate and work with each other, but because this is so fraught, nationalist noncombatants can provide an important intermediate step by working to understand the perspectives of nationalist paramilitaries and convey them to others. In many ways, the peace process in Northern Ireland is still not complete, as indicated by recent concerns that Brexit will re-inflame tensions over the border. Both "Naming the Names" and *House of Splendid Isolation* leave readers feeling that more work needs to be done to understand where paramilitaries are coming from, but both texts succeed in presenting that project as worthwhile.

Funding: This research received no external funding.

Conflicts of Interest: The author declares no conflict of interest.

References

Bunting, Brendan P., Finola R. Ferry, Samuel D. Murphy, Siobhan M. O'Neill, and David Bolton. 2013. Trauma Associated with Civil Conflict and Posttraumatic Stress Disorder: Evidence from the Northern Ireland Study of Health and Stress. *Journal of Traumatic Stress* 26: 134–41. [CrossRef] [PubMed]

Cleary, Joe. 2001. *Literature, Partition, and the Nation-State: Culture and Conflict in Ireland, Israel, and Palestine*. Cambridge: Cambridge University Press.

Devlin, Anne. 1986. Naming the Names. In *The Way-Paver*. London: Faber and Faber, pp. 95–119.

Dingley, James. 2009. Northern Ireland and the "Troubles". In *Combating Terrorism in Northern Ireland*. Edited by James Dingley. New York: Routledge, pp. 10–33.

Fitzduff, Mari, and Liam O'Hagan. 2009. The Northern Ireland Troubles: INCORE Background Paper. Available online: http://cain.ulst.ac.uk/othelem/incorepaper09.htm (accessed on 7 January 2019).

Heaney, Seamus. 1988. *Poems 1965–1975*. New York: Noonday Press.

Kennedy-Andrews, Elmer. 2003. *Fiction and the Northern Ireland Troubles Since 1969: (De-)Constructing the North*. Dublin: Four Courts Press.

Knobel, Ariel Heifetz. 2011. A Paradoxical Peace in Northern Ireland. *PRAXIS: The Fletcher Journal of Human Security* 26: 89–96.

Mahaffey, Vicki. 2013. Streams Beyond Consciousness: Stylistic Immediacy in the Modernist Novel. In *A Handbook of Modernist Studies*. Edited by Jean-Michel Rabaté. Hoboken: Wiley, pp. 35–54.

McCann, Fiona. 2012. The Good Terrorist(s)? Interrogating Gender and Violence in Anne Devlin's "Naming the Names" and Anna Burns' *No Bones*. *Estudios Irlandeses* 7: 69–78. [CrossRef]

O'Brien, Edna. 1994. *House of Splendid Isolation*. London: Phoenix.

O'Brien, Edna. 2011. Black Flower. In *Saints and Sinners*. New York: Back Bay Books, pp. 75–89.

Pelaschiar, Laura. 2009. Terrorists and Freedom Fighters in Northern Irish Fiction. *The Irish Review* 40–41: 52–73.

Ransirini, Shamara. 2015. Body, Violence, and Space: Anne Devlin's "Naming the Names". *Hecate* 41: 39–56.

Storey, Michael L. 2004. *Representing the Troubles in Irish Short Fiction*. Washington, DC, USA: Catholic University of America Press.

White, Timothy J. 2013. Lessons from the Northern Ireland Peace Process: An Introduction. In *Lessons from the Northern Ireland Peace Process*. Edited by Timothy J. White. Madison: University of Wisconsin Press, pp. 3–33.

© 2019 by the author. Licensee MDPI, Basel, Switzerland. This article is an open access article distributed under the terms and conditions of the Creative Commons Attribution (CC BY) license (http://creativecommons.org/licenses/by/4.0/).

Article

Translating the Enemy in the 'Terp': Three Representations in Contemporary Afghan War Fiction

Steven K. Johnson

School of Arts and Sciences, Southern New Hampshire University, Manchester, NH 03106, USA; s.johnson5@snhu.edu

Received: 10 February 2019; Accepted: 23 March 2019; Published: 27 March 2019

Abstract: This essay examines the ambivalent relationships between American soldiers deployed to Afghanistan and their unit interpreters in recent fictional works by Joydeep Roy-Bhattacharya, Luke Mogelson, and Will Mackin. In these works, the interpreter characters often occupy the liminal space between who is a friend and who is an enemy, serving as an ally to American military units while also reflecting projections of soldiers' assumptions about the enemy in relation to themselves. Most prominent in encounters with 'terps' are the discursive tactics employed intentionally and institutionally as boundaries by American forces that attempt to keep terps 'othered'—particularly tactics that prevent terps from exhibiting idealized American masculinity, and those of Islamophobic racism. The three terps in the study point to a rupture in the optimistic views about multiculturalism, where the terp translates an awareness of a cultural chasm instead of a bridge. In fictional narratives, more than finding agency in crossing boundaries, terps are fundamental in signifying where boundaries exist as they are caught in their interstices, as well as in critiquing the sources of those boundaries.

Keywords: war writing; war literature; masculinity; Islamophobia; interpreter; Joydeep Roy-Bhattacharya; Will Mackin; Luke Mogelson; Afghanistan

1. Introduction

Direct contact with the enemy in contemporary war fiction generally depicts encounters where weapons and technology keep most of the enemy physically distant, briefly glimpsed, or entirely hidden, and where techniques of propaganda and military training keep the enemy portrayed as a two-dimensional villain—the Other, *par excellence*. Michael Hedges notes that war-related othering of the enemy is a common ploy of nationalism, as "all who oppose our allies and us ... are lumped into one indistinguishable mass. They are as faceless as we are for our enemies" (Hedges 2002, p. 9). Indeed, crafting the enemy as the Other has a lineage that extends from practices of early warfare and which continues into contemporary world culture (Gay 1993; Hedges 2002). Beyond nationalism, Joanna Bourke recognizes that dehumanizing the enemy has maintained and spurred the will to fight wars in the 20th Century despite the desensitizing and machine-like aspects of modern war (Bourke 1999). And in the West, over the past twenty or so years, the othered enemy has shifted from the enemy of Communism to that of Islamic extremism (Büyükgebiz 2016). Indeed, the Islamic enemy continues to be narratively constructed as a two-dimensional Islamic terrorist Other whose singular purpose is to destroy the West. Such a narrative construction of the enemy in contemporary fiction about the wars in Iraq and Afghanistan extends well beyond the battlefield, and includes soldiers' encounters with foreign places, languages, religion, civilians, and death (Peebles 2011, pp. 101–3). Indeed, many recent fictional works and films about these wars readily reinforce such a simplistic narrative of American heroes battling villainous Islamic terrorists, or American heroes battling their own demons while an incidental terrorist enemy continually lurks as a threat to all in the war zone.

Three recent fictional works about the American wars in Afghanistan complicate this simplistic relationship to the enemy, however, through the use of characters serving in the role of interpreter, or 'terp' as American troops refer to them. The similarities between the terps in these disparate texts are surprising, and thus they are important narratives, as all three use the character of the terp to initiate more complex representations of Afghans and insert them into the written cultural memory of the war. In these narratives, the terp, a character type lacking adequate scholarship—especially in regards to contemporary writing—frequently emerges as one who is able to speak for and represent the enemy when the enemy cannot be found, critiquing the motives of American allies while likewise revealing the shortsightedness of their Islamophobic assumptions about their enemy. The terp adds depth and complexity to representations of the enemy, often simultaneously reinforcing and critiquing misguided beliefs about the enemy in the enemy's absence. In this way, the terp concurrently represents both an ally and an Other to American characters. While the role of real interpreters in Iraq and Afghanistan has been to assist American military units to bridge linguistic and cultural differences as they interact and engage with the local populace, the character of the terp also functions as a figurative boundary crosser who straddles languages, cultures, world views, religious beliefs, and sometimes sides. In this role of ambivalence, the terp sometimes mediates and sometimes reiterates the two-dimensional beliefs about the enemy's culture, race, and ethnicity. The terp thus serves as a trope, a turn in the liminal space where American soldiers encounter the Other, one with the possible risk of actually being the enemy disguised as friend (a spy), but also one who runs counter to soldiers' Islamophobic expectations, often foiling the preconceptions that American characters have about the enemy they are fighting. Such boundary crossing always comes with a cost for the terps, though. Not only are they are viewed with Islamophobic suspicion by the American forces they serve, but also as traitors and pawns of the occupiers to their countrymen, leaving the terp with an alienated and ambivalent identity. Terps often find themselves to be everyone's enemy, learning that there is inherent conflict with everyone in every act of interpretation. Mostly, in crossing boundaries, terps draw attention to the discourses of conflict initiated by American forces along with their ambivalent effects. In fictional narratives, more than finding agency in crossing boundaries, terps are fundamental in signifying where boundaries exist as they are caught in their interstices, as well as in critiquing the sources of those boundaries. In a world where the enemy is always already othered, the terp provides a literary engagement with the (im)possibilities of overcoming the other subject position.

This paper examines the role of three terps who experience the implications of alienation and ambivalence as a result of the boundaries they confront and attempt to cross. These stories employ the interpreter character in a role of new-found importance in American war writing, given the actual and frequent use of small unit interpreters by the US military in both Iraq and Afghanistan. These characters have not been adequately addressed in the critical analysis of contemporary war literature. *The Watch* by Joydeep Roy-Bhattacharya retells an updated version of Sophocles' "Antigone" set in a remote US Army outpost in Afghanistan ([Roy-Bhattacharya 2012](#)). The unit's new Dari interpreter, Farid Humayun Masood Attar—shortened to just "Masood" by the Americans—loosely follows the role of Antigone's sister, Ismene. Like Ismene, Masood would submissively follow the decrees of those in power, were it not for the dialogs he has with the novel's rebellious Antigone figure, Nizam, who arrives at the American outpost seeking to bury her brother who was killed in a battle with the Americans. Like Ismene, Masood struggles with the incongruity of stated American ideals (which he finds empowering) and the military practices and attitudes that often violate those principles, especially when non-Americans are involved. In his boundary crossing between American culture and the complex practices of Pashtun and Dari cultures in Afghanistan, Masood's hope in the American ideals of freedom and liberal democracy are confronted by the shortcomings of American soldiers, who are sexist, racist, Islamophobic, and homophobic. At the same time, Masood faces reprimand and rejection from his countrywoman Nizam for his disrespect to the Afghan dead—a betrayal of Afghan culture and Islamic belief—and for his inability to navigate the difference between morality and legality. As a terp, Masood copes his own ambivalence about the resulting miscarriage of justice.

Luke Mogelson's short story "New Guidance" is narrated by the Afghan-American interpreter Roohullah, whose name his American counterparts have shortened to "Roo" (Mogelson 2016). Raised in the United States by immigrants, Roo identifies with the American military, and with being American, even as he suffers from racist American attitudes. He also finds a strong identification with an Afghan soldier during his deployment who confronts Roo with the shortcomings of America's stated goals in Afghanistan. In the story, the American unit withdraws from its combat partnership with an Afghan infantry platoon in its fight against the Taliban, which leaves the Afghan National Army (ANA) unit in a precarious and ultimately losing position in its fight against the Taliban. At the story's end, Roo finds that his loyalty to the Americans has never been returned in kind, compounded by the fact he feels he has let down the Afghan platoon who, though abandoned by the American unit, continues to fight until it is destroyed. As with Masood, it is through Roo that American injustice is fully signified. After inquiring at a reunion about the status of the ANA platoon, Roo realizes not only the platoon's fate, but his own: "I waited for the major to tell me what had happened. I waited and waited and then, as I waited, I realized I didn't need to be told" (Mogelson 2016, p. 62).

In a variation of this theme, Joe (a name anglicized by Americans from Jamaluddein) operates as a SEAL Team terp in Afghanistan, and as a minor character in Will Mackin's story "The Lost Troop" (Mackin 2018). Joe haunts the narrator's thoughts as the bored SEAL team tries to generate meaningful missions in Afghanistan once the initial fighting appears to have subsided: "His voice, with its derived British accent and perpetual tone of disappointment, exactly matched that of my beleaguered conscience" (Mackin 2018, p. 8). While Joe helps the narrator grapple with his guilt about the loss of a comrade ("It wasn't your fault," says Joe to the narrator), the SEAL team and Joe are readily collaborating by story's end, undertaking a morally suspect revenge mission to detain a martinet school teacher from Joe's childhood who is quite uninvolved in the war (Mackin 2018, p. 13). Instead of simply recognizing the injustice of Americans, Joe willing joins the SEAL team in bringing unjust and violent action to his countrymen.

In these three fictional works, the terp mediates between languages, between cultural engagements, between religions, between violence and peace, between who is a friend and who is an enemy. Such mediation appears to result in ambivalent and melancholic self-hoods for the characters, even as the terps also mediate the injustice of America's role in the Forever War. And yet, something is lost in translation, and while the terps draw out the Islamophobia and the willful cultural ignorance of American forces in Afghanistan, they offer no insight for resolution or agency. The terps are key translators of critique even as they appear to reconstruct cultural difference. In all three stories, the character of the terp certainly engages American cultural assumptions about its enemy, but as a trope, the interpreter is a figurative turn against the dominant American narrative that insists the war in Afghanistan has been waged justly, and to the benefit of Afghans.

2. Interpreting Cultural Hybridity

The role of the terp as boundary-crosser and cultural intermediary is a realistic aspect of the stories examined by this paper and reflects the documented role of real interpreters who have participated in the Iraq and Afghanistan wars since 2001. Indeed, before the Forever Wars in Afghanistan and Iraq, interpreters have historically been used at high levels of command and for collecting military intelligence, while tactical roles on the battlefield have been uncommon (Baigorri-Jalon 2011; Campbell 2016, p. 63). Indeed, the consistent and intentional use of professional interpreters in small military units is relatively new to American military practice, and the role often results in social alienation for the terp. Mihaela Tălpaş notes the alienated role of the terp in her recent study, where professional interpreters in Afghanistan are seen as a danger "both by the ... coalition forces and by the local community," a risk both militarily and socially in their many roles—interpreting language and mediating culture and religion (Tălpaş 2016, p. 241). Thus, real interpreters' loyalties are often uncertain both to the military and to the local populace, even as they make important contributions and interventions that ease tension and that potentially reduce violence. This undervalued but important work carries personal costs for these interpreters. In her observations about interpreters serving in Iraq, Madeline Otis Campbell notes a complex situation, where the terp's crossing of linguistic borders exemplifies the "dilemmas of identification" as linguistic boundaries intersect with cultural ones (Campbell 2016, p. 61):

> [I]n taking on the language of the occupation, the subject finds recognition and a certain degree of freedom ... she asks to no longer be the other. Navigating the translation encounter thus raises questions of loyalty and identity on multiple registers for wartime interpreters: not only at the level of perceived political allegiances but also at the personal level of subjective recognition and interpellation into the dominant discourses of the occupier.
> (Campbell 2016, p. 80)

Campbell's recognition of this complex and ambivalent position of the interpreters in crossing languages and cultures follows Homi Bhabha's recognition of the ambivalence that is taken up in moments of cultural hybridity, moments that are both a product of colonization and simultaneously the potential locus for subversion, "where the construction of a political object that is new, *neither the one nor the other*, properly alienates our political expectations, and changes, as it must, the very forms of our recognition of the moment of politics"(Bhabha 1994, p. 25). Bhabha theorizes that agency in hybridity occurs when liminality results in the impossibility of identity, when "other 'denied' knowledges enter upon the dominant discourse and estrange the basis of its authority" (Bhabha 1994, p. 114). Campbell claims to be a witness to an act of subversive hybridity in one terp's use of cultural jokes that plays on the unwitting assumptions of American visitors who are trying to connect across cultural boundaries (Campbell 2016, pp. 64–65). As Campbell analyzes the interactions of interpreters in Iraq, she recognizes how they frequently take on varied subject positions and apply different strategies in achieving their goals. This hybridity that Campbell observes is not an aspect that emerges with the fictional terps.

Like their real counterparts, fictional terps take on the roles of cross-cultural mediators, but in moving from an observation of the real into a representation of the imagined, the three terps in this study never show the fluid hybridity that Campbell observes, as they do not work from positions that offer subversion or agency. In this way, the representative characters of terps diverge from Campbell's careful observations. In bridging the real to the fictional, it is important to consider the cross-cultural experiences of the terps, and whether they serve in furtherance of the dominant discourse of American military occupations of Afghanistan, or if they serve as critical resistance, as narrative subversion in the dominant discourse. It is fitting that such ambivalence is represented within the fiction of war and conflict, since, in its most generic sense, a war zone represents the space of chaos, a space where order is upended, where power is contested. Within such a narrative space, terps bridge the linguistic understanding of the characters who speak different languages, and can also interpret for readers the structures of social power through their own situational ambivalence. The ambivalence within the character of the terp exemplifies a pervasive anxiety about cultural identity, and it expresses its own ambivalence about cultural identity as resistant to both American Islamophobia and to the enemy motives of extremism in Afghanistan.

Such anxiety is connected to concerns about the stability of identity. Anthropologist Baruch Shimoni suggests that the boundary crossing of cultural hybridity is an individual balance of crossing and defending borders: "A sense of boundaries can be indicated by the extent to which people consciously or unconsciously want to keep or change what is perceived by them as their cultural borders" (Shimoni 2006, p. 217). Such borders are always imagined and subjectively experienced (Shimoni 2006). In this way, the character of the terp can be understood as a site where a culture war is actually being fought, addressing areas of perceived cultural danger in the signification of cultural boundaries, as well as being the interpreter of where such boundaries actually exist. A better understanding of hybridity in these narratives thus requires consideration of how the terp simultaneously critiques and exemplifies American perceptions of who (and what) is the enemy through the symbolic boundaries that terps confront. The most pronounced boundaries in these narratives include those of American gender norms, as well as ubiquitous American forms of racist Islamophobia. As terps interact with American characters, these particular areas are continually probed. The terps navigate their own encounters with the aggressive masculinity and racist attitudes of American soldiers and SEALs, often finding that while they are encountering these boundaries, no American truly reciprocates in the liminal space. Indeed, the actions of American military characters tend to resist crossing cultural boundaries, keeping themselves in and others out.

3. Interpreting Masculinity

Since *The Iliad*, the Western warrior has been measured against an idyllic aggressive masculinity that continues into representations of the American military. As Peebles notes, "Accounts from Homer to O'Brien ... reveal how life as a soldier affects his conception of manhood or masculinity. War can make (or unmake) the man—and today it is a proving ground for women as well" (Peebles 2011, p. 2). While Peebles finds varied American voices weighing in on the Iraq war experience—not just that of the white male—masculinity is nonetheless alive and well and dominant in the Iraq War (Peebles 2011, p. 100). Warfare's role in man-making is not surprising, as the narratives of war have long remembered fighting in war as a *par excellence* performance of masculinity (Braudy 2003; Ehrenreich 1997). Moreover, that idealized, aggressive masculinity in part perpetuates war: "Warfare and aggressive masculinity have been ... mutually reinforcing cultural enterprises. War making requires warriors, that is 'real' men,' and the making of warriors requires war" (Ehrenreich 1997, p. 129). Western war narratives continue to reconstruct a cultural memory that values and identifies with both patriarchy and aggressive violence. Thus, encounters between non-Western interpreters and American soldiers bring cultural boundaries of masculinity to the forefront, especially those that undermine the perceived masculinity of the enemy. And in narratives where the enemy is not present as a character, the terp comes to bear emasculation, thwarted from inclusion with American identifications.

In *The Watch*, the terp Masood confronts American gender norms upon his arrival at the fictional Tarsadan Outpost in Afghanistan. A helicopter delivers him shortly after a battle that killed and wounded of the Americans stationed there. And while Masood arrives ready to join with American forces and do his best, he is readily identified and degraded by the American soldiers for exhibiting effeminancy. As Masood walks across camp, one soldier shouts to the soldier escorting Masood, "Wo dat, Sarn't? ... Dude walks like a lady! Whoo, whoo ... " (Roy-Bhattacharya 2012, p. 98). Such observations confuse Masood, who, unlike the American soldiers, is quite comfortable describing American men as "beautiful" and admiring their physical forms in ways that surpass the boundaries of normalized American masculinity (Roy-Bhattacharya 2012, pp. 94–95, 107). Masood is further confused as he eats a meal alone with Simonis, the unit sniper who identifies himself as both gay and a killer. Through his conversation with Simonis, Masood struggles to navigate the Americans' binary boundaries, especially those existing at the intersections of homosociality and masculinity. Indeed, Masood expresses a deep and complex view of cultural friendship, which includes sexual attraction, but that does not rest in a singular sexual orientation. When Simonis' makes several passes at Masood, he misinterprets them as simply the overtures of friendship. In Masood's experience, a man is not either/or, but both/and. The dialog with Simonis leaves Masood "completely confused as if I have just had an encounter with a member of an alien race" (Roy-Bhattacharya 2012, p. 114). Other American soldiers are quick to deride Masood for what they perceive to be his sexual orientation: "Fruit's as gay as Father Christmas. Fuckin' loud and queer" (Roy-Bhattacharya 2012, p. 117). In the homosocial space of the all-male American camp, heteronormative masculinity is prized, and any male performance that signifies other possibilities is quickly derided and marginalized so as not to disrupt the dominant cultural belief in masculinity. Masood's signified femininity immediately reduces Masood's relevance and value, even as it critiques the American perspective. In the military community of Tarsadan outpost, heterosexual masculinity is a boundary that cannot be crossed easily, and it perpetuates a cultural belief of American superiority that permeates the unit.

Roo is similarly unrecognized as masculine by the Americans, treated like a child instead of as effeminate. And while he implicitly identifies with the American soldiers for whom he interprets, his childlike naiveté about the war around him and his own confusion about his motives in returning to Afghanistan underscore the childlike nickname the Americans have given him, "Roo," (who is also the toddler kangaroo from A.A. Milne's *Winnie-the-Poo*). Relegated to the subject position of the child, Roo frames the state of war through his own innocence. He not only interprets conversations between American Major Karzowski and Afghan Lieutenant Mustafa from this place, but also navigates between his identifications with both American and Afghan cultural values, as he physically crosses and recrosses through a boundary wall between the American and ANA barracks. Instead of resulting in hybrid agency for Roo, he finds only confusion as he is unable to live up to the ideals of either side. Americans and Afghans alike remind him of his inexperience and naiveté in emasculating ways, as Roo attempts to live up to the 'big brother' figures of both Major Karzowski and Lieutenant Mustafa. During a meal, Karzowski relegates Roo to the role of child by answering for him as adults are prone to do, and by defending Roo from the teasing of other American soldiers. Similarly, Mustafa scolds Roo throughout the narrative, as an older brother might a child, for not living up to Afghan cultural ideals: "He stared right at me until I literally hung my head [. . .] I understood that it was meant as a reminder, a rebuke" (Mogelson 2016, p. 49). Childlike, Roo's identity dwells in the interstices between American and Afghan ideals, unable to act like a man in either culture, and he is thus rejected by both.

Like Masood and Roo, Jamaluddein also has his name shortened: to "Joe" by the Navy SEALs for whom he interprets. Since he is "a middle-aged man," his age and experience are less of an issue to the SEALs, so instead of questioning Joe's masculinity, they generally ignore him (Mackin 2018, p. 8). Joe has a lesser role in the story than Masood and Roo, and he is nearly invisible until its end. Joe emerges as a character only as aggression emerges as the liminal space against which to signify his masculinity in relation to that of the Americans. In comparison to the SEAL team, Joe is generally ignored and irrelevant because he is not a warrior: "He wore armor on missions, but he carried no weapons" (Mackin 2018, p. 8). The narrator further states that Joe walks a little too close to the narrator for his own protection, indicating a lack of bravery by Joe while among a group of respected warriors. Though Joe enters the story as a disembodied voice, he becomes more present when he suggests that the SEAL team help him avenge a primary school teacher "who used to hit my knuckles with a ruler" (Mackin 2018, p. 14). Through this suggestion of gratuitous aggressive action, Joe becomes more embraced by the SEALs. When, at the end, the team surrounds the teacher's house instead of taking up a weapon, Joe raises a bullhorn and shouts the words from the end of Pink Floyd's "Another Brick in the Wall (Part 2)": "If you don't eat your meat, you can't have any pudding! *How* can you have any pudding if you don't eat your meat!" (Mackin 2018, p. 19). While Mackin does not provide readers with the first-person insights to Joe that Masood's and Roo's stories provide, there is an implication that Joe's bullhorn loaded with words are as weaponized as the rifles and grenades of the SEAL team, and that unlike Roo and Masood, he is accepted when he embraces aggression as one of the team (Mackin 2018). But as Joe does not reappear in any of Mackin's other stories like some of the other characters, the final analysis of Joe is unclear. He simply disappears. What is clear is that the SEALs and Joe alike relish the opportunity to take aggressive action against symbols of educational authority, though the SEALs have weapons and Joe has words.

If the terps mediate American beliefs about the enemy that are mostly unseen, that mostly blend in with the populace, all three terps do not measure up to the dominant belief about American masculinity represented through American characters—either as measured against indicators of femininity, adolescence, or aggression. In doing so, the characters complicate this American perspective by drawing attention to the inadequacy of such beliefs, while they are arguably more intuitive than the Americans in interpreting the complex situations in which they participate. Masood is more effective in understanding the American injustice to Nizam, Roo recognizes the American injustice of leaving the ANA platoon to fight on its own, and Joe joins the Americans in unjustly detaining his old school teacher. Through each, there is an estrangement of the dominant discourse of masculinity.

4. Interpreting Racism

Even more than drawing out beliefs of American masculine dominance, American military characters perpetuate Islamophobic racism—a pervasive cultural fear that ineptly conflates race, ethnicity, and religious practice into collective anti-Islamic beliefs. Islamophobia manifests in the recognition of hierarchic differences based on skin color, dress codes, cultural backgrounds, and religious beliefs (Büyükgebiz 2016, p. 230). Indeed, Western portrayals of Islam fundamentally misunderstand the existing diversity within the religion, assuming instead that it is a singular nation (Afshar 2013). Judith Butler writes extensively about the American relegation of Islam to a subhuman status through varied and various conceptual cultural frames that render dominant anti-Islamic discourse effective (Butler [2009] 2016). Butler analyzes American actions in the wars on Iraq and Afghanistan and considers the incongruities and various illogics that underlie such frames. Ultimately for Butler, Islamophobia stems from the frames that diffuse the national and cultural discourse of difference—one that is not always clearly or transparently racist, but one that articulates a sustainable cultural narrative of superiority over the othered enemy:

> When a population appears as a direct threat to my life, they do not appear as "lives," but as the threat to life (a living figure that figures the threat to life). Consider how this is compounded under those conditions in which Islam is seen as barbaric or pre-modern, as not yet having conformed to those norms that make the human recognizable. Those we kill are not quite human, and not quite alive, which means that we do not feel the same horror and outrage over the loss of their lives as we do over the loss of those lives that bear national or religious similarity to our own. (Butler [2009] 2016, p. 42)

In this concise statement, she explains the conditions for creating and sustaining a cultural narrative about an enemy that maintains discursive animosity through primitive characterizations of difference. As with masculinity, terps bear these two-dimensional Islamophobic projections in the narratives, both reiterating and complicating the Islamophobic assumptions of Americans within war narratives. Ultimately, reading Butler in the terps underscores that while terps are supposed to mediate cultures, they are instead caught in between cultures, wedged in the gulf that exists, unable to bridge it.

In *The Watch*, Masood draws critical attention to the callous Islamophobia of American soldiers. While he is not the only character in the narrative who bears racist comments and actions, his role as an interpreter gives him a unique perspective as American soldiers continually fail to live up to his expectations about their commitment to justice through "democracy, freedom, and the rule of law": "I don't do politics" says the American soldier Simonis to Masood's dismay (Roy-Bhattacharya 2012, p. 109). Arriving the day after several American soldiers have been killed or wounded in an attack on the base, Masood's experience with the American's is one of invisibility, and when he is finally seen by them, it is only and always sub-human, an object of derision and suspicion. In a very short span of time, Americans call him "raghead" and "Paco," and hears his countrymen referred to as "hajjis" (Roy-Bhattacharya 2012, pp. 102–9). The derogatory terms themselves show the Americans conflating skin color with dress, religious belief, and derisive terms for other ethnicities. This influence comes to bear on Masood when he views the corpses of the insurgents who attacked the Americans: "I begin to feel a reluctant kinship with them—one that I cannot but help contrast to the way I've been made to feel inside the base" (Roy-Bhattacharya 2012, p. 103). Combined with his femininity, Masood is constructed and framed by Americans as an object of derision, of lesser worth.

In his role as an interpreter, Masood straddles the boundary between his identities as an American supporter and as an Afghan. On the one hand, he attempts to help the Americans thwart Nizam—the book's Antigone—from burying her brother by manipulating his knowledge of Islamic burial rituals: "You are a woman. You have no role in a Muslim burial. We are many men here. We'll take care of it" (Roy-Bhattacharya 2012, p. 7). On the other, he is aware of his beliefs in the face of the unjust way in which the Americans treat Nizam. "You're a believer, aren't you?" Nizam asks Masood. "You know this is wrong" (Roy-Bhattacharya 2012, p. 14). Masood only responds with "a quick, anxious glance," and then avoids all eye contact altogether (Roy-Bhattacharya 2012, p. 15). Like Ismene, who gradually comes to share her sister Antigone's views about immoral laws and state sanctioned violence, Masood begins to recognize injustice through American disrespect of not the living but the dead.

In "New Guidance," Roo also bears racist attitudes from the soldiers with whom he serves. The Americans assume incorrectly that Roo is Muslim since he originally grew up in Kabul. In a culturally insensitive manner, the unit's commanding officer tries to grasp Islamic dietary practices regarding shellfish: "He frowned at [Roo]. 'Muslims,' he said. 'They eat lobster?'" Karzowski quickly points out that "Roo's no Muslim" as if being a Muslim is an issue or a surprise, and Roo then corrects the Commanding Officer: "You're thinking of pigs" (Mogelson 2016, p. 51). The short conversation punctures the simplistic lens through which Americans attempt to frame a complex and intricate culture as barbaric. Americans incorrectly understand the dietary restrictions of Islam, and incorrectly assume that Roo would know because he practices Islam. Karzowsky's quick response (speaking for Roo) feels as much like a protective defense as it does an explanation. Roo knows the answer because his parents were Muslim. "'If you're not Muslim,' the CO asked me, 'what are you?'" Roo has no answer to this insensitive question of identity (Mogelson 2016, p. 52). Indeed, Mogelson's story then further frames the Americans as the barbarians in the room as they quickly shift the dinner conversation to whether it would be easier to give up eating pork or to give up sex. Roo's character serves to interpret all that is racist and wrong in this conversation.

Coincidental to the plot of *The Watch*, the Americans for whom Roo works also bungle their response to Islamic funeral rites when an ANA soldier is killed in a Taliban ambush. Like Masood, Roo is caught in the middle, interpreting. As American forces refuse to evacuate the dead soldier's body due to command guidance, Roo attempts to convince Major Karzowsky of the urgency of the matter: "He should be buried soon . . . It's a Muslim thing" (Mogelson 2016, p. 55). Yet the Americans are unmoved and force the Afghans to wait four days for an Afghan Air Force helicopter to arrive. In the meantime, American helicopters arrive and depart from the base, bringing Roo woolen socks and chocolates from home, all of which he shares with the Afghan platoon. In response, Lieutenant Mustafa takes Roo to the truck where the dead soldier is being stored, and as a rebuke to the American injustice, he makes Roo look at and smell the corpse to help Roo understand that Rahim's death is of far less importance for Americans than chocolate and socks. In this moment, Mustafa confronts Roo with what amounts to Butler's point: it is Islam, not the Taliban, that appears to be the enemy, and that thus receive subhuman treatment from the Americans. It is in Roo's liminal position between the Americans and the Afghans that interprets this discrepancy, though Roo does not understand the magnitude and his role in it until the story's end.

Joe is absent for much of "The Lost Troop," floating in and out like a phantom. He is not mentioned until several pages into the narrative when, as the narrator minimally desecrates an Afghan cemetery by removing a rock from a grave and throwing it into a chasm, Joe emerges to scold, "I would expect such disrespectful behavior from the Taliban . . . but not from you" (Mackin 2018, p. 7). Where Masood and Roo passively accepted American injustice regarding burials, Joe actively confronts the SEALs. Chastened, the narrator recovers and replaces the rock back on the grave. And when the SEALs deposit the ashes of their dead comrade Yaz on the spot where he died, Joe again appears suddenly behind the narrator, unexpectedly, to clear the narrator's conscience. Joe remains a phantom until he assuages the narrator's guilt: "It wasn't your fault" (Mackin 2018, p. 13). Most notable here is that again funeral rites and their desecration are at stake. Joe, like Masood and Roo, has an active role in showing injustice to the Americans, declaring it to them in their own language, and then trying to comfort the narrator when the SEALs conduct their own funeral. And more than Masood and Roo, Joe turns American Islamophobic fears back on the Americans. The Americans are behaving like the Taliban, the worst version of Islam that Americans can imagine, and indeed playing to that assumption that all of Islam shares the Taliban's motives.

As noted earlier in this study, Joe also helps the SEALs plan a mission that ultimately harasses Joe's former school teacher who lives a solitary life deep in the woods, uninvolved in the war.

The subsequent mission unfolds with the building tension of a high school prank. With Joe shouting through his bullhorn, the SEAL team quickly capture the elderly school teacher, bind his wrists, and leave him kneeling on the ground asking the SEALs what he had done: "We didn't answer. Rather, we left him, knees bleeding ... Then we burst into his cabin to see how he lived" (Mackin 2018, p. 19). While Joe has joined the SEALs, it is a misguided and unjust use of force that leaves the 'barbaric' and 'pre-modern' Afghan teacher treated like an exotic animal, less than human.

5. Concluding Discussion

Three terps, one from a novel and two from short stories, do not make an overwhelming case, and they raise more questions than they answer. And yet, their similar roles in these different war narratives is remarkable. Of note, they represent a technique in recent war writing that enables American characters interaction with someone like the enemy, but who also claims not to be. While the majority of war writing about the Forever War focuses on American soldiers and their experiences, the interpreter allows for contact and dialogue with a representative of the 'enemy's' culture. In these interactions, the terps do not so much bridge culture as demonstrate the chasm between them. Instead of connecting cultures, Masood and Roo find themselves stuck in between, and Joe is mostly ignored until he participates with the American SEALs in wanton aggression against his old teacher. These three works of fiction reveal a seam in the writing about American wars since 2004, whereby Americans exhibit no interest in multiculturalism, but rather continue to extend the trajectory of domination. If the terp translates nothing else in these stories, it is this reiterative desire to want to be American or to be like America in the face of those who have no desire to connect. Even as Masood and Roo attempt to connect and identify, the Americans create and extend boundaries that thwart hybridity in these stories. While the terp offers an opportunity to consider boundary crossing amidst the chaos of war, what emerges instead is a projection, albeit sometimes critical, of American beliefs about their enemy, as seen through asserting American masculine ideals and through Islamophobic beliefs.

Terps appear in other recent works, too, including Robinson's and Kovite's *War of the Encyclopaedists* (Robinson and Kovite 2015) and Phil Klay's short story "Psychological Operations," in *Redeployment* (Klay 2014), and so there are certainly additional characters to consider in extending our understanding about how the terp functions in war writing. Moreover, there are many opportunities for additional research to understand the historical context of terps with other interpreters in Western war literature—not only how the literary interpreter differs from the historical one, but also how reading military interpreters open our historical understanding of cultural encounters. There is little detailed work that considers the representative role of interpreters in both fiction and non-fiction, those who live at the threshold between languages and cultures, between friends and enemies, as subjects of power. There is more work to be done in extending our understanding of the interpreter who continually inhabits the liminal space of intercultural work.

Funding: This research received no external funding.

Conflicts of Interest: The author declares no conflict of interest.

References

Afshar, Haleh. 2013. The Politics of Fear: What Does It Mean to Those Who Are Otherized and Feared? *Ethnic and Racial Studies* 36: 9–27. [CrossRef]

Baigorri-Jalon, Jesus. 2011. Wars, Languages, and the Role(s) of Interpreters. *Les Liaisons Dangereuses: Langues, Traduction, Interpretation*. Beyrouth, Lebanon, Dec 2010. pp. 173–204. Available online: https://hal-confremo.archives-ouvertes.fr/hal-00599599/document (accessed on 22 March 2019).

Bhabha, Homi K. 1994. *The Location of Culture*. New York: Routledge.

Bourke, Joanna. 1999. *An Intimate History of Killing: Face to Face Killing in 20th Century Warfare*. New York: Basic Books.

Braudy, Leo. 2003. *From Chivalry to Terrorism: War and the Changing Nature of Masculinity*. New York: Alfred A. Knopf.
Butler, Judith. 2016. *Frames of War: When Is Life Grievable?* New York: Verso. First published 2009.
Büyükgebiz, Mustafa. 2016. How the Enemy Has Changed: Islamophobia and Post 9/11 Syndrome in John Le Carre's Novel. *A Most Wanted Man*. *Pamukkale University Journal of Social Sciences* 25: 228–35.
Campbell, Madeline Otis. 2016. *Interpreters of Occupation: Gender and the Politics of Belonging in an Iraqi Refugee*. New York: Syracuse University Press.
Ehrenreich, Barbara. 1997. *Blood Rites: Origins and History of the Passions of War*. New York: Metropolitan Books.
Gay, Peter. 1993. *The Cultivation of Hatred*. New York: W.W. Norton and Company.
Hedges, Chris. 2002. *War is a Force That Gives Us Meaning*. New York: Public Affairs.
Klay, Phil. 2014. *Redeployment*. New York: The Penguin Press.
Mackin, Will. 2018. *Bring Out the Dog*. New York: Random House.
Mogelson, Luke. 2016. *These Heroic, Happy Dead*. New York: Tim Dugan Books.
Peebles, Stacey. 2011. *Welcome to the Suck: Narrating the American Soldier's Experience in Iraq*. New York: Cornell University Press.
Robinson, Christopher, and Gavin Kovite. 2015. *War of the Encyclopaedists: A Novel*. New York: Scribner.
Roy-Bhattacharya, Joydeep. 2012. *The Watch*. New York: Hogarth Press.
Shimoni, Baruch. 2006. Cultural Borders, Hybridization, and a Sense of Boundaries in Thailand, Mexico, and Israel. *Journal of Anthropological Research* 62: 217–34. [CrossRef]
Tălpaş, Mihaela. 2016. Words cut two ways: An overview of the situation of Afghan interpreters at the beginning of the 21st century. *Linguistica Antverpiensia, New Series: Themes in Translation Studies* 15: 241–59.

© 2019 by the author. Licensee MDPI, Basel, Switzerland. This article is an open access article distributed under the terms and conditions of the Creative Commons Attribution (CC BY) license (http://creativecommons.org/licenses/by/4.0/).

MDPI
St. Alban-Anlage 66
4052 Basel
Switzerland
Tel. +41 61 683 77 34
Fax +41 61 302 89 18
www.mdpi.com

Humanities Editorial Office
E-mail: humanities@mdpi.com
www.mdpi.com/journal/humanities

www.ingramcontent.com/pod-product-compliance
Lightning Source LLC
LaVergne TN
LVHW071956080526
838202LV00064B/6762